The J.D. Films

*Juvenile Delinquency
in the Movies*

by
Mark Thomas McGee
and
R.J. Robertson

Jefferson, N.C.   *London*
McFarland & Company, Inc.

Library of Congress Cataloging in Publication Data

McGee, Mark Thomas, 1947-
   The J.D. films.

   Filmography: p.
   Bibliography: p.
   Includes index.
   1. Juvenile delinquency films — United States —
History and criticism. I. Robertson, Randolph James.
II. Title. III. Title: The juvenile delinquency films.

PN1995.9.J87M33   791.43'09'09355   81-23616   AACR2

ISBN 0-89950-038-2

Copyright © 1982 by Mark Thomas McGee and R.J. Robertson

Manufactured in the United States of America

McFarland & Company, Inc., Box 611, Jefferson, North Carolina 28640

Table of Contents

A Word from Dick Bakalyan

When you're small in stature you always have to throw the first punch or be the first guy to break a window. Then the bigger guys will say, "Hey! He's okay!" You're accepted. Important when you're seeking some sort of identification. There were basics when I was a kid. For instance, you knew when you were doing something wrong. And you knew if you got caught you got your ass kicked.

Dope wasn't around then. It wasn't the thing. But if we could get a bottle of Pickwick Ale ... that was considered heavy. I remember breaking open a freight car once. Budweiser. My pals and I didn't even like beer but it was just the idea of having it.

I did a year's probation when I was fifteen. (Not something to brag about.) I had to be in the house by eight o'clock every night. Tough when you want to hang out. If I wanted to go to a dance on a Friday night I had to get a special permission. In addition I was not allowed to get into any street fights, frequent in my neighborhood.

At one Friday night dance a fight broke out between some of my pals and some guys from across town. I couldn't get involved. One of the other gang members knew that if I got into a beef I'd be sent to Concord Reformatory. He figured he had a soft touch so he really pressed me. I was fifteen years old and there were all these pretty girls around and I gotta eat this bull that the guy dished out. It was tough.

There were two off duty policemen there. When they realized what was happening they called me aside. "Listen, Bakalyan, you don't have to take that crap. We're not here. So do what you've got to do!" It was beautiful. They cut me loose and allowed me the freedom of doing what I had to do which was to kick this guy's ass and retain my self respect. I gained a great deal of respect for policemen that night.

Respect for self and others ... that's what's missing in young people today. Maybe because there are very few adult role models.

I played a delinquent in *The Cool and the Crazy* but not really. The kids in that film were actually okay. It was Scott Marlowe who led them astray. He was busy trying to get everybody hooked on marijuana and heroin. If you did the same story today you'd do it with cocaine or heavier drugs. *The Cool and the Crazy* is a cult film today; people laugh about it. It's a fun film. *Hot Car Girl* was another. *The Delinquents* on the other hand was trying to make a statement. That was Robert Altman's first film. It was also my first.

One day we got through shooting early and one of my costars, Peter Miller, said to me, "Come on, Dick. We're going to get a lemon icecream soda." No sooner had we walked into the shop than a police officer grabbed me, spun me around, and slammed me up against the counter. I thought it was a gag—that Peter had put him up to it. So I started to laugh. That made the cop angry. And once I realized that he was serious I settled down. It turned out that some guy had escaped from somewhere and was wearing similar clothes to mine. I told the cop that I was making a movie. "Nobody makes movies in Kansas City," he said. We all had a good laugh.

I knew from the beginning that I'd be typecast as an actor just as I was in real life. I always knew that I'd have a gun or a knife in my hand, so I always tried to find a different way of presenting that kind of character. When I did *The Delicate Delinquent* nobody had long hair yet. Trying to think like the character I was portraying, I thought to myself "Why should I cut my hair? They'll cut it when I'm drafted to be killed in some crazy war. The hell with them." It was that kind of attitude that justified the long hair and the negative behavior of the character I was portraying. Of course, by today's standards, my hair *wasn't* long.

I told my wife if I was going to do this sort of work I wanted to be the best. I wanted to make a name for myself. You don't accomplish it overnight, but over a period of twenty or thirty years. Then I'd have the respect of my peers which is more important than someone stopping you for an autograph. Of course, I like that too.

A lot of people were uptight about those juvenile delinquency films but we never told the true story of what was going on. We just brushed the surface. I never thought that kids would try to emulate us 'cause we never glorified the characters. *Dino* certainly wasn't glorified. He was a troubled kid. That picture reflected a time.

When I play a heavy I do not try to play him heroic unless the script calls for it. If he's a low life I try to portray him as the best, blackest low life. To make heroes out of irresponsible people is a disservice to the community and to self.

Los Angeles, 1981

Acknowledgments

Books of this nature are rarely the sole product of the author (or authors) listed on the title page. The assistance of several people, who have little or no vested interest, is usually required. So these authors want to take this opportunity to express their sincere gratitude to all those folks who were kind enough to take some time out of their lives to make this volume possible.

For sharing old memories with us, we want to thank Jack Arnold, John Ashley, Richard Bakalyan (he even supplied good hot coffee with his conversation), Edward Bernds (who never complained about the number of bothersome phone calls placed to him), Herman Cohen, Charles B. Griffith, Jacques Marquette, Dick Miller, Mamie Van Doren, and Mel Welles. And to Albert Zugsmith, thanks for not consenting to an interview. Your letter of refusal was the source of much merriment.

Information for this book came from the Academy of Motion Pictures Arts and Sciences, the American Film Institute, Ron Borst of Hollywood Movie Posters, Mike Hawks of Eddie Brandt's Saturday Matinee, and our heads.

We are also grateful to Denetia Arellanes, Kevin Fernan, Bob Greenberg, Martin Kearns, Bill Warren (who suggested a number of J.D. titles that most certainly would have slipped past us), Jim Wnoroski, and Wendy Wright.

And for loaning us some of those hard-to-see films, thanks to Kingsly Candler, Tom Dunahoo of Thunderbird Films, and Alex Gordon, a tireless film fan who was extremely helpful in putting together the history of American-International that appears in this text. Thanks Alex. Thanks to you all.

Most of the photographs for this volume come from the private collection of the authors. Those that do not, appear through the courtesy of the Academy of Motion Pictures Arts and Sciences, Allied Artists, American-International Pictures, Samuel Z. Arkoff, Bond Street Books, Columbia, Gaines Films, Hollywood Poster Exchange, Marty Kearns, Metro-Goldwyn-Mayer, New World Pictures, United Artists, and Warner Brothers.

Introduction

In 1955, on the opening day of the school year, an attractive female teacher was attacked by a student in the library of an inner city vocational school in New York. An English teacher was later threatened by a student brandishing a switch-blade knife in a classroom in the same school. Later that year, in an affluent California suburb, a high school student was killed playing "chicken" when the stolen car he was driving plunged off a cliff. A teenage witness to the incident was later killed by the police after he had shot and wounded a member of a local gang. The previous year, a small town was invaded by almost one hundred members of a motorcycle gang. Before the state militia could restore order, the town had been ravaged and a local citizen was killed.

These examples of teenage violence could have been culled from any number of newspapers or magazines published that year. Figures on the number of court cases involving juveniles had almost doubled in the years between 1948, the post-war low, and 1954. Although the causes behind the statistics were vigorously debated, there was little question that the juvenile delinquency problem in the United States was growing at an alarming rate.

This phenomenon was reflected in three significant and highly controversial films released in 1954 and 1955. *The Wild One, Blackboard Jungle,* and *Rebel Without a Cause* brought to neighborhood theatres the incidents described in the first paragraph. There soon followed scores of imitations, ranging from serious dissertations on juvenile delinquency as a moral and social issue, to crass and commercial programmers which exploited their audiences' quest for sex and violence. Our intention is not to critically evaluate the films of either category (although personal feelings have a way of coming through). The quality, or its absence, will certainly dictate the emphasis placed on individual films, but our primary goal is to study the J.D. films in the context of the cultural events which inspired them. We also hope that hindsight will nuture insight, about both the motion pictures and some of their creators. To this end we shall emphasize the most significant, or influential films and deal rather superficially with the lesser offsprings except in such cases where the minor efforts added some new perception to the original concept.

No art form is created in a vacuum. The J.D. films evolved from traditions already established in other motion picture genres. As we shall see, formulas were developed that would appear time and again.

More often than not, the juveniles were divided into two groups: thoroughly reprehensible "bad" teenagers and the basically decent if often misunderstood "good" teenagers. The latter group ran afoul of the law rebelling against the restraints and hypocrisies placed on them by society while the members of the first group engaged in violence and mayhem because of their total lack of conscience. The "good" teenager was often redeemed by a "good" teenage girl or an understanding adult figure. His evil counterpart was either killed, exiled to reform school, or worse, abandoned by his peer group.

The good delinquent was the evolutionary product of the "good bad guy" from the thirties and forties, when likeable actors like James Cagney would appear as a figure existing outside the law, still possessing a personal code of ethics. In films like *Public Enemy* and *The Roaring Twenties*, Cagney remained true to himself even during his inevitable downfall. Humphrey Bogart took over in the late thirties, replacing Cagney's wisecracking vitality with his own brand of world weary cynicism in *Petrified Forest* and *High Sierra*. In the forties, John Garfield embodied the loser hero who continued to play against a perpetually stacked deck in *Dust Be My Destiny* and *They Made Me a Criminal*.

After World War II, another trait was added to this style of hero — vulnerability. As personified by Montgomery Clift in *A Place in the Sun* and *From Here to Eternity*, this new character appeared to be in a state of constant inner conflict which alienated him from the rest of society. Wearing his inner pain like a new suit, Clift projected an introverted, introspective intensity which suggested a man unable to understand the inner workings of his own mind, let alone the complexitites of the outer world.

Although the juvenile delinquents of the mid-fifties (and subsequent decades) dressed and talked differently, the image of the good/bad guy or loser hero remained. The emphasis merely shifted to a younger figure. The "go your own way" spirit of Bogie, Cagney, and Clift were reincarnated in actors like Marlon Brando and James Dean who, in turn, served as role models for countless other actors to follow.

Undeniably, it was the period from 1955 to 1970 that provided the greatest number of films in this genre, but to exclude the films that came before and after would not have provided a cohesive framework for this study. So, they're in! Chapter One looks at the youthful rebellion of the "jazz" generation before moving on to the inner city delinquents from the thirties and forties, with a few odds and ends in between. Chapter Two covers the early fifties, focusing on the three influential films mentioned at the beginning of this introduction. Chapter Three continues the decade while Chapter Four explores the turbulent sixties, from the throw-backs to the earlier years to the motorcycle and youth rebellion films that ended that decade. The films of the seventies are summed up in an epilog.

Unlike the various other genres — western, science fiction, horror films — the J. D. film has not developed a cult following over the last few years. Relatively few of them have ever been seriously considered by either the critics or the public. Consequently, many of the films dealt with in this book have fallen into oblivion, unavailable for viewing since a number of years back. Attempting to jostle a twenty year old memory of an afternoon spent watching a thoroughly forgettable film like *Dragstrip Riot* is, at best, difficult. To insure as few errors as possible, we have poured over pressbooks, newspapers, and whatever scattered reference materials could be found. Some of the more obscure films released by independent companies received little or no documentation, as if they had never existed at all. So there will be some omissions and, we fear, some misinformation. Forgive us. We did our best.

Although juvenile delinquency, and films about it, were not confined to the United States, we have essentially limited our research to the more widely distributed films from this country. The few exceptions included were primarily to illustrate how U.S. products were imitated abroad. We have also attempted to restrict this volume to motion pictures that used juvenile delinquency as the main premise rather than a small aspect of another topic. Once again, though, there are exceptions.

Finally, there is the question of defining what constitutes a juvenile delinquency film. There were numerous films geared toward the teenage audience—rock and roll musicals, romantic dramas, comedies—and some of them had elements of delinquency and others did not. But it is difficult to discuss something like *Shake, Rattle and Rock*, which did contain teenage vandalism, without mentioning the film that inspired it, *Rock Around the Clock*, which did not. So often films like *Gidget* and *Blue Denim* will be mentioned as points of reference, indicating the shifts in audience interest which affected the J.D. films.

Another possible point of contention may be the inclusion of the motorcycle dramas and other films dealing with characters who have obviously long passed the age of consent. While the delinquents in *The Wild One* fall into this category, that particular film has always been discussed as a juvenile delinquency picture so we have chosen, unlike the law, to judge such characters on the basis of their actions rather than their age. Besides, the rebellious spirit inherent in *The Wild One* and others of that ilk is more crucial to the J.D. film than any arbitrary age distinction. Similarly, the degree of criminal activity may be questioned in some of the films included. Examples such as "drag racing" in the fifties and drug ingestion in the sixties may not be construed by most people as major crimes. Audiences for these films were not concerned with the extent of the illegal activities but rather the antiauthoritarian attitudes that instigated them.

Ultimately, it is the spirit of rebellion that made the best, and worst, of these pictures appealing. While adults decried that viewing such fare must invariably lead to emulation, for the most part teenagers used them as an excuse to pile into a car and spend an evening at a drive-in theatre, enjoying a vicarious thumb-of-the-nose at adult authority. Most of us who watched these films passed through our youth with little, if any, criminal activity, and have since grown into responsible adults, whatever that means.

While those wild, reckless years twixt twelve and twenty may now be way behind us, they still exist in our memories, vague recollections of sitting spellbound in the darkness watching James Dean express our inner anxieties about growing up. Memories of a shared defiance watching Peter Fonda flip the bird to The Man. Memories, if you were a girl, of standing in front of a mirror to see if anything could be done to make yourself look a little more like Sandra Dee, and, if you were a boy, Elvis Presley. Perhaps in these old memories we can still find that teenage rebel that exists in all of us, no matter what our age.

Chapter One

Whatever Happened to Andy Hardy?

"I think the young boy of fourteen or fifteen starts
out in life like that, say, in this area in Harlem,
poor, he sees something he likes and his parents
can't give it to him. He can't get a job and his only
alternative is to steal it. And if he wants it bad
enough he will do anything to get it." — Harlem
student, after viewing *The Devil Is a Sissy*.

Los Angeles Times movie critic Charles Champlin was speaking in
Century City, addressing a group of the Reiss-Davis Women's Club.
With the anarchistic happenings perpetrated by the teenagers in *Wild in
the Streets* (1968) still fresh in his mind, Champlin began his talk by
asking, "Whatever happened to Andy Hardy?" Now Andy Hardy was a
teenaged character portrayed by Mickey Rooney in a series of M-G-M
movies produced from 1937 to 1946. Andy lived in the small but comfortable midwestern town of Carvel, with his extremely understanding
father, Judge Hardy (Lewis Stone), his unbelievably sweet mother (Fay
Holden), and his older sister Marian (Cecilia Parker). Everyone was con-
sistently "nice" in the Hardy films, even Polly Benedict (Ann Rutherford)
who had to remain pleasant during those many periods when Andy's attentions would stray away from her to greener pastures.

Champlin's lamentation was not for Andy Hardy specifically but
rather for what the character represented. Andy was the perfect image of
an American teenager: sometimes misguided, often confused, but
basically decent, energetic, and obedient. When things got too anxious
for Andy he could always have a "man to man" talk with his father,
sequences that provided the backbone of the series' philosophy. In *Love
Finds Andy Hardy* (1938) Judge Hardy is concerned that a young man he
had previously sentenced for a petty crime might harbor some resent-
ment. "Why, Dad," Andy cheerfully remarks, "kids don't hold any
grudge against older people for punishing them. If they did, all kids'd
hate their fathers — and they don't." Uh-huh.

The traditional values expressed in the Andy Hardy series, that in
1942 earned M-G-M a special Academy Award for "furthering the

American way of life," had been eclipsed by a rebellion that more or less buried the former ideals in much the same way that weeds had long since obscured the Hardy's Carvel home on the studio's backlot.

Champlin's audience heaved a collective wistful sigh over the loss of Andy and other wholesome juveniles like Deanna Durbin, the young lady who spent ten years spreading good cheer with the same efficiency that spreads warm butter on toast. In films like *Three Smart Girls* (1936), *It's a Date* (1939), and *Can't Help Singing* (1944), this Pollyanna missionary sporadically burst into song between her incessant do-gooding. She too was honored by the Academy of Motion Pictures Arts and Sciences "for bringing to the screen the spirit and personification of youth." Typical of her vehicles was *That Certain Age* (1938) in which she forms a romantic "crush" on a worldly journalist, Melvin Douglas, a guest in her parent's home. Douglas, of course, discourages her advances. After all, what middleaged single man could be interested in an eager, ripening, nubile, attractive teenaged girl? Besides, Deanna couldn't really be in love; just a childish infatuation. So Douglas dampens her fervor by introducing his sometime fiancée as his wife. As expected, the masquerade becomes reality before the film concludes, and the sadder-but-wiser Miss Durbin returns to her dorky boyfriend, Jackie Cooper. Together they put on a musical benefit to send underprivileged Boy Scouts to summer camp.

Andy Hardy ... Deanna Durbin ... Henry Aldrich ... the youths of *reel* life. In *real* life things had always been a bit different. What Champlin and his audience had not yet come to grips with was the fact that it was not just the image of teenagers that had altered but their parents as well. There was no trace of Judge Hardy's benevolence in Edward Andrews when he played John Saxon's father in *The Unguarded Moment* (1956). Andrews divided his time between poisoning his son's mind against the opposite sex and grooming the boy for the athletic career that he never had. "If you knock down what I've spent years in building up," Andrews calmly tells Saxon, "I'll break every bone in your body." Nor is there a hint of Andy's mother to be found in Doris Dowling's boozy, adulterous mama in *The Party Crashers* (1958). And if critics like Champlin found such characterizations to be gross exaggerations, and exceptions to the rule, at least the pendulum had finally swung away from the completely unrealistic dogma of the Hardy films and their ilk. Teenagers after all did have real problems. Ideal role models were not always readily available. And sexual urges were often more than just puppy love.

Indeed, it may have seemed to the Reiss-Davis Women's Club that the juvenile delinquency problem had been spawned in the 1950s, both on and off screen. Nothing could be further from the truth. Oddly enough though, the concept of juvenile delinquency, like the motion picture, was primarily a product of the twentieth century. In less enlightened times all criminals, regardless of age, were judged according to the severity of their offenses. It was not until the 18th century that the more highly advanced civilizations established separate institutions for juvenile offenders. In 1854, England adopted the Reform Schools Act, legalizing the humanitarian concept of reformations rather than punishment. As young people might be incapable of distinguishing right from wrong, these schools were created to help lead them to become law-abiding citizens.

In the United States, the first reformatory school for juveniles was established in New York City in 1825. It was not until the last year of the 19th century that the first juvenile court was instituted in Cook County, Illinois. This concept of a separate judicial system lead to the administration of juvenile justice as practiced today.

Coincidentally, the motion picture as a public art form also gained acceptance in the early years of this century. It was not long before the issue of juvenile delinquency found its way to celluloid.

In *As the World Rolls On* (1921) Joe Walker's interest in Molly Moran nets him a beating from Tom Atkins' gang of hoods. Tom erroneously fancies Molly to be his girl. But Joe is not deterred so Tom frames him and Molly for a robbery that he, Tom, committed. It is not long before the truth surfaces during the trial and when Tom bolts from his courtroom seat, Joe thwarts his attempt to escape.

The Angel of Crooked Street (1922) is teenaged Alice Calhoun, working as a maid to support her mother. The rich woman for whom she works, Martha Mattox, mistakingly believes Alice to be responsible for a robbery and the girl is sent to a reform school where she becomes embittered. Once released she plans to frame Martha's son, Ralph Mc-Cullough, for revenge but ends up falling in love with him instead.

The Romance of a Million Dollars (1926) told the involved story of 17-year-old Breck Dunbarton (Glenn Hunter), paroled from a reform school to his rich Uncle Ezra's custody. Breck wants to go straight but everything seems against it. The first cog in the works is his expulsion from college following a theft for which he is blamed. He joins the Army and goes to France where he meets Marie Moore (Alyce Mills), an ambulance driver with whom he falls in love. Informed that his uncle has passed away, Breck returns home with Marie. Ezra's other nephew, West (Gaston Glass), also falls for Marie. To get Breck out of the picture, he robs one of the house guests. After a few suspenseful moments West confesses his crime and Breck's unusual bad luck does an "about face." He ends up with the girl and the family fortune.

While the new entertainment medium was still in its infancy, America entered a period which came to be known as the Roaring Twenties, the birth of the first youth rebellion. In this decade of flappers and drugstore cowboys, of "sheiks" and "shebas," teenaged girls patterned themselves after Theda Bera while the boys did their best to imitate romantic screen star Rudolph Valentino. Expressions like "bee's knees" and "cat's meow" were part of the new vocabulary. The Great War had left the nation unsure of itself while the newly emerging sexual theories of Sigmund Freud helped make everyone self-conscious. The "disenchanted" younger generation wanted to ignore it all and have a good time. Naturally, the methods used to have that "good time" — smoking, drinking, dancing — met with a storm of protest from angry parents who saw the whole business as a decline in morality. In the *Atlantic Monthly*,

John F. Carter responded thus to the adults: "I would like to observe that the older generation had certainly pretty well ruined this world before passing it on to us. They give us this Thing, knocked to pieces, leaky, red-hot, threatening to blow up; and then they are surprised that we don't accept it with the same enthusiasm with which they received it."

Our Dancing Daughters (1928) was one of the first films to capture the new Jazz Age philosophy, the studio's publicity department promising the movie-goer a firsthand look at those "scandalous" women who liked fast music and fast men. Former M-G-M bit player Joan Crawford got her first big break playing the "sheba" who lures Johnny Mack Brown away from Anita Page. F. Scott Fitzgerald claimed that Crawford was "the best example of the flapper, the girl you see at smart nightclubs, gowned to the apex of sophistication, toying iced glasses with a remote, faintly bitter expression, dancing deliciously, laughing a great deal, with wide, hurt eyes." And Fitzgerald should have known about such things. His own wild affairs were as heralded as his novels.

The clandestine drinking and dacing "exposed" in the film was the sort of stuff guaranteed to ruffle parental feathers. But it seems that throughout history the adults have taken some sort of perverse delight in being outraged, deriving almost as much pleasure as the kids who enjoyed outraging them. But as Walter Lippman noted, unlike the decades that would follow, the rebellion of the twenties was not against the religion or moral code of the parents, but rather the disillusionment with their own rebellion. "It is common for young men and women to rebel, but that they should rebel sadly and without faith in their rebellion, that they should distrust the new freedom no less than the old certainties — that is something of a novelty."

M-G-M's followup to *Our Dancing Daughters* was *Our Modern Maidens* (1929), again with Crawford only this time she was a flirtatious married woman, still seeking the company of fast men but with an interest in fast cars rather than fast dancing. It was somewhat of a novelty in that, contrary to the popular myth usually perpetuated by Hollywood, Crawford lived happily ever after. It was to be her last silent film. Hollywood was going through the transition to "talkies" which signaled an end to the silent screen; 1929 also marked an end to Johnny Weissmuller's professional swimming career as well as any doubts the public may have had about the feasibility of coast-to-coast airline service. Charles Lindbergh settled that issue with his July 8 flight. That year was also the beginning of the Great Depression.

Suddenly over 40 million people were looking poverty squarely in the eye. Factory output was cut in half. Millions were out of work. Dust storms, draughts, and floods crippled many farmers before the plummeting crop prices could. One of the only professions to prosper was crime. Newspapers regularly reported the exploits of notorious criminals like Clark "Ma" Barker and Charles "Pretty Boy" Floyd, then gave equal space to the outlaws' most active adversary, John Edgar Hoover. As the director of the newly formed Federal Bureau of Investigation, Hoover joined the ranks of the decade's most celebrated heroes — Tom Mix, Jack

Armstrong, Flash Gordon — to the point that a reporter for the *New York World-Telegram* stated: "Pick a small boy these days and ask him who of all the people in the world he wants to be like and ten to one he will reply — J. Edgar Hoover." Such a speculation may have been true, but there were just as many young men who admired the recklessness of John Dillinger, the nation's number one public enemy. Hardly oblivious to this fact, Hollywood began cranking out a series of gangster films which reinforced the belief that juvenile delinquents were spawns of the slums, nutured into a life of crime by hardcore adult delinquents.

Tom Powers, as enacted by James Cagney in *Public Enemy* (1931), exemplified the wisecracking opportunist determined to survive and make the best of a bad situation regardless of the moral or legal implications. Starting as a youngster in the impoverished environment of the Chicago slums in 1909, Tom earns nickels and dimes by running beer for a local tavern. During his teenage years, he graduates from petty thievery to grand theft, finally emerging as a full-fledged gangster during prohibition. Despite the fact that Tom meets a rather gruesome end, Cagney's vitality and personality made the character attractive, if not sympathetic, especially appealing to depression audiences who were feeling betrayed by the system.

The public's enthusiastic response to the gangster film alarmed numerous guardians of public morality who believed the genre tended to glorify the criminal. Pressure was applied to shift the emphasis from the hoodlums to the law enforcement officials. Movie tough guys like Cagney, George Raft, and Edward G. Robinson began wearing two different hats, hopping from one side of the law to the other.

One such example was Cagney's portrayal in *The Mayor of Hell* (1933). A former racketeer himself, Cagney's new committment is to improve conditions in a reform school mismanaged by a greedy superintendent. (The premise of this film would be repeated many times later in the decade.) Frankie Darro, the leader of the school's inmates, appeared in another delinquency film that year, *Wild Boys of the Road*. He and two other juveniles leave their homes during the Depression so as not to burden their parents with the responsibility of feeding them. Hopping freights and dodging railroad detectives on their cross-country odyssey, the youths experience firsthand the rampant poverty which had crippled the country. Dragged into court for vagrancy, Darro delivers an impassioned speech to the judge:

> I'll tell you why we can't go home. Because our folks are poor. They can't get jobs, and there isn't enough to eat. What good will it do to send us home to starve? You say you got to send us to jail to get us off the streets. Well, that's a lie! You're sending us to jail 'cause you don't want to see us. You want to forget us. Well, you can't do it. 'Cause I'm not the only one. There's thousands just like me and more hitting the road each day.

Taking another look at the horrors of poverty, *Dead End* (1937) was based on Sidney Kingsley's play about people who live, metaphorically, on a dead end street facing the river. Baby Face Martin (Humphrey Bogart), a notorious criminal, returns to his old New York East Side

tenement home to briefly escape from his unhappy existence. To Dave Connell (Joel McCrea) and many of the other inhabitants of the neighborhood, Martin is a not so gentle reminder of what the current crop of street urchins, seen in various stages of mischief throughout the film, might become. Martin's sentimental sojourn becomes a cruel slap in the face, literally when his mother (Marjorie Main) delivers a quick blow to his cheek, denouncing him, and figuratively when he learns that his childhood sweetheart has become a tramp.

Director William Wyler wanted to add to the story's intensity by shooting on location, but producer Samuel Goldwyn insisted on keeping it studio bound. To placate Wyler the budget was extended to build an enormous set. But like many members of the audience, Goldwyn didn't want too much realism in his film. Strolling onto the set one afternoon, the producer asked why the hell everything looked so dirty. Wyler reminded him that it was supposed to be a slum. "Well, this slum cost a lot of money," Goldwyn snapped. "It should look better than an ordinary slum." His desire for beautification would have been better served outside the confines of the studio. As one *New York Post* critic observed, *Dead End* would have been an ideal film to screen for the committee that had crippled the Wagner Housing Act.

The group of young actors portraying the street punks — Billy Halop, Leo Gorcey, Bobby Jordan, Huntz Hall, Bernard Punsley, and Gabriel Dell — moved to Warner Brothers where they made a number of films, collectively billed as "The Dead End Kids." The first and most entertaining of their efforts was *Angels with Dirty Faces** (1938), the story of Rocky Sullivan (James Cagney) and Jerry Connolly (Pat O'Brien), chums since childhood, one a crook, the other a priest. An opening sequence suggests that the boys were cut from the same cloth, both of them running from the authorities after breaking into a boxcar. Only Jerry's successful escape spares him the criminal influence that Rocky suffers in the reformatory. The newspaper accounts of Rocky's illegal activities stresses the urgency to Jerry, now Father Connolly, of reforming the local juveniles, dissuading them from following in Rocky's footsteps. But the kids admire Rocky. To them he is a hero, which is why, during the remaining minutes before Rocky is to be executed, Father Connolly begs him to die a coward. "You've been a hero to these kids and hundreds of others all through your life," he tells the gangster. "Now you're going to

---

Edward Alperson, the president of Poverty Row's Grand National Pictures, had purchased the rights to the Angels with Dirty Faces story in 1936. At that time, Cagney had quarrelled with Warner Brothers and was making pictures for Grand National. Alperson was set to use the property as a vehicle for Cagney when he was talked into making Something to Sing About (1937) instead. It was a mistake which caused Alperson's company to go bankrupt but fortunately left the story to more capable hands.

The Dead Ends Kids in the movie that started it all, Dead End (United Artists 1937). They were tough cookies before Sam Katzman de-clawed them.

be glorified in death and I want to prevent that, Rocky. They've gotta despise your memory. They've got to be ashamed of you.... I know what I'm asking and the reason I'm asking is because being kids together sort of gave me the idea that you might like to join hands with me and save some of those other boys from ending up here." But Rocky feels Jerry expects too much of him; asking him to throw away the only thing he has left — his self-respect. Father Connolly spends several tense moments as Rocky is being strapped to the chair but his old pal does the right thing — he turns yellow before they pull the switch. The film ends with Father Connolly asking the sour-faced, betrayed group of kids to join him in a prayer "for a boy who couldn't run as fast as I could." He then leads the boys out of their cellar hangout, up a series of steps to the accompaniment of choir music, a scene that more than suggests that the stairs lead to heaven.

Crime School (1938), a semi-remake of *Mayor of Hell*, placed the Dead End Kids in a reform school where the staff was more criminal than the inmates. Humphrey Bogart was the idealistic young Deputy Commissioner of Correction, appalled by the beating of Billy Halop by a sadistic guard. Believing that brutal discipline breeds hardened criminals, Bogie initiates a series of modern reforms which lead the young lawbreakers into becoming responsible citizens. Bogie also discovers that the reformatory superintendent has been embezzling school funds. Between straightening out the boys and jailing the crooks, Bogie finds time to romance Halop's sister, played (as usual) by Ann Sheridan, more or less a standard subplot for these pictures. In fact, the formula was immediately repeated, almost verbatim, for *Hell's Kitchen* (1939). The boys graduated from reform school only to be placed in another institution run by crooks. Their only hope rests with Ronald Reagan and Margaret Lindsay, two honest social workers with whom they join forces to rid the place of the bad guys.

As these films continued, the Dead End Kids moved farther away from their original image to become merely misunderstood victims of official ignorance, indifference, or corruption. (The Fonzie character on television's *Happy Days* suffered a similar overhaul.) By the time *Angels Wash Their Faces* (1939) rolled around, the young group not only had cleaner faces, they also wore suits and ties, moved to a slightly better neighborhood, attended school regularly, and softened into responsible, if rambunctious, young citizens. Once again with a little assistance from Ronald Reagan, Halop and the gang put some corrupt officials behind bars and clear one of their gang members of false arson charges.

Before teaming with the Dead End Kids Reagan had cut his teeth on another J.D. drama, *Girls on Probation* (1939). He helped Jane Bryan regain her respectability after she too was falsely accused of a crime she did not commit. But the actor was reluctant to accept a role opposite the Dead End Kids because of the "lurid tales" told about them by his fellow actors. Cagney set Reagan straight. He told the future president to politely inform the boys that unless they behaved he'd "slap hell out of them."

John Garfield, something of a misunderstood, overaged kid himself, joined Halop and the gang in *They Made Me a Criminal* (1939). As a boxer falsely accused of murder, Garfield finds the seclusion he needs on a desert ranch operated by Ann Sheridan and May Robson, a home for stray boys. His whole life spent looking out for himself, Garfield risks exposure by entering a boxing contest so that he can raise money for the ranch.

The Dead End Kids on Dress Parade (1939) presented the once-feared streetfighters as cadets in a military school. Watching them knock one rebellious kid into line was disconcerting, as if the whole lot of them had been given a lobotomy. Not long after that the boys, minus Halop, moved into a new home, Poverty Row's Monogram Studios. Leo Gorcey took over as leader of the East Side Kids. They still hung around the streets, occasionally insulting a policeman or two, but the boys had been de-clawed. For some reason they went through another name change in 1946 – "The Bowery Boys." Of course, no member of the cast had been a *boy* for a decade and the results were embarrassing. After his father died, Gorcey abandoned the series, leaving Huntz Hall to captain the sinking ship.

On his own Billy Halop appeared with Bogart in *You Can't Get Away with Murder* (1939), yet another yarn about a hardened criminal grooming a younger boy for a life of crime. Everything goes sour when an innocent man is convicted of a crime that Halop and Bogie committted. Fearing his threats won't keep the boy silent for long, Bogie shoots Halop. But before Halop dies he sets the record straight and all but hands Bogie a ticket to the electric chair.

The brief success of the Dead End Kids prompted an early if short-lived vogue in juvenile delinquency films. Metro-Goldwyn-Mayer, the most prestigious of the movie studios, produced a fictionalized account of Father Edward Flanagan, the priest in Omaha, Nebraska, who sponsored a home for juvenile offenders. Flanagan's home, and the movie, was called *Boys Town* (1938). The film opens with a young boy walking the "last mile," explaining the circumstances that brought him to such a tragic end. "Just before we got out of the reformatory we made up a gang.... One of them turned rat, an' I killed him..."

"There isn't any such thing in the world as a bad boy," Father Flanagan often said. "But a boy left alone, frightened, bewildered ... the wrong hand reaches for him ... he needs a friend ... that's all he needs...."

Actor Spencer Tracy spent weeks at the real Boys Town, preparing for the role of Father Flanagan. When he received an Academy Award for his performance, he forwarded the statuette to the priest with the following inscription: "To Father Edward J. Flanagan, whose great human qualities, timely simplicity, and inspiring courage were strong enough to shine through my humble effort."

In the film, Tracy is asked to take care of Mickey Rooney, a young trouble-maker who disrupts Boys Town with his efforts to impress the other lads with his "tough guy" act. Eventually Mickey flees to the city where he coincidentally passes by a bank being robbed by his brother's gang. Mickey is wounded and while recovering in the hospital learns that his inadvertant involvement in the crime has reflected badly on Tracy's school. Feeling pangs of regret, Mickey locates the gang's hideout and demands that the gang clear him of any wrong-doing to vindicate Boys Town. The hoods turn on Mickey and his brother, holding them both captive. When the kids back at Boys Town learn of Mickey's predicament they hurry to the rescue. The popularity of this film gave M-G-M ample cause to crank out a sequel, *Men of Boys Town* (1941).

Nineteen thirty-eight proved to be quite a year for the J.D. film. There was *Reformatory* with Jack Holt and Frankie Darro, a rehash of Warner Brothers' recipe. *Rebellious Daughters* was the old chestnut about a high spirited girl driven out of her home by unsympathetic parents to the sin and corruption of the big city. *Delinquent Parents* told of a trouble-prone young lady who finally gets some help from her mother, now a judge, who had placed her in an orphanage at infancy. And in *Little Tough Guys*, Billy Halop once again found himself in close quarters with law breakers, causing the National Council of Jewish Women to complain that "the continual portrayal of boys in their teens carrying guns and employing them to commit crimes" was bad psychology. They might have taken some solace in the fact that it was one of the few pictures to show a boy being reformed by a reform school.

Still lower on the quality scale were the pure exploitation films which dealt with subjects forbidden by the Production Code. Consequently, these pictures received limited distribution, usually run in small urban area theatres.

Sex Madness (1937) quickly dismissed its social obligation with a prologue about the dangers of venereal disease, then took relish in recounting the trials and tribulations of a small town girl corrupted by fast living in the big city. An easy mark for unprincipled men seeking cheap thrills and tawdry pleasures, the once naive heroine quickly learns the evils of aroused lust.

"Exposing" drug abuse, *Assassin of Youth* (1935), *Marijuana* (1936) and *Reefer Madness* (1938) were each loaded with plenty of misinformation and scare tactics, illustrating the horrors that the evil weed can cause. Again the films dealt with innocent kids manipulated by older drug pushers into a life of degradation, culminating in shame, crime, murder, and occasionally suicide. The lack of effectiveness of such warnings is evident by the fact that when these films are shown in revival theatres, many members of the audience are passing around joints.

One of the more unique youth films during the thirties was Cecil B. DeMille's *This Day and Age* (1938). Five thousand high school boys take the law into their own hands when a gangster is unjustly acquitted for the murder of a shopkeeper. The boys kidnap and suspend the killer over a pit of rats to make him confess. Although their illegal activities were done in the name of justice, the boys' actions were ultimately more frightening than anything perpetrated by the Dead End Kids.

For the most part, this spasm of juvenile delinquency films in the late thirties was an exception to the rule. Hollywood, being primarily a family oriented medium, chose to ignore, minimize, or restrict these problems to the inner city. Films that came too close to home on the subject of youth rebellion met with protest from adults who did not wish to acknowledge the problem. Since teenagers were unable to support their own sources of entertainment, Hollywood's image of youth was, essentially, what adults wanted to see, i.e. Andy Hardy and Deanna Durbin. But those days were coming to an end. The forties gave birth to the teenage revolution, essentially a byproduct of World War II. With so many adults off to various battle fronts, young people began taking part-time and full-time jobs. Teenagers obtained status. Industries catered to them. Various magazines began devoting columns to them. *Seventeen* magazine was created. Soda shops sprang up like weeds, each housing a jukebox stocked with the kind of records that would attract the bobbysoxers.

Margaret Mead found nothing puzzling about the fact that juvenile delinquency increased during this period. According to her, it is only from older brothers and older companions that boys learn how to be boys. This social development is distorted in slum areas where the older boys were unable to reinterpret their fathers' failures to guide them toward more successful roads. "They become gang leaders, in turn effectively short-circuiting the development of their younger brothers in society," wrote Miss Mead in her book *Male and Female; A Study of the Sexes in a Changing World.*

Indeed, the Depression may have been put to rest but juvenile delinquency had not. *Look* magazine was inspired to explore the possible causes, eventually publishing a picture story "Are These Our Children?" Essentially the article made the point that wartime America was doing a superb job of producing planes, guns, and ships but was botching the raising of its young. "As boys, they deserve sympathy," *Look* declared. "As symbols, they deserve alarm." The response to the article was overwhelming. Most of the letters that flooded the magazine's mailroom suggested social and community programs as a way of curbing juvenile delinquency, the basis for Columbia's *Juvenile Court* (1938) in which Paul Kelly, as a Public Defender, struck a blow against teenage crime by organizing a Police Athletic League. Eleanor Roosevelt had still another solution: "If every effort were made to fit the job to the child, I think we would move to productive work some of the youngsters who become most dangerous when idle."

As part of their *This Is America* series, RKO produced a two reel documentary, "Children of Mars." *New York Times* critic Bosley Crowther felt the film was sincere but a little simplistic. According to the film, the blame for juvenile delinquency rested entirely on the shoulders of the mothers whose jobs in war plants made it impossible for them to devote all of their time to their children. "The home of the children under scrutiny seems otherwise a happy, normal one," wrote Crowther, "which is far from a typical example of a home from which the bulk of cases come."

Immediately after reading *Look's* picture story, Charles Koerner, the vice president of RKO Radio Pictures, fired off a letter to the magazine in which he stated that he was "inspired" by the "dramatic treatment" of the problem to the extent that he wanted to make a movie based on the article. "We are prepared to throw our entire production resources behind the filming of 'Are These Our Children?'" Koerner boasted, then turned the assignment over to one of the studio's low-budget units headed by Val Lewton. Lewton was a producer who, at that time, had already achieved minor miracles by making intelligent, effective horror dramas written around the ridiculous "studio-tested" titles that Koerner dreamed up like *The Leopard Man, I Walked with a Zombie* (both 1943), and *Curse of the Cat People* (1944). Manny Farber was so impressed with Lewton's abilities that he once stated that the producer escaped the corruption of Hollywood by his own integrity. "In another set-up, I think Lewton would probably make extremely good movies; he may eventually do that even in Hollywood."

Lewton attempted to bring his customary high standards to *Are These Our Children?* but the odds were against him. In the first place, he was unable to fully endorse the solutions to the problem that the film offered—youth clubs, closer supervision, and playgrounds. He recalled a conversation he had once had with a real teenage delinquent during which he asked the boy if there were any playgrounds in his neighborhood. "Sure," the youth replied, "but you can't play baseball all the time."

Even before production could get underway the State Department reminded the studio that such a film might give other nations the impression that the United States did not know how to handle its youth. Then the Hays office ordered the removal of a subplot in which one of the abused minors in the script is forced to kill his sadistic father. Then several people from *Look* magazine, from which the studio naturally expected to receive a lot of free publicity, expressed a dislike of the picture. Coupled with a bad preview, the film was re-edited and new scenes were shot. It went through several title changes*—*Are These Our Children?, This Dangerous Age*—before finally emerging as *Youth Runs Wild* (1944), a title that belied Koerner's supposed serious intentions.

By the time everyone had finished tampering with the picture, Lewton felt it had suffered irreparable damage. In a letter to his mother and sister, the beleaguered producer said that RKO had removed all of the good things and left only the "banal and silly" elements that had more or less become clichés of the genre. Lewton's request that his name be removed from the credits was denied.

Unfortunately, the film has not been seen by these writers and for the synopsis we are relying on Joel Siegel's wonderful biography of Lewton, *The Reality of Terror*. According to Siegel, the story takes place in a small American town during World War II where 24-hour defense

*In 1931 RKO had made another J.D. film under the title of Are These Our Children? which had been a youth-led-astray-by-a-flapper yarn, the couple's affair brought to a disturbing crescendo when the boy (Eric Linden) killed someone over a bottle of gin. This may account for the title change.

plant schedules have disrupted normal family life. Returning from the war, a soldier finds that his brother-in-law is becoming a delinquent. Another home hides the mistreatment of a young girl who eventually runs away and falls in with a bad crowd. The soldier, and his young wife, eventually open a day-care center for children and a job training center for teenagers. From the information available, *Youth Runs Wild* was just an extended version of the studio's own "Children of Mars."

Monogram quickly released their own version of the problem, *Where Are Your Children?* (1944) with poor Gale Storm inadvertently getting mixed up with criminals on her way to join her lover, Jackie Cooper, serving a tour of duty in the Navy. One sequence depicting the beating of a gas station attendant by a teenager had to be altered so that the boy's age was 21.

The suggestion that something other than slum conditions accounted for teenage crime — parental abuse or neglect, for example — linked both *Where Are Your Children?* and *Youth Runs Wild* to Leo McCarey's *Wild Company* (1930) in which neglectful parents allowed their son to run amok to the point that he becomes involved with a bunch of crooks. PRC's *I Accuse My Parents* (1944) followed much the same story line.

On trial for killing a man, James Wilson (Robert Lowell) responds to the judge's request for some words in his own defense by accusing his parents. A series of staccato closeups, accompanied by startled gasps cause the judge to angrily bring down his gavel. He then asks the boy for some sort of explanation, which he gets (as does the audience) in detail. Via flashback, we are told the boy's heart-wrenching tale of bickering parents, the nightclub singer with whom he falls in love, the racketeer who tricks him into a life of crime, and the struggle that ended with Jimmy killing the racketeer in self-defense. The story is told with all the delicacy of an elephant stampede with one sequence a particular standout. Jimmy rushes home to tell his parents he has won first prize in a national contest with his essay, "My Country, My Home." His folks are gone. The camera slowly moves through the living room, highlighting the ash-trays filled to overflowing and past enough liquor bottles to put the entire Marine Corps out of action for a month, coming to rest on a note from his mother which reads: "You'll find ten dollars in the drawer. Take care of yourself until I get home." During this slice of poignancy the soundtrack has been supplying strains of "Home Sweet Home."

When Jimmy's parents do arrive they all but ignore his good news, plunging right into their nightly argument. Jimmy's despondency is matched only by his embarrassment when his mother shows up at school the next day plastered to the gills.

Jimmy tells the judge that had he not been ashamed of his homelife, he is convinced that he wouldn't have started lying to his classmates and sought refuge in the sort of company that coerced him into trouble. The judge dismisses the murder charge, gives Jimmy a suspended sentence for his participation in some robberies, then wheels on the boy's parents. In a burst of unbridled sermonizing, his Honor cautions Mr. and Mrs. Wilson that they must learn from the tragedy brought about by their son's neglect. "I speak to parents everywhere when I say that if in the pursuit of your own pleasures and occupations, you neglect your children, realize now, before it's too late, that this might have been *your* boy!" The irony of it all is that parental neglect wasn't so much responsible for Jimmy's criminal activities as was his unbelievable naivete. The movie's final cautionary note comes after the "end" title, an announcement that *I Accuse My Parents* will be shown to our armed forces overseas, a sure-fire morale killer if ever there was one.

Possibly for the same reasons that pornography novels and exploitation films like *Sex Madness* often opened or closed with some trumped up moral message that supposedly gave everything social redeeming value, many J.D. films contained long stretches of embarrassing moral diatribes, the action grinding to a halt, often in some courtroom, while somebody beat their gums.

Where Are Your Children? concluded with a probation officer asking: "What makes you think that the youth of the 'better families' are immune to these bad influences?" She goes on to explain how foolish it would be to lose our young people in our efforts to win the war. "And won't the Nazis make great use of such shortsightedness in our democracy?" (For some unknown reason this was the first Monogram film to have the distinction of playing the top half of a double bill in three Fox West Coast Theatres, held for four weeks in Chicago.) *The Devil on Wheels* (1947), as concerned with speed-demon parents as it was with their offspring, concluded with a repentent father sharing the blame for the death caused by his hotrodding son. Even more pointed was the revelation in *Dangerous Years* (1947) that the boy on trial (Billy Halop) was actually the prosecuting attorney's son, placed into an orphanage when he was a baby. (Shades of *Delinquent Parents*.)

Gun Crazy (1949) opened with a youngster (Russ Tamblyn) breaking into a shop to steal a much coveted handgun. Scurrying from the scene of his crime, the boy tripped, the gun sliding from his hands to the feet of a police officer. After a term in reform school and a stint in the army, he returned as a young adult (John Dall) with his obsession for firearms still strong. This fixation is largely responsible for his introduction to a thrill-seeking female carny sharpshooter (Peggy Cummins) who unfortunately does not share his reverence for life. Like Bonnie and Clyde the two embark on a life of crime, poignantly ending with the young man's shooting the woman (with whom he is deeply in love) to stop her from killing two of his old friends. Two years earlier John Dall was involved in another unhealthy relationship which also led to murder. In Alfred Hitchcock's *Rope* (1947), Dall and Farley Granger were two perverted college students who commit a murder for the thrill of it, similar to the real life Leopold-Loeb case. The two homosexuals invite several people to their apartment and use the trunk which houses their victim's body as a table for their guests to set their drinks.

Audie Murphy, the baby-faced soldier who emerged the most decorated soldier of WWII, made one of his first motion picture appearances in *Bad Boy*, also known as *The Story of Danny Lester* (1949).

On the run from the law are John Dall and Peggy Cummins, two Gun Crazy
(United Artists 1949) delinquents.

Murphy played the title role, a rebellious youth who is sent to a
rehabilitation ranch where Lloyd Nolan wins him over with kindness and
understanding.

Returning to the concept of slum-bred delinquents, *Knock on Any
Door* (1949) chronicled the life of Nick Romero (John Derek), a character
whose miserable life has caused him to adopt the philosophy "live fast,
die young, and have a good-looking corpse." A series of flashbacks
enables the audience to piece together Romero's traumatic childhood,

not the least of the tragic events being Romero's presence during the murder of his best friend during his stay in a reform school. Nick's petty crimes predict a sorry end until his love for the girl he eventually marries, Emma (Allene Roberts), gives him the desire to go straight. But he seems unable to hold a job and one night, after gambling away his paycheck, Emma tells him she is pregnant. Nick sees no alternative but to return to his thieving ways. Arrested for murder and on trial for his life, Nick pleads guilty to robbery but insists that he is innocent of killing a police officer. An unsympathetic District Attorney (George Macready) badgers the truth out of him by inquiring about the cause of Emma's death. Nick comes apart and admits that she committed suicide and he had shot the officer out of frustration. Nick's lawyer (Humphrey Bogart) is shocked by this revelation. He had believed in his client's innocence. In much the same way that Clarence Darrow had once defended Nathan Leopold and Richard Loeb, the lawyer shifts the spotlight away from the crime toward the causes leading to it. He tells the jurors that if slum conditions are allowed to continue, a knock on any door might find another Nick Romero. His plea for mercy falls on deaf ears. Nick is sentenced to death much to the relief of most of the movie critics who felt the character would have been a worthless bum no matter where he had been raised. Regardless, the film can be considered as a sort of trial run for director Nicholas Ray who six years later would make a juvenile delinquency drama that would eclipse all that went before it and shape most of what would come after.

1949 was also the year that Maxwell Shane completed his film version of Irving Shulman's novel about street gangs, *The Amboy Dukes*. Specifically, Shulman's story was about Frank Goldfarb (the last name changed to Cusak for the movie) who, embittered by his impoverished surroundings, sinks deeper and deeper into criminal life. A contributing cause is the lack of guidance from his parents who must both constantly work overtime just to make ends meet.

Frank and the gang spend most of their waking hours hanging around the local pool hall when they're not running errands for the small-time hoods who occasionally employ them. But during one of the rare occasions that Frank decided to attend school, he and his best friend, Benny Semmel, cause such a disturbance that the entire class is placed under suspension until they each bring one of their parents to the school. Fearing reprisal from their parents, Frank and Benny return later that afternoon to beg the teacher to give them a break. When he refuses the three of them get into a scuffle. The teacher is shot with Benny's zip gun and dies. As the police begin closing in the boys become distrustful of one another. Frank places an anonymous call to the police and names Benny as the murderer. But the lieutenant in charge of the case knows it's Frank on the other end of the phone and says, "You better come in, Frank. We want to talk to you too." Frank hurries back to his apartment, grabs a few things and attempts to make an escape from the rooftop. There he encounters "Crazy" Sachs, another member of the Dukes who had been waiting for a chance to get even with Frank for stealing his girl. Knowing that Frank has squealed, Crazy feels perfectly justified in hurling Frank over the edge of the roof. The last line of the novel describes Frank's fall, his body hitting the rail of the third-story fire escape, bouncing off in an arc toward the street, "screaming his life away."

To make Shulman's novel acceptable for the screen, Shane had to make several concessions which were, unfortunately, detrimental to the finished product. From the outset, the Breen office stated they could in no way approve of a story that concerned juveniles mixed up with raping 12-year-old girls, consorting with whores, performing brutal sex acts, smoking reefers and engaging in murder and vicious violence. So Shane bartered. The rape became a mild beating. The whores, the reefers, and the novel's strong language were eliminated. Frank's brutal death was changed to incarceration. The violence was toned down to such an extent that the Dukes emerged as only slightly more intimidating than the Dead End Kids. The film's title became *City Across the River*.

As a further note of placation, to prove the whole business had been "just a movie," each member of the cast portraying one of the Dukes was introduced to the audience. Years later, and for the same reason, the murderous little child in *The Bad Seed* (1956), Patty McCormack, would be spanked by Nancy Kelly as an epilogue to the movie.

But even this weak brew proved to be too strong for the PTA and other civic groups who were furious because of the sequence showing the students constructing zip guns in metal shop. Further outrage against the picture came after one high school teacher asked his students what they thought the message of the film was. The general consensus was that squealing was dishonorable. This was in spite of the picture's prologue in which Drew Pearson suggests that juvenile delinquency might be abolished by cleaning up the slums. Pearson's sentiments were similar, though much kinder, to the shop teacher in the film who remarked: "Sometimes I think the only solution is to clear out all the people and drop an atom bomb on that whole slum."

Whatever the merit or faults of *City Across the River*, it should be noted that it was slightly ahead of its time. The Dukes may have worn gabardine suits instead of black leather jackets but their speech had the sound and the picture had the feel of the sort of movie that would not be made for another six years. At last the focus was off the adults and on the delinquents as it would be in the films of the fifties, a decade in which the young people of the nation finally spoke so loudly that the adults could no longer ignore them.

Chapter Two

Brando, Dean and Daddy-O

"Teenagers — we never had 'em when I was a kid."
— From *Crybaby Killer*.

There was a rather shocking bit of business in Lippert's *For Men Only* (1952)* wherein a fraternity pledge was ordered to shoot a small dog as part of his initiation. The student refused and ended up dead. It was pretty strong stuff for its time but relatively tame when compared with the antics of the Black Rebels in Columbia's *The Wild One* (1954) just two years later. The days when a young man's only concern was to race his *Hot Rod* (1950) on an official track were but a memory. The precredits sequence in *The Wild One* — the tranquility of a quiet afternoon shattered by dozens of thundering motorcycles and their black-leather jacketed riders — was a dramatic metaphor illustrating the emergence of a teenage counter-culture. Teenage rebellion had moved out of the big city slums all the way into suburbia. Teenage crime was on the rise. What had happened to bring about the change? Well, a whole lot of threatening events had transpired since the Amboy Dukes violently protested their impoverished environment but one of the most significant contributing factors was that the Russians had their own atomic bomb.

The word hit Washington one August afternoon in the summer of 1949 and three weeks later it was public knowledge. The news was no less than terrifying to a nation just recovering from World War II. Suddenly the horror that had struck Hiroshima and Nagasaki five years before no longer seemed as distant. Government officials and scientists argued the practicality of a more powerful bomb, the hydrogen bomb, a trump card to hold against Russia. Most of the scientists were morally opposed to the idea. Then one of the physicists who had worked on the Los Alamos A-bomb project, Dr. Klaus Fuchs, admitted that he had been giving atomic secrets to the Soviet Union. That bit of information more or less put an end to further discussion. President Harry Truman ordered work on the H-bomb to begin immediately and on November 1, 1952, a couple of years after the "police action" in Korea began, the first one was exploded on an atol in the Pacific. The force was equivalent to five million

**The film was retitled* The Tall Lie *when it was discovered that female moviegoers were taking the original title too literally.*

tons of TNT, capable of starting fires for 300 square miles and causing damage to an area of 140 square miles. Radioactivity resulting from the bomb could lethally poison the atmosphere for years.

Even after the Korean War ended in a stalemate, the fear of communism lingered, and so the threat of annihilation. The American Communist Party, a recognized political party during the depths of the Depression, was branded with a subversive stigma that tainted anyone who had been remotely involved with the organization. The public became concerned that a network of communist agents were involved in some Kremlin-instigated master plan to undermine the American way of life from without and within. Seizing the opportunity to ride the public's paranoia all the way to the White House, Joseph McCarthy, a previously obscure senator from Wisconsin, launched a mighty battle against an enemy who, for all practical purposes, was not there. What his investigations did accomplish, besides furthering the mass paranoia, was to cast suspicion and distrust on intellectuals, integrationists, dissidents, "one world" pacifists, atheists, nonconformists, and liberals, and to ruin several lives in the process.

Rebellion against parents by their children is a natural, healthy way of youngsters establishing their own identities. But the impending threat of nuclear holocaust caused young people to dissociate themselves from the authority figures that had placed the entire world in jeopardy in a more aggressive manner than ever before. Like their Roaring Twenties counterparts, they began to dress differently, adopt a new vocablulary and indulge their own tastes for fast cars and fast music. The realization that there might be no tomorrow, however, took the edge off some of the fun which soured into hostility.

M-G-M's *Blackboard Jungle* and Warner's *Rebel Without a Cause*, both released in 1955, may have been the decade's two most demonstrative statements on the new youth culture, but *The Wild One* had a notable influence, evidenced by the countless imitations of Marlon Brando's character in the film, Johnny. In fact, Vic Morrow was criticized for copying Brando for his Artie West role in *Blackboard Jungle* although the actor may have been justified in doing so. Many real-life delinquents were doing the same.

Brando's Johnny was one of the movies' first antiheroes, at times reminiscent of the lonely wanderers who used to drift through western movies, often portrayed by John Wayne or Randolph Scott; the do-gooder who cleaned up the town then went riding off into the sunset without ever enjoying the fruits of his labors. Yet, unlike those concerned knights without armor, the lead character of *The Wild One* is contemptuous of or indifferent to the society in which he was born. Early in the film Johnny and his gang are relaxing in a tavern, he keeping time to a be-bop jazz record by tapping the jukebox like a percussion instrument. A local floozie reads the "Black Rebels" insignia on the back of his leather jacket and jokingly inquires what he is rebelling against. Johnny turns to her with a look of sullen disdain and replies, "What have you got?" This pretty much reflected the sentiment of the nation's young.

Donning their tight jeans and black leather jackets (the official costume of many a real-life delinquent), the Black Rebels appear more like the villains of those old westerns than heroes, but when contrasted to the "square" populace that constitute the town they invade, the bikers almost seem preferable. At least they are alive. They are not impotent like the sheriff. They do not put money ahead of their better judgment as do the businessmen of Wrightsville who see a quick buck to be made from the beer-guzzling cyclists. And because of this rather unfavorable portrait of middle-class America, coupled with the film's lack of a moral stand, many critics accused it of inspiring anarchy. The film's director, Laslo Benedek, dismissed such an idea. "On the contrary," he claimed, "incidents that happened were based on actual fact. Before writing the screenplay, John Paxton and I spent weeks in research." So did the producer, Stanley Kramer, who interviewed a number of actual gang members, much of their conversations used verbatim in the film.

Kramer pretty much functioned as America's liberal conscience during the fifties and sixties. He continually tackled controversial subjects including racism, isolationism, mental illness, and miscegenation in films like *Home of the Brave* (1949), *High Noon* (1952), *The Sniper* (1952), and *Guess Who's Coming to Dinner?* (1967). His usual tolerant, forgiving attitude may have fallen a little short when discussing the war crimes in *Judgment at Nuremberg* (1961), but no matter. He was one of the few outspoken liberal voices working within the largely conservative major studio structure. It is unfortunate that he was unable to alter his techniques to change with the times. His heavyhanded, liberal moralizing became as outdated as his middleaged liberal professor alienated by radical students in *R.P.M.* (1970). A quick review of his output leads one to conclude that he fared far better as a producer than he did as a director. At least such is true of *The Wild One*, which Kramer had no idea was going to cause such a ruckus.

The picture was based on an incident that occurred on July 4, 1947, in the small town of Hollister, California, fictionalized by Frank Rooney in "Cyclists' Raid," a short story that appeared in a 1951 *Harper's* magazine, told from the perspective of an intelligent, introspective hotel proprietor named Joel Bleeker. He is vaguely disturbed by the motorcycle gang's disciplined military precision. The cyclists think and act as one, further accentuated by the similarity of their clothing. As a former lieutenant-colonel during the war, Bleeker "had always hated the way men surrendered their individuality to attain perfection as a unit."

Bleeker takes the precaution of hiding his attractive 17-year-old daughter, Cathy, in her upstairs bedroom. Later Bleeker joins the group's leader, Simpson, for a drink in the hotel bar. The two men begin talking about the gang which Simpson describes as a constantly expanding unit encompassing the youth of America. "Our hope for the future." After a few beers the group becomes rowdy. Simpson tells Bleeker that although such a large and selective group must insist on discipline, it was equally necessary to "allow" a certain amount of relaxation. Bleeker soon learns the full implications of Simpson's remark.

Drunk and violent, the bikers embark on a destructive rampage through the town. Two of them come crashing through Bleeker's hotel doors astride their bikes. Cathy comes downstairs to investigate the noise and is run over and killed. Simpson quickly hurries his group away from the town.

Later, one lone, repentant member of the group returns to plead forgiveness. Bleeker flies into a blind rage and delivers a brutal beating to the boy. By the time he has returned to his senses and a doctor is treating the injured boy, Bleeker finds that his grief for his dead daughter is compounded by an inner loathing for his own capacity for violence.

There was no equivalent of the Bleeker character in Paxton's screenplay. Although the townspeople eventually erupt into violence, there is no evidence of one of them suffering any inner turmoil over the experience. The introspection of Rooney's story was transformed into cinematic action. The neofascist regimentation of Simpson's group was replaced by a more sporadic gang of bikers, their leader an inarticulate rebel. Cathy is elevated from a victim to one of the central characters. Played by Mary Murphy, Cathy is a waitress and it is through the sequences between her and Johnny that the audience is given some key to understanding the biker's mystique. Cathy is hypnotically drawn to Johnny and his unconventional "we just gotta go" lifestyle, refreshingly intoxicating when compared to her own mundane existence.

The film begins with a series of seemingly scattered thoughts narrated off-screen by Johnny. His tone is portentous, referring to "the trouble" and "the girl," which evolve as the two significant elements of the story. His admission, "I was just going with it" suggests that both elements were out of his control instead of being an attempt to absolve himself of blame. Johnny rarely instigates anything. He merely reacts. When, at the end of the story, Johnny rides back into town alone, he has taken his first step toward controlling his life.

After the opening credits, Johnny and his gang encounter a motorcycle meet where "recognized" clubs compete in races. The Black Rebels disrupt the event, establishing themselves immediately as outsiders, contemptuous of organized standards of behavior, instinctively rejecting the society that will not accept them. However, before riding away, the Black Rebels steal a symbol of society, the second place trophy, which they award to Johnny. By mounting the stolen object on his handlebars, Johnny openly defies convention. But by accepting the award in the first place (feeling he would have won it had he been allowed to participate in the contest), Johnny acknowledges a recognition of society's values. And this dualistic attitude towards acceptance and rejection follows the character throughout the film.

The Black Rebels' next stop is the quiet, rural town of Wrightsville (a name surely intended as a pun). Soaking up suds at the local tavern, the gang take over the place and soon are aware of the local police officers' inability to interfere with their reveries. While racing for beers, one of the bikers breaks his leg, extending their stay to allow time for his recovery. Later, a member of a rival motorcycle gang (Lee Marvin) is

arrested, events that seem to conspire to keep them in town until the situation can grow out of control.

Meanwhile, Johnny encounters Cathy, a pert, wholesome waitress working in the coffee shop which adjoins the tavern. Their relationship initially stems from the attraction of opposites. In one of their first scenes together, it appears as if they are not even speaking the same language, with Johnny attempting to explain his philosophy in an early example of "jive" talk.

> *Cathy:* Where are you going when you leave here? Don't you know?
> *Johnny:* (bored) Oh, man, we're just gonna go.
> *Cathy:* (defensively) Just trying to make conversation. It means nothing to me.
> *Johnny:* Well, on weekends we just go out and have a ball.
> *Cathy:* (interested) What do you do? I mean, do you just ride around or do you go on some sort of picnic or something?
> *Johnny:* (incredulously) A picnic? Man, you are too square. I have to straighten you out. Now, listen. You don't go any one special place — that's cornball style. You just go. (Snaps his fingers.) A bunch of us get together after all week and it builds up. The idea is to have a ball. Now, if you're gonna stay cool, you've got to wail. You gotta put something down. You gotta make some jive. Don't you know what I'm talking about?
> *Cathy:* Yeah. Yeah. I know what you mean.
> *Johnny:* Well, that's all I'm saying.
> *Cathy:* My father was going to take me on a fishing trip to Canada once.
> *Johnny:* (pause) Yeah?
> *Cathy:* We didn't go.
> *Johnny:* Crazy.

Later, Johnny offers her the pilfered trophy as an expression of his feeling for her. Clearly, she is more than just another potential sexual conquest but as a symbol, Cathy is everything that the Black Rebels ride to escape from. Johnny's conflict of feelings cause him to fluctuate, alienating and rejecting her while at the same time he is drawn to her.

Cathy initially declines Johnny's gift. She too is both attracted and repelled. To her Johnny symbolizes freedom from her repressed lifestyle, the stranger in her dreams who would one day drive into town, order coffee and take her away with him, and to a place in her mind further away than Canada. But Johnny cannot be molded into her dream, for she is not seeking freedom so much as she is trying to exchange one limited, but secure lifestyle for something similar, but somehow different. So she reacts to Johnny with anger. "You've impressed everybody now, big motorcycle racer," she tells Johnny, referring to the trophy. "Why don't you take that back so they can give it to somebody who really won it." Both Cathy and Johnny are adept at puncturing the hypocrisies of each others' lifestyles without acknowledging their own.

That night Johnny rescues Cathy from the bikers who attempt to gang rape her. Riding away on the back of Johnny's motorcycle, Cathy

---

Marlon Brando and the gang from The Wild One (Columbia 1954).

feels the sexual exhilaration of speed and freedom. When they stop at a deserted park, Cathy takes the initiative, asking Johnny if he still wants to give her the trophy. His brutish attempts at affection frighten and anger her once again and it is apparent that the two can find no middle-ground on which they can relate. "The girl" runs away while back in town "the trouble" explodes.

Cathy's father (Robert Keith) is the town's sheriff, an ineffectual man seeking to avoid confrontation with the gang. The local businessmen have also been placating the Black Rebels as they have been spending a lot of money. But with the coming of nightfall, the bikers are drunk, rest-less and bored. They disconnect the telephone lines then go on a destruc-tive rampage through the town's business section. Since the bikers' presence is no longer profitable, the businessmen transform into an angry, vigilante mob. Their first target is Johnny whom they capture as he tries to follow Cathy from the park. They subject him to a brutal beating until Cathy's father summons the courage to intervene. Johnny attempts to escape from the town but is cut off by still another group of townspeople. Someone hurls a tire iron at him. It hits Johnny on the back of his head. His motorcycle goes out of control, striking and killing an old man. By the time Johnny regains his senses the mob is accusing him of murder. At this point a county sheriff (Jay C. Flippen) and his men arrive. They disperse the mob, round up the gang, and restore order.

Johnny is held in jail on manslaughter charges. Cathy is instrumen-tal in convincing one of the witnesses to the event to admit the accident was caused by the thrown tire iron. Johnny and the others are released and given a stern warning that they will all be thrown in the cooler for good if any one of them returns to the county.

Time passes. The town returns to its sleepy existence. In the coffee shop Cathy hears the familiar roar of a lone motorcycle. Johnny enters, takes a chair, but finds himself unable to express his feelings so he places his trophy down on the counter and smiles. Cathy returns the smile. Realizing they can never fulfill each others' needs, the two have at least achieved a mutual respect. Johnny exits the coffee shop and rides out of town for the last time.

It might be interesting to note that before *The Wild One* was even in release it was the recipient of adverse reactions. Kramer's original inten-tion had been to show the intolerance of middle America to anyone who varied from the public norm, a concept too radical for the censors to ac-cept. Emphasis was, instead, shifted to the violence of the gang, and at-tempts to justify their attitude were blunted. The hypocrisies of the businessmen were downplayed. Even diluted, the film was hardly designed to endear itself to the family audience. Harry Cohn, the dic-tatorial head of Columbia Pictures, reportedly hated the picture but released it on the basis of Kramer's and Brando's track records. It was banned in the United Kingdom for 14 years out of fear that it might incite violence and inspire delinquency. At home, many national magazines and newspapers panned the picture on moral grounds, seldom attempting an objective, critical evaluation.

Whatever other criticisms might have been hurled at the picture, *The Wild One* could not be accused of being the catalyst for other motorcycle dramas. There were but one or two until the release of *The Wild Angels* over ten years later. It should also be noted that with the exception of AIP's *Motorcycle Gang* (1957) biker films in general never dealt with juveniles. The gangs were always comprised of members well into their twenties, often in their thirties. But because the genre expressed the rebellious attitudes of the younger generation, they are usually thought of as *juvenile* delinquent stories.

Far more accurately, *The Wild One* conveyed the sentiments of a breed of bohemians that came to be known as the Beat Generation, a disenchanted group of dropouts who hung around coffee houses smoking marijuana, listening to jazz and freeform poetry. The bearded men in their khaki pants and sandals, and the women in black leotards wearing too much eye shadow were immortalized in Jack Kerouac's novel *On the Road*, written in three weeks. Allen Ginsberg, Gregory Corso, and Kenneth Rexroth were some of the others who put the "beatnik" philosophy on paper. Hollywood attempted to cash in on the topicality of the event — *The Rebel Set, The Beat Generation* (both 1959), *The Subterraneans* (1960) — without even a token effort to explain it. Most of these pictures were simple crime dramas with beatnik characters peripheral to the plot. One such silly effort had *Get Smart's* Ed Platt disguised as a beatnik to escape police detection. He then recruits some of the embittered patrons of the espresso joint he owns to join him in a major crime. Only *Bucket of Blood* (1959), a satire written by ex-beatnik Charles B. Griffith and directed by Roger Corman in five days, seemed to capture a little of what Kerouac had talked about in his novel.

The violence depicted in *The Wild One* turned out to be little more than a primer to the potential threat portended in *Blackboard Jungle*. Based on Evan Hunter's sensational novel of one teacher's war with his classroom of young criminals, the story was no less sensational when it was transferred to the screen, a task completed in three quick months from the moment producer Pandro Berman laid his eyes on the book. As an illustration of cultural upheaval, the film contained a sequence that rivalled the opening of Kramer's picture. School teacher Richard Kiley attempts to communicate with his students by playing for them his prized collection of swing records. His students don't want to hear Bix Beiderbecke. While the soundtrack throbs to the beat of a new sound, rock-and-roll, the kids make quick work of Kiley's music, leaving him alone to search through the pieces of the broken 78's, shattered memories of a once popular culture.

Blackboard Jungle was the first major motion picture to use a rock-and-roll musical soundtrack. It introduced a song that would become the national anthem for teenagers, "Rock Around the Clock." Sung by Bill Haley and the Comets, the recording would disrupt the entire record industry by being the first of its type to occupy the "Hit Parade" for 15 weeks. The music, later dubbed "rock 'n' roll," was the illegitimate

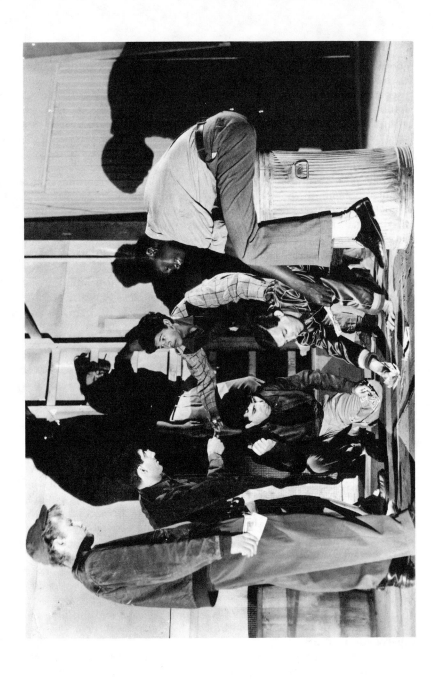

offspring of white country music and black rhythm and blues. With the release of *Blackboard Jungle* the music and juvenile delinquency became inseparable bedfellows. Many people were firmly convinced that the music actually caused delinquency.

M-G-M executives could not possibly have anticipated the antagonism that the picture would suffer from critics and the public alike. True, the project had met with some mild opposition from the censors who were not happy about words like "dago" and "nigger" in the script, or lines like the one spoken by a teacher about how a prostitute makes more money than they do. Writer-director Richard Brooks refused to insert a line of dialogue about the juvenile delinquency problem being much worse in Russia. But some compromises were made. Much of the novel's offensive language and violence were deleted which was all censor Geoffrey Shurlock felt he could ask for lest it be suggested that the board frowned upon movies that tackled contemporary problems. However, cognizant of the touchy nature of their subject, it might have behooved the studio to exploit the picture in a less sensational manner. The ads for *The Wild One* avoided references to motorcycles or gangs, containing instead nondescript catch-lines like "That 'Streetcar' Man Has A New Desire." But *Blackboard Jungle* boldly announced "A drama of teen-age terror! They turned a school into a jungle!" Of course, the picture delivered exactly what those advertisements promised.

Idealistic Richard Dadier (Glenn Ford) accepts a teaching position at a large city vocational training school. He has heard about the school's discipline problem and asks the principal, Mr. Warneke (John Hoyt) about it. Warneke becomes angry and flatly denies any problem. Dadier quickly learns that his job is more that of a warden than an English teacher. His pupils are all potential hoodlums, disruptive, ignorant, indifferent, and hostile. The school is little more than a dumping ground designed to retain the youngsters until they reach legal age. The veteran teachers are either ineffectual, cynical, or blind to the problem; satisfied to process the students through the system with little pretense of actually teaching.

During the first day of class, Dadier's pupils derive an inordinate amount of pleasure from calling him "Daddy-O." He forces himself to laugh along with them then starts to write his name on the blackboard to set them all straight. A baseball zings past his head, taking a large chunk of the board with it. Hefting the ball, looking with awe at the room full of unsympathetic faces, Dadier wins a minor victory by not losing his cool. Instead of delivering a lecture he simply tells his class that whoever threw the ball would never pitch for the Yanks. But when one of the students attempts to rape one of the female teachers (Margaret Hayes), Dadier explodes. He chases the student who tries to leap through a win-

---

Vic Morrow (left), Sidney Poitier (right), hanging out in Blackboard Jungle (M-G-M 1955).

dow. He is badly injured by the broken glass but the students think the damage was done by Dadier which creates a further division between him and his class.

"Don't be a hero and never turn your back to the class," advises Jim Murdock (Louis Calhern), an embittered fellow teacher who thinks of the whole school as one giant garbage can. And Dadier begins to agree with him. After being mugged and his pregnant wife (Anne Francis) unnerved by a series of nasty notes and phone calls, he is ready to resign. He is offered a more tempting position at another school where the students are well-mannered and eager to learn. But he cannot accept his failure. The real test of his ability waits for him back at Mr. Warneke's horror high.

Dadier is aware that every class has at least one leader and his class contains two. One is Artie West (Vic Morrow), a bigoted bully. The other is Gregory Miller (Sidney Poitier), a quiet and sensitive youth with a better-than-average I.Q. Miller plans to quit school at the end of the year and predicts that Dadier will do the same. Dadier proposes a pact whereby neither of them will quit. The teacher asks Miller to help him lead the others away from the path of abysmal ignorance toward the more productive road to knowledge. With Miller's help, Dadier manages a small breakthrough by getting his students to discuss the morality of a cartoon short, "Jack and the Beanstalk." This hint of interest terrifies Artie who quickly steps up his campaign to send Dadier packing by driving the teacher's wife to a nervous breakdown. Dadier eventually confronts Artie with his suspicions about the notes and phone calls to his wife. Artie pulls a knife. Miller warns Artie's gang to stay out of the duel or risk more trouble than they can handle. Without the support of his gang Artie's cowardice is revealed. Dadier tells the others that there's no place in the classroom for troublemakers like Artie. The film ends with Dadier marching the delinquent to the principal's office with the full approval of the others.

"We educators who have previewed the picture have been disturbed by the picture's exaggeration and its probable effects upon the public attitude toward the students and teachers," wrote Edward N. Wallen, the principal of a vocational and technical high school in the Bronx. His feelings were shared by Superintendent C. Frederick Pertsch who insisted that the film constituted "a grave disservice" to the nation's youth by "misrepresenting and sensationalizing the situation." Columnist Hedda Hopper said it was the most brutal film she had ever seen and was convinced it would frighten many would-be teachers away from the profession as well as giving delinquents "new ideas about how far they can go." Desperate M-G-M executives tried to counter charges that the film gave a distorted account by reprinting the following newspaper articles:

Vic Morrow, with Switchblade, tries to give teacher Glenn Ford a lesson, in Blackboard Jungle (M-G-M 1955).

New York City — "Brutal Murder by Three Youths Baffles Everyone Involved."

Los Angeles — "Youth Beats Up Teacher in Class." The teacher,
who reprimanded a 16-year-old student for creating a disturbance, suffered fractures of the nose and cheekbone.

Washington, D.C. — 14 year old arrested on 14 counts of robbing
his fellow junior high students.

San Francisco — a battle between two gangs resulted in two dead,
three wounded and one boy sent to prison for life.

Another juvenile crime was committed the day prior to the opening
of the picture in New York. A high school teacher was stabbed to death
by a student in the Bronx. U.S. Ambassador Clare Booth Luce threatened
to leave Venice and "cause the greatest scandal in motion picture history"
unless *Blackboard Jungle* was withdrawn from the Venice Film Festival.
Arthur Hornblow told reporters that Miss Luce had merely said she
would not attend the showing. Whatever the truth, the film was pulled
and *The Kentuckian* (1955) was substituted. This action caused one
weary reviewer to defend *Blackboard Jungle* on the grounds that, by the
very fact it could be made, the picture was a testament to a country's
greatness while *The Kentuckian* was more a testament to its silliness.

A high school teacher by the name of Rose Zeitlin spoke favorably of
the picture. "Take it from a teacher whose experience has been fairly fortunate," she wrote, "the film may be sensational, but it is hardly possible
to exaggerate the conditions in the public high schools of this and
presumably other cities across the country." Another champion of the
picture was Hazel Flynn whose column appeared in *Daily News Life*.
She felt it was time everyone "woke up" to what was really going on
among a certain slice of the nation's youth.

But mounting protests all but forced M-G-M to make special trailers
to be run at the conclusion of the picture, an example of which goes:

> To our patrons: the school and situations you have just seen are not to be
> found in this area! We should all be proud of the facilities provided for
> our youth by the public schools of New Brunswick and the Middlesex
> County vocation and technical high school. We suggest a visit to any of
> the fine schools in our city and county. You will be cordially welcome.

The above foolishness was in addition to the prologue already
spliced ahead of the credits, which stated that all the scenes and events
depicted in the film were fictional and that the United States was fortunate to have a school system that was a tribute to its faith in youth.

Still the picture was chastised. *Los Angeles Times* columnist Phillip
Scheuer wrote a scathing review of the film which suggested that it might
damage our cause in foreign countries, "particularly if it ever fell into
Communist hands." Directly beneath Scheuer's tirade was a small four-
liner about director Nicholas Ray who had been conducting tests of
young actors for his movie *Rebel Without a Cause*.

While many found *The Wild One* disturbing, motorcycle gangs
existed outside mainstream society and, as such, were an isolated
phenomenon. Similarly, *Blackboard Jungle* restricted its activities to an

inner-urban area, something unique to larger cities. *Rebel Without a Cause* took these themes away from such peripheral areas and set them down on the doorsteps of middle-class America. The problem was no longer some unknown gang member on some distant tenement street. The problem was the stranger in your own home. More importantly, the film took that stranger's point of view.

The story centered on Jim Stark (James Dean), a high school student whose middle-class parents were forced to move to a new city after his seemingly unprovoked acts of violence. On his first day at the new school Jim attracts the attention of Buzz (Corey Allen), the leader of a group of toughs. Buzz challenges him to a "chickie run," in which stolen cars are driven toward the edge of a cliff, the first one to jump out branded "chicken." Jim reluctantly participates, leaping from his vehicle at the last possible moment. Buzz fails to get out in time and plunges to his death. Jim, Buzz's girl friend Judy (Natalie Wood), and a neurotic teenager nicknamed Plato (Sal Mineo), return to their respective homes where their parent's lack of understanding drives them back into the night. Meeting at a deserted mansion, Jim, Judy, and Plato are threatened by Buzz's gang who are fearful that Jim will reveal their participation in the accident to the police. Plato shoots one of the punks with his handgun just as the police arrive to investigate the disturbance. Plato flees to a nearby planetarium with Jim and Judy chasing after him. Jim secretly removes the clip from Plato's gun then convinces him to give himself up to the police who have surrounded the building. On the planetarium's front steps, Plato becomes frightened by the abundance of lights trained on him and panics. He attempts to run but is gunned down by the police who are unaware that the gun he is brandishing isn't loaded. Jim's parents have witnessed his futile attempt to save the other boy. As the film closes there is an indication that both he and they have come to a better understanding of each other.

The genesis of *Rebel Without a Cause* began more than ten years prior to its making. In 1944 Dr. Robert M. Lindner published a book under that title, a case history of a psychologically disturbed young delinquent who Lindner had treated at a federal penetentiary. Warner Brothers purchased the screen rights to the book in 1947. Marlon Brando was optioned for the lead role on the basis of his stage success in *A Streetcar Named Desire*. The studio took the project no further. Brando eventually made his screen debut in Stanley Kramer's *The Men* (1950). Meanwhile, the studio held onto the rights to Lindner's book.

In the summer of 1954 director Nicholas Ray informed a Warner's executive, Lew Wasserman, that he was interested in making a film dealing with juvenile delinquency. Ray had previously directed another film on the subject, *Knock on Any Door* and had built a reputation on off-beat dramas like *They Live by Night* (1949), *In a Lonely Place* (1950), and *Johnny Guitar* (1954). Wasserman suggested Lindner's book (which had been gathering dust for seven years on the studio's shelf) as a possible property. Ray had his own treatment in mind, based on his own research conducted in local juvenile halls. The title of his treatment, *Blind Run,* was taken from a proposed sequence in which two teenagers play "chicken" by driving towards each other in a dark tunnel. Eventually, it was decided that only the title of Lindner's book would be retained and a new screenplay would be developed from Ray's own ideas.

Clifford Odets, a personal friend of Ray's, was the director's first choice to write the script. The studio insisted on Leon Uris, author of *Battle Cry* and *Exodus*. Artistic and personal differences soon arose between Uris and Ray so Irving Shulman, who had authored the novel *The Amboy Dukes*, was called in. Shulman was responsible for setting the story in middle-class suburbia and the development of the story's basic structure. The "chickie run" sequence replaced Ray's "Blind Run" after several local newspapers reported a similar event that had ended in tragedy. Shulman also found it difficult to work with Ray and left the project before the year's end. Leonard Rosenman, who would eventually write the musical score for the film, suggested Stewart Stern, a young writer with only one minor film credit, as a replacement for Shulman. He proved to be a good choice for he worked well with Ray and the final screenplay was completed in the first months of 1955.

James Dean was Nicholas Ray's choice for the lead role from the beginning. Earlier in his career, Dean had tried unsuccessfully to break into films, finding only bit parts in *Sailor Beware*, *Fixed Bayonets* (both in 1951), and *Has Anybody Seen My Gal?* (1952). Following the advice given him by actor James Whitmore, Dean left for New York to study at the Actor's Studio and eventually established himself in a handful of volatile performances in Broadway plays and live television dramas. Elia Kazan, who had previously directed some of Marlon Brando's most successful pictures, saw Dean on stage in New York and signed him for the role of Cal in his adaption of John Steinbeck's novel *East of Eden*. Despite second billing below Julie Harris, the film was an ideal showcase for Dean's talents, earning him the first of two posthumous Academy Award nominations.

Having seen Dean's work in Kazan's film, Nicholas Ray immediately sought him for *Rebel Without a Cause*. Although *East of Eden* had not yet been released, Dean was considered a "hot" property so Ray followed him to New York where he convinced him to accept the part without even seeing a completed script. Fortunately, *Giant* (1956), which had been scheduled to begin filming in April, and for which Dean had been signed, had been postponed until June due to Elizabeth Taylor's pregnancy. Dean and Ray returned to Hollywood for final preparations on *Rebel*.

During rehearsals, the primarily young cast was encouraged to experiment and improvise within the framework of the script. Scenes were altered or omitted, depending on the creative input the director received. This created an infectious communal feeling towards the film as well as the improvisational quality giving the final product a spontaneous emotional urgency that was well suited to the subject matter.

Ray also imbued the film with a sense of authenticity by employing actors who were playing roles close to their actual age. The lead female part of Judy was given to former child actress Natalie Wood who was 16 years old at the time. The demanding role of Plato was played by the diminutive Sal Mineo, looking younger than his scant 16 years. The other teenage roles were taken by unknown teenage actors, Nick Adams and Dennis Hopper among them. Only the casting of 24-year-old James Dean followed the Hollywood tradition of placing older actors in teenage parts.

Principal shooting on *Rebel* began late in March of 1955 amid apprehension among Warner executives who were concerned about the subject matter. Ten days into filming the front office threatened to shut the production down. Ray offered to purchase the rights and continue on his own. After viewing the rushes, the studio gave him the go ahead. Two days later the director was summoned to the front office again and told to scrap the black and white footage already shot and begin again in Warner-Color and CinemaScope. This new found faith in the project may be attributed to two factors. *East of Eden* had just been released in early April and Dean was proving to be a critical and popular success. Also, the similar themed *Blackboard Jungle* was showing a profit for M-G-M since its release the month before. Whatever the reasons, *Rebel Without a Cause* was promoted from a vehicle for its new young star to a more respectable "A" picture.

In the original black and white footage, the movie opened with a typical middle-class adult returning home late at night, loaded with presents for his family. The man is intercepted by Buzz and his friends who work the man over, causing him to drop his packages as he runs for the safety of his home. Buzz and the gang split. A few second later a drunken Jim Stark comes staggering along, discovers the mechanical toy monkey which the man had dropped, and lies down on the pavement next to it as the police sirens approach. Possibly feeling that the violence of the sequence was too strong to appear so early in the proceedings, the released color version begins with Jim's entrance, the explanation for the presence of the toy monkey or a later reference to "that beating on 12th street" is never made clear.

After the credits roll Stark is taken to the police station's juvenile division. While waiting for his parents to arrive, Jim notices two other teenagers who will figure prominently in the events yet to happen; Judy, a girl detained for wandering the streets after curfew, and Plato, who for no apparent reason shot some puppies. All three are eventually released to the custody of their parents (or guardians), although it is obvious that this visit to juvenile hall has succeeded in doing little more than keeping them off the streets for one night.

Within this sequence the dividing lines between the teenagers and the adult authorities (which include their parents as well as the police) are immediate drawn. Suburban parents verge on caricature, totally ineffectual or oblivious to their children's needs. Jim's father (Jim Backus) is a failure at everything except making money. He emerges an impotent figure, dominated by an emasculating wife (Ann Doran) and a meddlesome mother-in-law. Judy's father (William Hopper) refuses to return her need for affection, instinctively rejecting his daughter's blooming sexuality, while her mother (Rochelle Hudson) offers little comfort or

guidance beyond platitudes about growing up. Plato is the product of a broken home, both parents having deserted him to pursue nonfamily pleasures while regularly sending generous checks for his support to a caring but inadequate governess. While these inept parental figures veer perilously close to parody, this media image provided a welcome insight in the days of *Father Knows Best*.

The other adult authority figures are equally ill-equipped to cope with their young charges. A teacher abandons the pretense of discipline during a field trip to the observatory where the kids suffer the prophecies of doom from an elderly lecturer. The teenagers mock a security guard with Nazi salutes and derision and he seems powerless to stop them. The police are a faceless entity, continually arriving at the scenes of violence a day late and a dollar short. And when they do finally arrive their feeble efforts are aimed only at the sick and frightened Plato who one of the officers refers to in such enlightened terms as a "Cookooboo." Another officer, on the trigger happy side, almost shoots Jim as he races into the planetarium to help Plato. The fact that Plato is killed is no more shocking than the fact that there is no indication that the teenagers whose violence motivated his actions will ever be taken into custody.

The one exception to this rule is Ray Framek (Edward Platt), an officer at juvenile hall. Tough enough to command Jim's respect yet compassionate enough to be genuinely concerned about his feelings, Framek embodies the perfect father figure. His understanding leads Jim to confess his self image as an outsider. "If I didn't have one day when I didn't have to feel all confused and didn't have to feel that I was ashamed of everything...," Jim explains, "... if I felt I belonged somewhere, you know." Framek *does* know and tells Jim, "If the kettle starts boiling again, will you come and see me before you get yourself in a jam. Even if you just want to come in and shoot the breeze. It's easier sometimes than talking with your parents. Anytime night or day." However sincere his intentions, Framek is on another assignment when Jim needs him the most. Although this may seem a dramatic necessity (for if Jim had talked with Framek the events which would ultimately lead to tragedy may have been averted), Framek's absence illustrates that, despite the altruistic intentions and extraordinary dedication of an outsider, he or she is no substitute for parental understanding or guidance.

For the most part, the teenagers protect themselves behind a guise of toughness and indifference. Even Plato, whose pain and vulnerability are immediately obvious, initially rejects Jim's offer of his jacket to keep him warm. Judy rebukes Jim's initial contact, referring to him as a "real yo-yo" and a "new disease." She tells Jim "I go with the kids," preferring the protective anonymity of the gang. Buzz guarantees a confrontation with his potential rival by slashing Jim's tires and challenging him to a series of duels. The other members of the gang jockey for rank and position by

---

British censors scissored this scene with James Dean in Rebel Without a Cause (Warner 1955).

putting each other and everyone else down. Even a relatively "straight" art student severely admonishes Jim for accidentally stepping on the school symbol. The teenage society is comprised of cliques, each with their own language, rules, and social mandates that one must follow in order to belong. Even Jim, desperately craving to be a part of some kind of family, hides behind an indifferent facade, telling Plato that he doesn't want to make friends.

Plato seems the most unstable of the group, yet he is the first to deal honestly with his feelings. He begins almost to worship Jim once he senses his sincerity. Before the "chickie run," Judy lets her guard down a bit and questions Plato about his "friend," obviously attracted to Jim for much the same reason that Plato was. Even Buzz breaks down the barriers while engaging in some existentialist philosophy with Jim as they stand on the edge of the cliff they are about to drive towards.

"'That's the edge,' Buzz chuckles. 'That's the end.'

"'Yeah,' Jim responds. 'It certainly is.'

"Buzz takes a puff from Jim's cigarette. 'Know something? I like you. You know that?'

"'Why do we do this?'

"'Well,' Buzz shrugs, 'you gotta do something now, don't you?'"

Like Brando's disjointed dissertation in *The Wild One*, Buzz's rationale for this rite of passage expresses everything while explaining nothing. It is the conviction with which the characters act which make their beliefs real and urgent. Even as Buzz expresses his feelings for Jim, the forces that brought them to the test cannot be stopped. Perhaps, after the ritual, Buzz and Jim could have dissolved their rivalry in mutual respect. This, however, is not to be. For even though they both leap from their respective cars at approximately the same moment, Buzz catches his jacket's arm on the door handle which prevents his escape. Buzz's death destroys any chance Jim had of being accepted by the gang; they hold him responsible. The gang disperses, leaving Judy behind. For a moment she contemplates joining Buzz but Jim reaches for her and the touch of his hand brings her away from the cliff's edge. It is at this moment that Jim has unwittingly "won" Judy from his vanquished rival. Her ties with Buzz and the other kids have been severed. Her hardedged facade swiftly dissolves.

Later that night Jim confesses to Judy his earlier attraction to her. She apologizes for her behavior. "You shouldn't believe what I say when I'm with the rest of the kids," she tells him. "Nobody is sincere." His honesty permits her to express her real feelings for the first time. They have nothing left but each other. They flee to a deserted mansion which Plato had pointed out earlier.

Shortly after they arrive, Plato appears to warn them that the others are searching for Jim. Then, feeling secure in their sanctuary, Plato assumes the role of guide while Judy and Jim pretend that they are newlyweds. Ensconced in their own private world, they form their own family unit with Jim and Judy as the parents and Plato their child. As the evening wears on Plato contentedly drifts into sleep. Jim and Judy cover

The reception committee for
the new kid on the block!

JAMES DEAN

The overnight sensation of 'East of Eden'

Warner Bros. put
all the force of
the screen
into a challenging
drama of today's
juvenile violence!

'REBEL WITHOUT A CAUSE'

CINEMASCOPE
WARNERCOLOR

...and they both come
from 'good' families!

NATALIE WOOD SAL MINEO

James Dean as Jim Stark in Rebel Without a Cause (1955), became an eternal
symbol of alienated youth. The movie was released less than a month after the
young actor's untimely death.

him with a blanket and wander off to explore other rooms in the house. When Plato awakens he finds himself surrounded by Buzz's gang who have traced Jim's car to the mansion. Plato makes good an escape, shooting one of the boys with his handgun. By the time Jim decides to investigate Plato is in a state of hysteria. Jim can do nothing to stop him from running away to the nearby planetarium. Jim manages to make his way inside where he attempts to regain Plato's trust. But the frightened youth is suspicious and petulant. Once again Jim offers him his jacket to keep warm. Plato accepts it. Jim asks to see his gun for a moment and surreptitiously removes the clip before returning it. Jim then guides Plato safely outside to the waiting authorities. At the last minute Plato panics and breaks into a run. Jim makes a desperate attempt to stop him but cannot. The police open fire and Plato falls dead.

The last sequence of the film, with Jim and his parents reaching a new understanding, has been criticized as a concession towards a Hollywood happy ending. It certainly strains credibility to believe Jim's parents should emerge from the events with any more insight or strength than they had already displayed. Jim, however, has failed in his own brief experience at being a father, if only a surrogate one, and this recognition may have allowed him to better understand his own parents' shortcomings.

In the last scene of the film the camera pulls back as the characters depart. One lone figure arrives in the predawn light, walking up the steps of the planetarium. The figure has been identified as director Nicholas Ray. His appearance, signifying the beginning of a new day, serves to remind the audience how little of the story's time frame has elapsed, approximately thirty hours.

Principal photography was completed late in May of 1955. Four days later, James Dean was on his way to Texas to join the location unit for *Giant*. From June to late September, Dean appeared in the coveted role of Edna Ferber's fictional oil tycoon, Jett Rink. A clause in Dean's contract prevented him from indulging in his new passion for race car driving until completion of his part. After his final scene, filmed on the Warner's lot, Dean and a friend departed for a weekend race at Salinas. By 6:00 that evening James Dean was dead. His neck had been broken upon impact when his lightweight racing car, speeding up the inland route, collided with another vehicle outside Paso Robles, California.

Even though newspapers carried the story of his death, the public's exposure to Dean had been limited. There was considerable pessimism at Warner Brothers concerning Dean's yet-to-be-released films, *Rebel Without a Cause* and *Giant*. (*East of Eden* had been released five months earlier.) The deaths of other actors had spelled disaster for their posthumous releases. "Nobody will come to see a corpse," Jack Warner reportedly stated.

In late October, less than a month after the accident, *Rebel Without a Cause* was released to theatres across the nation. In a remarkable turn of events, predated only by the hysterical public reaction following the death of Rudolph Valentino, the movie became a wild success and Dean was hailed as a major star. *Giant* was released more than a year after his death. By that time he had become a cult figure of almost mythical proportions. He had metamorphosed from an image on film into an eternal symbol of alienated youth. Dean would never grow old or disappoint his fans by appearing in listless productions ill-suited to his talents as other former "rebels" eventually did. His three starring films continue to be shown on television and play to appreciative audiences in revival theatres more than a quarter of a century after his death.

Of the three films, James Dean continues to be most closely associated with his role in *Rebel* although his performances in *Giant* and *East of Eden* are similar. The setting for the latter film was a rural farm community during World War I which created a distance in time and space, separating the character from contemporary audiences. Dean's role was secondary, left off-screen for long periods of time. Despite the deck being stacked against him, Dean manages to evoke some sympathy, reinforcing the belief that he may have been capable of more versatile roles.

In *Rebel Without a Cause* the man and the myth become fused into a single identity. As Jim Stark, Dean became the ultimate reflection of the emerging youth culture. His untimely death merely solidified this image, a rite of passage similar to the "chickie run," in which Jim Stark survives while James Dean did not. If his goal had been to "live fast, die young, and leave a good looking corpse," then he certainly succeeded on all three counts, both personally and professionally. More importantly, he left a cinematic legacy for each successive generation of young "rebels."

Chapter Three

Smorgasbord

"Lord knows I'll never make an Academy Award movie, but then I am just as happy to get my achievement plaques from the bank every year."
— Sam Katzman, motion picture producer.

"When we made these pictures I assure you that the farthest thought from our minds was that they'd wind up in a museum."—Samuel Z. Arkoff, V.P. of American-International.

"What the kids of today want to see is a dramatic solution to their own problems, enacted by players of an age in which they can relate."—Albert Zugsmith, motion picture producer-director.

It appears that most movie producers in Hollywood are eager to be the first to be second. That is to say that once the foundation has been laid by the creative few, the architects of imitation rush forward, usually carrying rotten timber. So it is hardly one for Ripley that once *Blackboard Jungle* and *Rebel Without a Cause* began turning a profit, filmmakers focused their attention to the genre. From 1956 to the mid-sixties the J.D. film enjoyed its most prolific period.

First to cross the finish line in second place was "Jungle" Sam Katzman, so named for his "Jungle Jim" series of features which ran from 1948 to 1954. Working with Fred F. Sears (his favorite director during the fifties), Katzman cranked out *Teenage Crime Wave* (1955), in theatres scant weeks following the release of *Rebel Without a Cause*. It proved to be a landmark picture for the producer, his first brush with "topicality" and the youth market. Afterward, he kept his eyes and ears open to current trends and fads, usually the first to capitalize on it. Any new dance craze was certain to get the Katzman treatment: *Cha-Cha-Cha Boom!* (1956), *Calypso Heat Wave* (1957), *Twist Around the Clock* (1961). The latter film was in theatres while Dion DiMucci's "The Wanderer," sung in the film, was still on the charts.

It was Katzman who first heard the distant sound of money in the throbbing beat of rock 'n' roll music. The music had been created as a result of black artists' experimenting with sounds and structures associated with up-tempo white bands. Simultaneously, country artists began affecting a blacker, more soulful sound in their music, accentuating the beat with added percussion. When these two musical forms converged the result was a noisy, infectious sound which captured the pulse and pocket money of teenage America.

Katzman had a screenwriter hastily prepare a scenario which incorporated a brief and inaccurate history of the new phenomenon into a trite storyline which was later modified to showcase Chubby Checker and a dance called "The Twist." Fred Sears directed his cast of unknowns through the motions of pretending their material was credible and the result was *Rock Around the Clock* (1956). The real stars and the movie's raison d'être was, of course, Bill Haley and the Comets. The picture became an instantaneous success, recouping most of its modest budget within the first few weeks of its release. It was also something of a cause célèbre in England where teenagers had not previously been exposed to the new sound. They rioted and ravaged cinemas during the running of the picture. These sorts of actions irrevocably linked rock 'n' roll to juvenile delinquency as if the music was some Godless communist conspiracy to undermine the family unit and sabotage the appreciation of "good" music. This is a slight exaggeration but there were many parents, teachers, religious leaders, politicians, and other professional meddlers who sincerely believed that rock 'n' roll was an evil, corrupting influence that led to deafness, promiscuity and, of course, juvenile delinquency.

Supposedly in response to such allegations, but primarily to capitalize on the success and controversy of the first picture, Katzman hurried to release a follow-up film, *Don't Knock the Rock* (1956). This time rock 'n' roll idol Alan Dale (curiously patterned after Frank Sinatra) returns to his hometown only to find the inhabitants therein divided on the issue of rock music. During an out-of-town rock show, Jana Lund, who had previously been spurned by Dale, vindictively incites a brawl that supplies fuel to the belief that the music has a disruptive influence. With the help of disc jockey Alan Freed, the singer convinces the oldsters that the new music is no more evil than the jazz music of their generation. Bill Haley and the Comets join in for a big rock 'n' roll show and everyone has a swell time. So much for controversy.

Inspired by the success of Katzman's films, both major and minor studios mounted their own productions dealing with the new musical trend. By comparison, Fox's *The Girl Can't Help It* (1956) and U-I's *The Big Beat* (1957), both in color, seemed like extravaganzas after Katzman's impoverished offerings. Both movies sought to consolidate adult-oriented artists with the rockers in the hope that the films would appeal to someone other than just the teens. Alan Freed starred in a number of lower case productions such as *Mr. Rock and Roll, Rock, Rock, Rock* (both 1957), and *Go Johnny, Go* (1959). He always played an idealized image of himself — the altruistic adult intent on giving the kids what they wanted to hear. For the most part, these films were flimsy excuses to showcase the musical interludes which, after all, were their primary appeal. If these productions have any validity, it lies in their presentation of the founding fathers of rock 'n' roll at the peak of their creative and popular success.

Some rock films were so threadbare that they could only afford one rock 'n' roll star. Roger Corman's *Rock All Night* was a perfect example. It was based on a television play, "The Little Guy." Writer Charles Griffith was given 24 hours to expand it into feature length. He cut up the original script with a pair of scissors and pasted the pieces before and after his added material. The film was shot in six days on a set left over from another picture. The story takes place in a nightclub where Abby Dalton's singing debut is interrupted by the appearance of two armed hoods who terrorize the patrons. Eventually, a diminutive loner (Dick Miller) overcomes the thugs, giving Abby the reassurance she needs to face her audience.

"It was a little bit strange from the standpoint of music," confessed Corman in a recent interview, "because the group I had was the Platters and they were available for one day but it wasn't the day I was shooting." Corman quickly revised the script so that all of the scenes of the Platters came during the first ten minutes of the picture. After that, in spite of the advertisements claiming that the singing group were the film's stars, they never appear again.

Although rock films flourished in the mid-fifties, there was no single superstar in the field. Bill Haley was a little too old and stocky for the role. Chuck Berry, Little Richard, and Fats Domino had hit records but many people still found blacks unacceptable as "idols." Staid, sexless singers like Eddie Fisher and Vic Damone were too closely associated with adult-oriented "pop." James Dean's death had left a void and there seemed to be no single, unifying image for teenage America.

Then, a 21-year-old former truck driver from Memphis, Tennessee, burst forth on the scene, combining Brando's sneering defiance with Dean's brooding vulnerability. As if that was not enough, all hell broke loose when this young man sang rock 'n' roll. Elvis Presley's contribution to the evolution of rock should never be underestimated, but of equal importance was the fact that he was the first white singer to give the music a definite visual appeal. When Elvis was on stage or television, he looked and moved the way the music felt. This explicit interpretation of rock 'n' roll's more erotic aspects outraged adult critics who had almost succeeded in removing all the sexual implication from popular music. The resulting controversy propelled Presley to the forefront in the battle of "us" vs. "them."

Producer Hal Wallis signed the volatile new talent with an eye towards casting him in a supporting role in *The Rainmaker* (1956). For whatever reasons, Wallis held Presley back, replacing him with Earl Holliman. In the meantime 20th Century-Fox inked Presley to a three picture contract but were still unsure of his potential. So they gave him third billing in an otherwise forgettable western to be titled *The Reno Brothers*. By the time the picture was ready for release, Presley's popularity had risen as a result of his highly rated appearances on Ed Sullivan's TV show. The studio renamed the film, *Love Me Tender* (1956), after Presley's hit song from the movie. The singing idol was featured prominently in the advertising as the "star," despite the fact that he did not appear in the film until nearly 30 minutes had elapsed.

Hal Wallis gave Elvis top billing in *Loving You* (1957), a sparkling technicolor showcase in which he basically played himself. He was then cast in M-G-M's *Jailhouse Rock* (1957) as a pseudo-juvenile delinquent named Vince Everett, a hot-blooded construction worker sentenced to prison on manslaughter charges. Vince develops a musical talent in prison, under the tutelage of Hunk Houghton (Mickey Shaughnessy), a former country-western singer. Once he is released from prison, Vince embarks on a singing career. He gets some pointers from Peggy Van Alden (Judy Tyler), an employee with a record company. She recognizes his potential and becomes professionally and romantically involved with him. Vince and Peggy start their own record company and Vince becomes rich and famous, sacrificing everything, including Peggy, along the way. Hunk is finally set free and is given a job by Vince as a high-priced flunky. Hunk realizes how much Vince's attitude has hurt Peggy and decides to beat some sense into his former protégé. Refusing to protect himself, Vince is injured in the windpipe by one of Hunk's upper-cuts. After the surgery, Vince forgives the remorseful Hunk and realizes his true feelings for Judy. The picture ends with Vince proving that his voice is as good as ever by singing the picture's love theme, "Young and Beautiful."

Jailhouse Rock was the most contemporary of Presley's early vehicles and, as such, is the most dated in terms of looks, fashions, and attitudes. The early part of the picture, dealing with Vince's brief incarceration, manages to dust off almost every "prison movie" cliché. Once he is released, the picture evolves into another variation on the "rags to riches" theme, elevated only by Presley's playing the role with a Brando-ish insolence. Naturally, Elvis is basically good. He just needs a little beating now and then to help him see things more clearly. But whatever its faults, the picture was the first and one of the few Presley movies to explore the darker side of his image.

Presley's final picture before entering the Army in 1958 was *King Creole* (1958). This time he played a more traditional juvenile delinquent, a high school student named Danny Fisher growing up in one of New Orleans' shadier districts. After one of his many violent outbursts, Danny learns that his poor conduct will prevent him from graduating again. Quitting school, he falls in with a street gang led by Shark (Vic Morrow). They pull off a few petty crimes before Danny finds legitimate work as a singer in a Bourbon Street nightclub. Gangster, and rival club owner Maxie Fields (Walter Matthau) uses his moll, Ronnie (Carolyn Jones) to entrap Danny into signing a contract. When Danny refuses, Maxie employs Shark and his friends to find something in Danny's past or present to use as blackmail. Shark convinces Danny to join them in the robbery of the drug store which belongs to the bullying boss of Danny's father (Dean Jagger). During the robbery, Danny's father is badly injured and Maxie pays his medical expenses. Indebted to the mobster, Danny signs the contract, then learns that it was Maxie who set the whole thing up in the first place. In a rage Danny beats Maxie senseless and later defeats Shark in an alley scuffle. Injured, Danny is taken by Ronnie to an out-of-town

HIS FIRST BIG DRAMATIC SINGING ROLE!

ELVIS PRESLEY AT HIS GREATEST

Jailhouse Rock

hideout. Recovering from his wounds, Danny briefly enjoys a romantic interlude with Ronnie until Maxie shows up and kills her. Before Maxie can give Danny a dose of the same he is shot in the back by a mute henchman who Danny had previously befriended. Danny returns to his family, his singing career, and the wholesome girl he left behind, Dolores Hart.

Producer Wallis obviously intended the picture to be more than just another vehicle for Presley's musical talents. The story was based on Harold Robbins' novel, *A Stone for Danny Fisher*, changing the lead character from a boxer to a singer for obvious reasons. Michael Curtiz was hired to direct, his list of credits including *The Adventures of Robin Hood* (1938) and *Casablanca* (1942), as well as *Angels with Dirty Faces*. An impressive lineup of actors supported Presley, including *Blackboard Jungle* alumnus Vic Morrow. Wallis even arranged for part of the film to be shot on location, a logistics nightmare due to Elvis' enormous popularity at the time. This sort of attention made *King Creole* one of the relatively few "real" movies in which "The King" appeared. Many critics were forced to admit that he showed some potential as a dramatic actor. Indeed, Presley's borderline J.D. pictures met with far more approval than did Sam Katzman's early genre efforts, a comparison made only to bring the text back to where it began before it became sidetracked.

"Jungle Sam" was a producer who managed to move comfortably from genre to genre with equal aplomb, giving the same care and attention to detail to every film, which is to say that each of his productions were treated with comparable disdain. He became legendary in the industry for his frugality (a nice word for "cheapness"), his breakneck production schedules, and the complete absence of artistic pretension.

Prior to Katzman's becoming the movies' equivalent of the newspaper, he built his reputation on nonsensical serials—*Congo Bill* (1948), *King of the Congo* (1952), *The Lost Planet* (1953)—undistinguished horror films—*Bowery at Midnight* (1942), *The Ape Man* (1943), *Voodoo Man* (1944)—and the East Side Kids series. By 1955 he was firmly entrenched at Columbia's studios, which existed in the Hollywood twilight between the major and minor studios. There he specialized in assembly-line programmers, starring has-been performers spouting dialogue from juvenile screenplays, directed by some studio hack. Because of their bargain-basement budgets, even a relatively small financial return guaranteed black ink in Columbia's profit column. Of his inventory of films, writer Richard Thompson once remarked that no serious scholar could possibly sit through more than ten minutes of any given title without ceasing to be a serious scholar. Nevertheless, it is with "serious" regret that your authors admit to not having seen *Teenage Crime Wave*, surely one of Katzman's least documented efforts. Our information, brief as it may be, comes from exhibitor magazines and the vague memories of a few close friends.

In Jailhouse Rock (M-G-M 1957), Elvis Presley spends a term in prison before rising to fame and fortune.

The picture opens with Tommy Cook springing his "hard-as-nails" girlfriend, Molly McCart, from a prison farm. While waiting for a third member of their gang, the two hole up in a farm house, encountering a religious, elderly couple. Cook vents a lot of his pent-up anger on his captives. They, in turn, attempt to bring the gun-toting youth to his senses. The old woman asks Molly if she has ever read the Bible. She shakes her head. "Nah. I read comic books. I need laughs." A neighbor drops by to pay a friendly visit and is shot. Tommy and Molly learn that the friend they were waiting for has been killed by the police who are closing in. The two race up a mountain road, pursued by the cops. They hope to become lost in the crowd at the Griffith Park observatory but the park is closed because of a holiday. Molly is killed during a shootout and Tommy, in handcuffs, starts bawling like a baby.

Other producers, however, were not as eager to exploit the more violent possibilities of the juvenile delinquency drama as Katzman had been. In Andrew Stone's *The Night Holds Terror* (1955) a youthful John Cassavetes leads a trio of young thugs invading the middleclass home of an only slightly older couple (Jack Kelly and Hildy Parks) but this was basically a variation on *The Desperate Hours* (1955). What had happened to curb other producers from following Katzman's lead was a Senate subcommittee, headed by Senator Estes Kefauver, formed to investigate the causes of juvenile delinquency in America. Kefauver was the Tennessee senator who had already made a name for himself when his organized crime hearings were televised in May of 1950. Seeking to connect the problem to the mass media (always the easiest target), the committee looked back on the film *City Across the River* and concluded that while the film purportedly was made as a deterrent, "we have seen the delinquency rates rising since 1948, and, while we cannot say what effect this film had, if any, we may assume that it was hardly one of reducing delinquency." Such a responsibility was pretty heavy to attach to any one film much less Shane's little drama which had, after all, been so watered down by the censors that any chance it may have had to make an effective statement had been nullified. Regardless, according to Kefauver and his brood, the film was guilty because it did not succeed in what it was not allowed to do. The message was clear: If the media were not part of the solution, they were part of the problem.

The Kefauver committee published a 122 page report of their findings but the whole business came to very little really, more the cause for laughter than anything else. At one point someone, in an accusing tone, told Jack Warner that they had already received a call about *Rebel Without a Cause*. Since the film had not even been completed at that time the perplexed studio boss could only shrug his shoulders and suggest that the caller must have been using mental radar since he had not yet seen the picture himself. And when Dore Schary was asked if he had heard about the group of school girls who had set fire to a barn after seeing *Blackboard Jungle*, he snapped back that there was no fire in his picture. "They can't pin that on us!" Oddly enough it was the conservative Ronald Reagan who came to the picture's defense by pointing out that while there was violence in the film, it was more important to look at the end result. "Any juvenile seeing it would have to have a feeling of disgust for the bad boy," Reagan told the committee. "And I got something else out of it. I found in it a great tribute to a group of persons who seldom get much credit — the schoolteachers of the country."

But Kefauver was not upset by just the content of the films but the advertising for them as well. The campaigns, to use his own words, were "supercharged with sex! Purplish prose is keyed to feverish tempo to celebrate the naturalness of seduction, the condonability of adultery and the spontaneity of adolescent relations."

During this period of repression, when the House on Un-American Activities (HUAC) was actively discouraging filmmakers from realistically confronting contemporary or controversial subjects, another medium came under attack — comic books. Yes, those ten-cent staples of childhood were indicted for a multitude of sins, including the promotion of juvenile delinquency. Dr. Fredric Wertham, a psychiatrist specializing in the problem of delinquent children, authored a landmark book on the subject, *Seduction of the Innocent*. As the title implies, Wertham denounced the comic book industry for corrupting the American youth and sought to link increasing delinquency statistics to violence and horror in comic books. Few would deny that a number of the books in question had become increasingly graphic in their depictions of violence and sexually stimulating females. However, Wertham's contention that such material serves to instigate violent behavior seems as baseless as the similar accusations recently aimed at television. It appears that the public continues to seek simple solutions to complex problems, usually choosing the most conspicuous target to attack. Still, the hoopla caused by Dr. Wertham's book forced the comic book industry to adopt the Comic Code Authority, a self-imposed and regulated censorship board. Educational Comics (EC) refused to knuckle under and discontinued their line of horror, science fiction, crime and war comics. After that, comic books were pretty dull and the kids were left to find a new source of entertainment.

Ironically, as the comic books were tightening their constraints, the motion picture industry was hesitantly embarking on its first steps toward an unparalleled era of freedom. Another self-imposed regulatory board, the Production Code, had been instituted in 1933 as an alternative to government enforced regulation. As movies became the most accessible art medium, Hollywood formed the Motion Picture Producers and Distributors of America to placate critics. Basically it was a political and public relations organization headed by former Postmaster General Will H. Hays. The Hays office set the guidelines for what they considered to be suitable motion picture entertainment. And the suitability of content was based on the fact that motion pictures appealed to every class, "mature, immature, developed, undeveloped, law abiding, criminal." It became the business of Mr. Hays to protect the lowest common denominator, recognizing differences between sections of the country, "small communities, remote from sophistication and from the hardening process which often takes place in the ethical and moral standards of groups in large cities." Still, under pressure from the less flexible Legion of Decency (the watchdog committee of the Catholic Church), the Hays office instigated the Production Code Administration, with Joseph Breen as executive censor. It was his job to read scripts and view completed films to make certain writers and producers were complying with the rules. Once passed, the films were awarded a seal of approval.

The enforcement of the code was dependent on two factors: the public's acceptance of the code and the motion picture industry's adherence to it. The second factor was insured since the major distributors also owned many of the theatres in which their films were run. In 1948 this monopoly was broken. The studios were restricted to production and distribution. The theatres were then purchased by independent companies who were under no obligation to exhibit only Code approved entertainment.

Although most producers continued to meet Code standards, Otto Preminger did not. He refused to remove "offensive elements" from his sex comedy, *The Moon Is Blue* (1953) which was released by United Artists without the seal. Audiences did not seem to miss it. The film's success forced Hays and his cohorts to reevaluate their outdated restrictions. In 1956 the Code underwent extensive revisions, allowing previously forbidden subjects to be depicted on the screen "within the careful limits of good taste."

Another contributing factor to this new freedom was television. Movie attendance dropped as TV sales rose and the censorship spotlight shifted to the more accessible free entertainment. Hollywood attempted to lure audiences back into theatres by producing more lavish spectacles, color films, and adding gimmicks like Cinerama, CinemaScope, Vista-Vision, 3-D, stereophonic sound, SmelloVision, and so on. Once the novelty wore off, few of these new processes would survive the decade. But audiences still sought what they could not get at home and one answer was a more "adult" approach to controversial subjects.

The new freedom did not give the motion picture "carte blanche" to fearlessly tackle new subjects. The controversy surrounding *Baby Doll* (1956), Tennessee William's study of down-home degeneracy, proved that the guardians of public morality could still raise a ruckus over something that outraged their sense of decency. As early as 1936, Pope Pius XI pretty much summed things up when he said, "Everybody knows what damage is done to the soul by bad motion pictures. They are occasions of sin. They seduce young people along the ways of evil by glorifying the passions. They show life under a false light. They destroy pure love, respect for marriage, and affection for the family...."

There is little doubt that Hollywood can expedite changes in such superficial aspects as fashion, hairstyles, language, etc. But could this same influence be extended into emulating antisocial behavior not compatible with the viewer's basic psychological make-up? In terms of cause and effect, do the media influence the public or vice versa? Dore Schary, a respected film producer and the head of M-G-M studios in the mid-fifties, offered one theory. In a speech before the National Conference of Controllers, Schary remarked that "movies seldom lead opinion, they merely reflect public opinion and perhaps occasionally accelerate it.... No motion picture ever started a trend of public opinion or thinking. Pictures merely dramatize these trends and keep them going."

As the controversy continued, most movie producers, with the exception of Sam Katzman, approached the juvenile delinquency issue with extreme caution. The hazing suffered by both *Blackboard Jungle* and *Rebel Without a Cause* had served as a warning. It was probably no accident that Fox's *Teenage Rebel* (1956), which may have been sincerely motivated, was far too respectable to be any fun. Its three principals — Ginger Rogers, Michael Rennie, Mildrid Natwick — were all over thirty and their presence in the cast promised much more in the way of adult conversation than teenage rebellion. True to one's worst suspicions, such was the case, based as it was on Edith Sommer's play, "A Roomful of Roses." Ginger was a divorced mother attempting to rekindle a relationship with her teenage daughter who had been living with her father for eight years.

More interesting, though equally dull, was Warner Brothers' adaptation of Maxwell Anderson's play, *The Bad Seed* (1956), taken from a novel by William March. Several concessions to the Code were made, the first being to advance the age of the prepubescent murderess. In the original play, Rhoda (Patty McCormack, who also appeared in the film version), is a precocious eight year old girl whose engaging smile belies a cold-blooded killer. When she loses a coveted penmanship award at school, Rhoda arranges the "accidental" death of the winner. A handyman comes too close to uncovering her secret so Rhoda locks him in a barn and sets it on fire. Rhoda's mother (Nancy Kelly) discovers the truth, gives Rhoda an overdose of sleeping pills then shoots herself. Rhoda survives the ordeal with no indication that she will ever alter her murderous ways. This being too shocking for motion pictures, the film version has the mother surviving her suicide attempt while Rhoda is conveniently struck by lightning. This contrived retribution, from the "hand of God" no less, succeeded only in casting dispersions on the credibility of the entire story. Adding insult to injury, the studio added a supposedly "cute" curtain call in which Nancy Kelly takes Patty McCormack over her knee and gives her a good spanking, as if old-fashioned discipline could in any way compensate for her monstrous activities. This sort of mental retardation might account for the one critic who applauded *The Restless Years* (1956) because "the necking" was "toned down to something almost healthy," as though the denial of normal sexual feelings was some cause for celebration. The picture was completely void of any of the conventional elements that might appeal to the audience for which it was supposedly intended, save whatever attraction John Saxon and Sandra Dee might hold for the younger female members in attendance. The film's high point came when Saxon was challenged to a drag race. After one or two suspenseful moments he declines the offer and robs the film of its only potential action sequence.

The Restless Years was derived from Patricia Joudry's play, "Teach Me How to Cry," which, incidentally, would certainly have been a far more suitable title for the film. Teresa Wright played the frightened recluse of the play, stubbornly refusing to admit that her lover of years before has deserted her. Her only appearance to the world is her daily sojourn to the mailbox to check for the letter that will never come. Sandra Dee, her daughter, has become an emotional recluse, caused by the shame of being born out of wedlock. She is saved from her life of celibacy and surpressed emotions by John Saxon. He loves her, despite the urgings of his status-seeking parents to marry "the right kind of girl." Saxon gives his heart to the girl from the wrong side of the tracks and his devotion and love permit Sandy to display her feelings for the first time. She buries her head in his chest and weeps. This breakthrough for Sandy causes her mother to face reality at last; she puts an end to the letter charade. John's parents conclude money is not all and they live happily ever after.

The same studio's *Running Wild* (1955), ostensibly a crime drama, was, by contrast, closer to home. Middleaged Keenan Wynn may have been the chief villain but he did employ teenagers to strip cars and there were several sequences of juke joints blasting rock 'n' roll music. William Campbell played the rookie cop out to bust Wynn. Campbell's brooding, dark appearance often cast him on the opposite side of the law. That year he also appeared as the young delinquent in *Cell 2455, Death Row*, a story loosely based on the early exploits of convicted sex-offender Caryl Chessman. The film ends with Campbell in prison, preparing his own legal defense for an appeal. The actual Chessman, maintaining his innocence to the end, was eventually executed in the gas chamber.

Sandra Dee may have welcomed John Saxon's attentions but Esther Williams is not nearly so enthusiastic with him in U-I's *The Unguarded Moment* (1956). A devoted school teacher, Esther begins receiving anonymous, lewd notes from Saxon, one of which suggests the desirability of a nocturnal meeting in the school stadium. She accepts the invitation in the hope of talking some sense into the misguided youth. Hidden by darkness, Saxon attacks her. She manages to escape before he can get down and dirty and is conveniently picked up by a patrol car. After filling out a report of the incident, Esther returns home only to find the sex maniac has broken into her home. She opens the front door and begs him to leave, which he does. His identity is revealed when he becomes caught by an automobile's headlights while racing across the street. Still he denies the event ever took place and the school principal, Les Tremayne, seems inclined to believe him. Why, he questions, would "a minor god" like Saxon, and a football hero at that, need to throw himself at an older woman. The reason is made quite clear to the audience who, by this time, have already seen how crazy Saxon's father is. Played to the hilt by Edward Andrews, Saxon's old man is sexually warped, believing all women to be "dirty" liars and cheats, and who "ought to be wiped off the face of the earth!" It is never quite made clear whether his attitude is the result of his wife's leaving him or if she took off because of it. No matter. This is a soap opera so the focus of the drama is on Esther's plight.

An ad for The Unguarded Moment (U-I 1956).

For a while it appears that Miss Williams can convince no one that the incident ever took place. She becomes the target for malicious gossip and the principal begins to fear a scandal. Her only support comes from a soft-boiled policeman, George Nader. But while he attempts to get at the truth, Esther makes every effort to protect young Saxon because he's "just a boy." Nader dully remarks, "I ought to drag you up to the reform school and show you some of the angel faces roosting there." Later, when Saxon attempts to absolve himself of suspicion by reminding Nader that he is, after all, only eighteen, Nader snaps, "So was Billy the Kid." Through it all, Esther continues to try to help Saxon realize what he has done without persecuting him. Her unrelenting kindness eventually causes him to confess. "There's something about her that gets under your skin," Saxon tells Nader on the way home after a police grilling. "Who else after you played her a lousy trick would worry about you getting a lift home." Nader hurries to Esther's house to tell her the good news and none too soon. For Saxon's father, fearing the police might be on to something, had broken into Esther's house to search for something in her past with which he might blackmail her into calling off the investigation. But while looking for skeletons in her closet he ends up hiding in it instead when Esther returns home sooner than he thought. Peeking through the door he becomes aroused by her as she undresses and by the time Nader arrives on the scene he is chasing her all over the front room, wheezing and slobbering. (It's the film's finest moment.) Andrews suffers a fatal heart attack from the extra-curricular activity and Saxon joins the Army. The film's closing line is from Miss Williams who tells Nader, "I guess if you love them they grow up."

It is difficult to determine exactly what the critics thought about *The Unguarded Moment* as they all seemed far more concerned about the fact that Miss Williams was in a nonaquatic role than they were in the film.

With the major studios trying to keep a low profile it was up to Katzman and Sears to set things right again. Although *Rumble on the Docks* (1956) owed more to *On the Waterfront* (1954) than its J.D. predecessors, it was, at least a down payment. It was one of James Darren's first features, the actor who became Gidget's companion in a series of wholesome teenage comedies. In fact, despite their Geritol tone (even the song "Gidget" sounded like something written for Frank Sinatra), *Gidget* (1959), and its two sequels, were enormously popular with teenagers, predating the surfing movies which emerged during the mid-sixties.

As the leader of a gang called the Diggers, Darren ironically admires the union boss who crippled his father during a union brawl. This seemingly insensitive behavior is better understood once the audience realizes that Darren's hateful father blames him for his disability, telling the boy that he would not have had to become a longshoreman in the first place if he hadn't had Darren to support.

Unique among the early J.D. films were three projects involving Reginald Rose, a writer who came to prominence during the "golden age" of live television dramas. Following the success of *Marty* (1955), a teleplay adapted into an Academy Award winning motion picture, producers sought out other original television dramas as potential film properties. An added advantage to such stories was that they were tailored to the confines of television budgets, making them economic to produce as features. Rose's *Crime in the Streets*, successful on television, prompted Allied Artists to engage John Cassavetes and Mark Rydell for two of the leads from the original presentation to come to Hollywood for the movie version. Sal Mineo, fresh from *Rebel Without a Cause*, and James Whitmore were added to the cast for boxoffice insurance. Almost the entire film was shot on a large soundstage, built to represent a New York tenement street. Sidney Lumet, the director of the television version, refused to come west to make the movie. Don Siegel replaced him, a director who would later gain notoriety for films like *Invasion of the Body Snatchers* (1956), *Flaming Star* (1961), and *Dirty Harry* (1971). Although Rose was credited as screenwriter, Siegel made several alterations in the material which created a rift between the two men during the shooting of the picture.

The story centers around Cassavetes, the psychopathic gang leader who utters volatile remarks like: "I feel loose. Like I was made for getting even." And getting even is exactly what he wants to do to Malcolm Atterbury for telling the police that the boys had roughed him up a little. Cassavetes wants the old man dead and nothing that social worker Whitmore can say or do will change his mind. Only when Peter Votrain suddenly appears and cries, "I'm your brother! I love you!" does Cassavetes have a change of heart.

For all the high powered talent employed, the movie is a lifeless affair. Perhaps the milieu suffered from overfamiliarity. James Whitmore's understanding social worker was already a cliché. Rose fared better with *Dino* (1957), again featuring Mineo, this time in the title role.

The picture opens with Dino's release from reform school serving a three year sentence for participating in a robbery which led to murder. The stretch in reform school merely hardened the boy, indicated in a scene where he must defend himself against a knife-wielding opponent. Released to the custody of his parents, Dino finds his home environment little improved since his incarceration. His father, a violent, insensitive man is instinctively suspicious of his every move. The old man beats Dino regularly. It looks as if the boy will return to his old gang, the Top Hats, but complications set in. Brian Keith, a settlement house case worker, keeps filling his head with ideas about going straight and Susan Kohner believes that Dino is more than just a petty crook. Dino forsakes his old life, hustling his brother away from a planned robbery to pay a visit to Keith.

The jury that must decide the fate of a boy on trial for the murder of his father become the *12 Angry Men* (1957) of Rose's most successful and powerful screen adaptation. Each character in this brilliant drama represents a different flaw in human nature that might contribute to juvenile delinquency. One of the jurors has a pair of basketball tickets burning a hole in his pocket. He can't wait to vote, hoping to be on time for the game. Another condemns the boy out of hatred for his own son.

Still another votes "guilty" because he is prejudiced against Hispanics. Other jurors take the roles of cowardness, ignorance, fear, and indifference. Only juror number eight, played by Henry Fonda, possesses the compassion necessary to force the others to give the youth a chance. "Look, this boy's been kicked around all his life," he reminds them, recounting the boy's impoverished living conditions, the nightly beatings suffered at his father's hands, the death of his mother when he was nine, and the year and a half spent in an orphanage while his father served a jail term for forgery. "I think maybe we owe him a few words." By the time he's finished, Fonda has put a reasonable doubt in everyone's mind about the boy's guilt.

Another television drama dealing with delinquency, "Deal a Blow," became *The Young Stranger* (1956). The author, Robert Dozier, was the son of William Dozier who had just taken the position of RKO studio head. RKO produced the film version, with young Dozier adapting his teleplay. James MacArthur and John Frankenheimer, star and director of the original teleplay, repeated their respective roles for the big screen. It was a rare instance of the writer and director, both in their mid-twenties, being close in age to their young lead, as opposed to most writers and directors working in the genre. The disclosure that the story was based on a true incident from Dozier's own life gives some added significance to the elder Dozier's decision to make the movie.

The story focuses on Hal Ditmar (MacArthur), a 16-year-old boy who is finding it increasingly difficult to communicate with his ambitious father (James Daly). Early in the film Hal and a friend cause a minor disturbance in a local movie house. The theatre manager (Whit Bissell) overreacts and deliberately provokes Hal into a fight. The police are called in and Hal is released to the custody of his parents. His father uses his influence as an executive in the film industry to convince the manager to drop all charges. In spite of his efforts on his son's behalf, it is obvious that the father believes Hal was totally responsible for the incident, and the boy can say nothing to alter his opinion. As their relationship becomes increasingly strained, Hal returns to the theatre to ask the manager to tell his father the whole story. The manager attempts to throw him out and the fight that results sends Hal once again to the police station where a sympathetic police officer (James Gregory) uncovers the truth. When his father hears what actually happened, the two reach a better understanding.

The Young Stranger was one of the more restrained entries in a field noted for sensationalism and exploitation. Daly's portrayal of the father is not another bizarre caricature. His treatment of his family is much like another business dealing, both understandable and believable for an overly occupied, success oriented businessman. His anger over a basically trivial incident stands as an example of what happens when parents expect the worst of their children. Quite often, that is exactly what they get.

Also notable for its low key approach was *The Young Don't Cry* (1957). Sal Mineo was back as a youngster subjected to continued brutality in a Georgia based orphanage. He becomes friends with an escaped convict (James Whitmore), who, like the boy, was initially trapped in a violent environment through no fault of his own. The experience gives Mineo the inner strength to walk out of the orphanage and make a new life on his own.

Insensitive, impotent, and often downright mean parents and authority figures crept into the scenarios of many early J.D. dramas, most likely because such characters provided an easy, knee-jerk cause for bad boys and girls. We have already discussed the hostile parents in *Dino, Rumble on the Docks,* and *The Unguarded Moment* but there were others.

The audience is given only a glimpse of the father-son relationship in *The Cool and the Crazy* (1958) but it was just long enough for the boy to shove his father's face in a mirror and say, "Look at you! You're a mess! You stink!" To which the old man replied, "Get outta here you bum!" One of the worst of the lot was Jack Kruschen in *Reform School Girl* (1957). The film is barely underway when Kruschen is shown gazing lustily at his niece, Gloria Castello, who is ironing a dress, wearing only a slip. Her aunt makes a brief appearance before trotting off to work just to utter a few nasty remarks to the girl and provide the implication that Kruschen is nothing but a leech. This impression is given reinforcement by the fact that he is unshaven and wearing a tank top. An off-stage horn signals Gloria that her date has arrived. Kruschen intercepts her at the door. "Tell them you're staying home tonight," he says, gripping her shoulders. "Look, Rita won't be home 'til midnight. We can have a ball." From the expression on Gloria's face it is quite obvious that the proposition is as repulsive to her as it is to the audience. But by the time *The Party Crashers** (1958) arrived on the scene, it was almost unnecessary to explain that it was Mark Damon's slutty mother and drunken father that made him a mess. Except that in this particular case, their appearance is crucial to the plot. Damon crashes one party only to discover that his mother is to be the evening's entertainment. When he attempts to remove her from the premises, the old broad takes a fatal tumble down a flight of stairs. This tragic event cures Connie Stevens' infatuation with Damon, makes his father go on the wagon and serves as a cue for Bobby Driscoll's parents to spend more time with him.

By 1957 the time was right for an incisive satire on an already overworked subject. Instead, audiences got Jerry Lewis as *The Delicate Delinquent*. More serious in intent than usual for the comedian, the film vacillates between maudlin drama and frenetic comedy. There is a nice bit, before the opening credits, with two street gangs ritualistically preparing for a rumble. They meet in an alley and at the point of conflict, Lewis comes stumbling through a side door carrying armloads of

An otherwise forgettable film, The Party Crashers deserves some place in motion picture history as being Frances Farmer's one attempt at a comeback after being maliciously tossed into a sanitorium where she was sexually abused and secretly given a lobotomy.

One of the last of AIP's early J.D. double features: Dragstrip Riot and The Cool and the Crazy (both 1958) entered an already glutted market.

Hollywood still found audiences for reform school movies, especially when the inmates were well developed young starlets like Yvette Vickers in *Reform School Girl* (AIP 1957).

garbage. Seeing the switchblades and chains, he screams in abject terror, drops his garbage cans and makes more than a sufficient amount of noise to bring the fuzz down on all of their heads. Unfortunately the film went downhill from there. After crying his way through a police lineup, Lewis is taken under the wing of a sympathetic cop, Darren McGavin, who makes a policeman out of Jerry. The moment of truth comes during Jerry's first night on patrol. But he comes through for his partner, demonstrating courage and ability to everyone's satisfaction except Dick Bakalyan and his gang of toughs who Lewis and McGavin render helpless.

Dean Martin, originally slated for McGavin's part, cancelled out, terminating a ten year partnership with Lewis. It then became Jerry's first solo effort and was quite profitable, as were all of his pictures during this period.

Released the same year (with a similar title) was Robert Altman's first feature, *The Delinquents*. It was filmed two years earlier, in the summer of 1955, when a farsighted investor handed Altman $63,000 to make a picture about juvenile delinquency. Altman wrote the script in five days and produced and directed the film in his home town, Kansas City. United Artists picked up the releasing right for $150,000 and made a considerable profit when it was finally released.

Tom Laughlin starred as a good boy from the wrong side of the tracks, forbidden to see his sweetheart, Rosemary Howard. So Laughlin persuades one of his buddies to fake a date with the girl and drive her to a rendezvous at a deserted mansion where a party is to be held. Things get a little too rowdy for Tom and Rosemary so they duck out. The police show up soon after and it looks to the others like Laughlin blew the whistle on them. He's forced to drink a bottle of Scotch then left to take the rap for a dead gas station attendant, his head smashed by a pump nozzle during a bungled robbery. Staggering home, Laughlin learns that his girl has been abducted. A few well-placed blows to the proper jaws nets him information as to where she is being held and, in no time at all, he and Rosemary are headed for the police station.

United Artists followed the course of least resistance by tacking on a prologue to the film which implored citizens to work against "the disease of delinquency" by working with church and community groups.

Tom Laughlin was one of the few professionals in Altman's cast, though according to the director he was "an unbelievable pain in the ass." Altman believed that Laughlin's troublesome behavior may have resulted from the actor's frustration at not being a priest. To use Altman's words, "Big Catholic hang-up." This religious fanaticism may have prompted Laughlin to produce, direct, write, and star in *The Young Sinner* (1965), completed five years prior to its release. Filmed under the title *Christopher Wotan*, it was intended as the first part of a projected trilogy, *We Are All Christ*. The story is told in a flashback framework as Chris Wotan (Laughlin, of course) confesses his sins to a Catholic priest. Chris is the product of an unhappy homelife—alcoholic father, working mother, etc. He loses his opportunity for a college diploma after an argument with a teacher. He then rejects his wholesome girlfriend for a casual affair with a wealthy socialite whose father might help him regain his chance for a scholarship. Chris screws this chance up, figuratively and literally, when he and the girl are found in bed together by her parents. Alone and dispondent, Chris joins some of his friends in a joy ride which leads to some trouble at a drug store and his final expulsion from school. Not one to sit idle, Chris becomes involved with a sexually precocious 14-year-old who takes him to her secret loft above a church. Repulsed by what he has become, Chris goes on a destructive rampage inside the church. He later returns to that church to seek spiritual guidance from a priest who promises to help redeem his life through Christ.

Attempts to explain the causes of delinquency were all but swept under the carpet by Allied Artists and American-International Pictures, the two companies most prolific in the production of J.D. dramas and teen oriented motion pictures. Laughlin's meticulous account of the events that shaped Chris Wotan would have been only too excessive to the folks at AA and AIP. Such attention to cause and effect was unnecessary. Their writers and directors cared little about psychological explorations. The teenage characters were little or nothing more than stereotypes, all good or all bad, the way B-westerns once presented their heroes and villains. In *Dragstrip Girl* (1957), bad guy John Ashley is not the product of a broken home or even a bad environment. He makes only the vaguest reference to his wealthy parents when he repeats one of his father's favorite expressions: "What's in it for me?" The results of these "black and white" views of the world, while ultimately grotesque, achieved a sort of surreal quality that could often be extremely entertaining without once ever being mistaken for art.

Allied Artists was established in 1929 as Monogram Pictures, its founder Iowa-born Ray Johnson. For a time the studio was located on Las Palmas during a brief union with Republic Pictures. Later the company occupied space on the Universal lot before finally settling into its own facilities on Sunset Drive. Under the leadership of Steve Broidy the company changed its name to Allied Artists, hoping to attract better stars and directors to the lot. This ruse proved successful for a brief time, resulting in films like *Friendly Persuasion* (1956) and *Love in the Afternoon* (1957), both starring Gary Cooper, the first directed by William Wyler, the second by Billy Wilder. John Huston was supposed to film *The Man Who Would Be King* but nearly two decades passed before that project would be realized, coming as it did just about the time that the company headed into bankruptcy.

But Allied Artists' prestigious days were numbered. Their backlog of B-westerns, tawdry melodramas, and Bowery Boys comedies eventually caught up with them. From time to time an *El Cid* (1961) or *Billy Budd* (1962) would carry the AA logo but the company's real image more comfortably rested with *Attack of the Fifty Foot Woman* (1958).

In contrast, American-International flourished during Allied Artists' struggle for survival, a time when both RKO and Republic folded. AIP's secret for success was more or less to follow Sam Katzman's blueprint for specializing in the transitory tastes of young audiences who, according to the surveys, constituted the largest percentage of the ticket-buying public. AIP movies were inexpensive, black and white "quickies" tailored especially to fill double-feature slots at drive-ins and second run grind houses.

American-International was founded by James Harvey Nicholson, an ex-theatre manager, and Samuel Zachary Arkoff, a lawyer. They first met while Nicholson was working for Jack Broder. Broder's company, Realart Pictures, was a small outfit that earned most of its revenue by rereleasing old Universal movies. Arkoff came to Broder's office to demand some restitution for one of his clients, Alex Gordon. Gordon had submitted a script to Broder, *The Atomic Monster*, which Broder promptly rejected, then used the title on a rerelease of *Man Made Monster* (1941). When Arkoff managed to extract $500 from the tight-fisted Broder, Nicholson was impressed. After emitting a surprised whistle he told Arkoff to leave his card. "There are an awful lot of people in this town who could use you!" A few months later the two men joined forces and with the meager sum of $4500 (or $3500, the story varies from telling to telling) they formed the American Releasing Corporation which became American-International three years later. Joseph Moritz, a veteran exhibitor, was their third partner. Five years after the release of their first feature, AIP moved into a new office building on the site where Charlie Chaplin had once filmed his *City Lights* (1931).

A few months prior to that company event, Nicholson and Arkoff had hosted a luncheon in Miami for exhibitors. Producer Jerry Wald chose the occasion to challenge the two men's morality. He begged Nicholson and Arkoff to lift their horizons. Pictures like *Hot Rod Girl* (1956) and *I Was a Teenage Frankenstein* (1957) were not, Wald told them, the sort of pictures that would build a market for the future. "While they make a few dollars today they will destroy us tomorrow." Many critics supported Wald. Writing about one of AIP's efforts, *The Hollywood Reporter* noted: "A few weeks ago a Brooklyn school principal committed suicide because he could not suppress the rape and hoodlumism in his institution. *The Cool and the Crazy* is a badly written, sloppily edited, poorly directed, low-budget film that may well inspire more such tragedies."

In their defense, Nicholson rose to his feet and stated that he would prefer that his own children see an AIP picture than something like *God's Little Acre* (1958), which was hardly the issue. To Wald, Nicholson's remark was about as relevant as a father declaring that he would rather see his child shot than hung. But then Wald had little business attacking Nicholson and Arkoff on a morality issue since his own *Peyton Place* (1957) had contained elements of rape, incest, and murder. Besides, as a general rule, AIP pictures were pretty harmless. Teenagers were rarely seen smoking, drinking, or taking drugs, at least not during the fifties. Herman Cohen, the producer of *I Was a Teenage Werewolf* (1957) and other youth-oriented epics, was quite proud of this fact. "My teenagers were clean teenagers. They never took heroin up-the-arm; they weren't involved in any illicit sex things, and my films always received PG ratings, when the ratings did start."

In truth, the most provocative element of American-International's pictures were the titles and advertising campaigns, usually conceived before the scripts were even written. The contents of the pictures were quite often dull by contrast, and always very moral. "I personally felt that the kids never took those pictures seriously," said John Ashley whose first film appearance was in *Dragstrip Girl*. "I think they went to those pictures and laughed at them. They didn't really get that involved because the pictures were not well made. They were written by men who were in their late thirties or forties. The stories were pretty standard stuff. The wildness in those days was pretty mild. The kids got off on them but didn't think they were any better than I thought they were. To me the picture that had the most impact was *Rebel Without a Cause*, strictly because Dean was so charismatic. I was no kid at the time but I went out and got me a red jacket. I saw his pictures over and over again because I could identify with Dean. Between he and Brando, if you couldn't figure out who you wanted to be you were really out to lunch."

Still the controversy continued over the possible damaging effects of AIP's product. Producer Alex Gordon, Arkoff's former client, volunteered to discuss the matter on Paul Coates' *Confidential File* television, a sort of forerunner to the currently popular *60 Minutes*. After a Mike Wallace-type grilling, Gordon was able to convince Coates that the pictures were quite harmless. "I don't think he'd even seen any of them," Gordon said and he was probably right. Like many others, Coates was probably responding to the advertisements. But it hardly mattered. Nicholson and Arkoff were not about to change their profitable ways. After floundering during their first two years in business, the company had found its niche in teenpix.

It was 1956 when American-International Pictures released their first "Twin Bop Rock 'n' Sock Show!" The first feature was *Shake, Rattle and Rock* which boasted of Fats Domino and Big Joe Turner in the cast. A quip from the poster pretty much summed up the story: "Rock 'N' Roll vs The 'Squares'." What it actually was was a rehash of Sam Katzman's *Don't Knock the Rock*.

Michael "Touch" Connors starred as the likeable host of a rock 'n' roll television show, patterned after Dick Clark's "American Bandstand." Margaret Dumont, once a straight-woman for the Marx Brothers, appeared as the leader of a comically indignant group of oldtimers who are protesting rock music for want of something better to do. During one of Connors' local dances several unruly teens engage in some petty vandalism* and Connors gets into a bind when he refuses to name the youngsters involved. The kids rally to his side when "Touch" decides to put rock 'n' roll on trial. With television cameras rolling, he interrogates his hipster sidekick (Sterling Holloway) whose "jive talk" responses are

*Such events always transpired during the performances of tepid white singers, a possible attempt to avoid attaching any racial significance to these actions.

translated into English subtitles at the bottom of the screen. Connors finally calls himself as a witness, acting as the interrogator simultaneously as Woody Allen would do fifteen years later in *Bananas* (1971). To wrap up his case, he runs an old film of kids in the 1920s dancing wildly to the Charleston. Miss Dumont is recognized as one of those frantic dancers so she agrees to stop complaining. Fats Domino arrives to perform "I'm in Love Again" while youngsters and oldsters alike rock out until the closing credits.

Whatever else might be said of this picture, it was at least novel in that it approached the subject matter with humor, pale as it may have been.

The companion feature was a throwback to the forties and movies like *Delinquent Daughters* and *I Accuse My Parents*. It starred Marla English, Mary Ellen Kay, and Gloria Castello as the *Runaway Daughters* of Lou Rusoff's script, three high schoolers from troubled homes. It was still early enough in the game for Rusoff (Arkoff's brother-in-law) to feel obliged to show some motivation for his teenaged characters by offering glimpses of their individual home lives. Marla's folks give her everything but the love and understanding she needs, a cliché that harkens all the way back to *Wild Company*. Mary's father wants to be certain she does not disgrace him the way her mother had (shades of *The Unguarded Moment*) so he puts the nix on her dating. Lastly, and taking a cue from Plato's invisible parents in *Rebel Without a Cause*, Gloria's mother is living abroad, in the process of divorcing her third husband. When the girls head for Los Angeles to start a new life they run headlong into trouble. Nothing, however, to equal the real life trouble that befell actor Tom Conway who suffered a hemorrhage two days into the picture. This sort of setback on a fast schedule picture is tantamount to a major blockbusters's being delayed by five or six weeks of bad weather. As a matter of fact, bad weather threatened an earlier AIP picture, *Girls in Prison* (1956), filming on location in Chatsworth. The unexpected series of minor tornadoes nearly shut production down until director Edward L. Cahn decided it would add to the realism of the picture and forged ahead. But Cahn could do nothing about Conway's condition. He was instructed by the film's producer, Alex Gordon, to shoot around the actor until a replacement could be found. Gordon was fortunate in securing the talents of John Litel. Litel arrived on the set at ten o'clock the next morning, took twenty minutes to look over the script and finished the day without so much as fluffing a line. And at AIP if you didn't fluff a line the scene was considered a take. Between Litel and Ed Cahn, Gordon was able to complete his picture in nine days as originally scheduled, despite the two day setback.

"Eddie was an old pro, said John Ashley. "I remember there was one

From left: Marla English, Mary Ellen Kaye, Gloria Castello, and Adele Jergens in **Runaway Daughters** (AIP 1957).

day when we shot 56 set-ups.* But I think Eddie had reached the point in his life where he knew that these pot-boilers that he was knocking out weren't going to get him established."

In such a frenzied atmosphere, Anna Sten seemed quite out of place when she arrived on the first day of shooting with her champagne and caviar sandwiches. She was upset when she first learned that she would be sharing a dressing room with Adele Jergens. The producer had to politely explain that things were a little different at AIP than they had been when she worked for Sam Goldwyn, the producer who had given her the royal treatment after importing her from Russia in the hope that she would be another Greta Garbo. After all, *Runaway Daughters* was not a Sam Goldwyn production. It was nine days and $94,000.

Mobility being a major asset in any teenager's quest for independence, it only stood to reason that any motor vehicle, especially cars, played a large role in teenage folklore. Part of the prevailing competitive attitude was: the faster the car, the more prestige it held. Older cars were often given modified engines and called hot-rods, yet another symbol of contempt for adult conventions. Having always been a favorite subject for the camera's eye, vehicles in motion became the focal point of numerous films aimed at young audiences.

AIP's *Hot Rod Girl* became, in many respects, the archetype of the genre. John Smith was the influential leader of a group of hot-rodders. Chuck Connors was the obligatory friendly police officer, the initiator of a racing strip to keep the kids off the streets. When John's younger brother is killed in a race, John withdraws from the group. Without his leadership the other kids soon abandon the strip and return to racing on the public streets. John's girl, Lori Nelson, cannot understand his attitude and shifts her attention to newcomer Mark Andrews who, to prove Lori made the right selection, challenges John to a hot rod race. Another youngster is killed and John is held to blame. Connors launches an extensive investigation which points the finger of guilt at Andrews. John and Lori discover their true love and, presumably, hot rod into the sunset.

The old romantic triangle got another fuel-injected workout in AIP's *Dragstrip Girl* (1957), reuniting Edward L. Cahn and Alex Gordon, the director and producer of *Runaway Daughters*. And once again Lou Rusoff penned the scenario, attempting to make his teenage dialogue as realistic as possible by taking notes whenever his own kids and their friends were within an earshot.

The plot was pretty simple. Fay Spain moves into town and immediately attracts the attention of Steve Terrell and John Ashley. Not wishing to become involved with either boy, she instead enjoys playing one against the other. To Ashley she represents far more than just another conquest. In a not too brief sequence with Fay he confesses that

*A major studio average was more like four or five set-ups a day.

Frank Gorshin and Judy Bambar in Dragstrip Girl (AIP 1957).

Terrell has always has his "number" even when they were just kids. "We'd both go after the same thing and somehow he'd always get it." So much for motivation. From this point on Ashley will stop at nothing to defeat Terrell, both on and off the race track. To vent some of his rage, he challenges Terrell to a series of dangerous drag races. When one of the suicidal contests causes an injury to one of the bystanders, Ashley's indifference to the wounded party makes Fay think twice about him. Earlier in the film she had told her mother that "serious" was the last thing in the world she wanted to be. "All that jazz comes soon enough." The dangerous reality of her speed crazy search for kicks begins sinking in.

Not satisfied with the outcome of the chicken runs, Ashley decides to enter the U.S.A. Regional Sweepstakes. Being from a rich family he has little need for the scholarship prize being offered but he knows Terrell must win it in order to continue his schooling. Ashley wants some idea of what he is up against so he breaks into the garage housing Terrell's hot-rod and takes it for a ride. He accidentally kills a pedestrian and is later content to let Terrell take the blame for it when the police arrest him on the day of the race. Fay jumps into Terrell's car and finishes the race for him. Not only does she win the scholarship but supplies the police with evidence that puts Ashley in the car on the night of the hit and run. Clearly she has not only chosen the right guy but a more responsible lifestyle as well.

Terrell, Ashley, Gordon, Cahn, and Rusoff joined forces again for *Motorcycle Gang* (1957). So as not to tamper with success, Terrell played the hero again with Ashley his nemesis. Ashley recalled that his early typecasting as a villain upset his mother. "My mother, who was a Baptist midwestern lady, always felt she had to defend me to all of her friends. She didn't understand why I had to play all those evil roles and told her friends that I really wasn't like that."

Since the film opens with Ashley returning from jail after a fifteen month stint for hit and run, *Motorcycle Gang* seems, at first, to be a sequel to *Dragstrip Girl*. Once the plot begins to unfold it appears to be more of a remake. Instead of Fay Spain's acting as the catalyst for the rivalry between Terrell and Ashley, Anne Neyland takes over the chore. And the test of manhood is accomplished on motorcycles instead of hot-rods. Only the climax deviates slightly. Ashley and his gang are disqualified from the PMT races so they decide to vent their rage on a few citizens in a small town, a shoestring version of *The Wild One*. Terrell and his gang of "good" boys quickly restore order.

Adept at speed, director Cahn was able to shoot the picture during the two week furlough Ashley was given following his basic training at Fort Ord. More than aware that juvenile delinquents and "skin-heads" did not mesh, Ashley had convinced an understanding second lieutenant to let him start growing his hair. But one determined sergeant used a full field inspection as an excuse to march Ashley, and several others, to the company barber shop one day prior to Ashley's furlough. Equally determined, the actor positioned himself at the back of the column and during the march spotted a young man delivering newspapers. "I called him over, handed him a couple of bucks and traded my fatigue jacket for his sack of papers which I quickly threw over my shoulder. He took my place in line. When the rest of the group did a 'column right' I executed a left flank and returned to the barracks with my hair intact."

Another romantic rivalry formed the basis of *Teenage Thunder* (1957) with the smaller Howco-International cutting in on AIP's and AA's turf. Chuck Courtney and Robert Fuller were the hot-rod enthusiasts who competed with each other on and off the track. Melinda Byron, an attractive girl working as a waitress at the gang's hangout, shows Chuck some attention so Fuller challenges him to a chicken race. Both drivers speed toward each other with Melinda attempting to stop them by standing in the middle of the road at the point of impact. Chuck and Robert swerve to avoid hitting her. The police arrive. This scrape with the law causes an argument between Chuck and his father. He leaves home but pops up later for the big drag race against Fuller. As expected, Chuck wins the race, the girl, and his father's respect. He rounds off his perfect day by beating the tar out of Rob Fuller.

Not to be left at the starting line, Allied Artists entered the competition with *Hot Rod Rumble* (1957). "Big" Arny (Richard Hartunian) joins a hot rod club but turns everybody off with his loutish behavior. Leigh Snowden played Arny's girlfriend who gives him the heave-ho for another guy. On their way home from a party, Leigh and her new beau are run off the road by a car resembling Arny's. The boy dies and Arny is ostracized until the real culprit is discovered, another member of the club who was deliberately trying to smear Arny. The club welcomes Arny's return as does his girl. Unfortunately, Arny is still a lout.

The repetition of the unjustly accused hero theme was, understandably, quite popular. It supported the fantasy element of these pictures. Suffering the prejudice of the narrowminded adults (and often peer group), the catharsis of this fantasy would always occur at the climax of the story when the authority figures would come to realize that they had been mistaken in their feelings all along. Teenagers were not so bad after all.

Dragstrip Riot (1958), another AIP picture, followed the formula to the *n*th degree. As the new kid in school, Gary Clark is immediately at odds with an entire cyclist gang and Bob Turnbull, the leader of some car racing fanatics. Turnbull teams with the bikers. Together they attempt to run Clark and his date into a ditch. One of the bikers is killed instead which only makes things worse for Clark. Not only are the bikers angrier than ever but the police, to whom Gary reports the accident, suspect him of having caused it. It seems that Clark is haunted by his past, having spent six months in a house of detention for hurting an innocent boy during a fight. It will come as no surprise to learn that before the film's 68 minute running time has expired, Clark is vindicated of any wrongdoing and gets the girl in the package.

John Ashley was back in *Hot Rod Gang* (1958) which featured his friend, Gene Vincent. As John Abernathy III, Ashley was under the strain of maintaining his grandfather's oppressive life standards in order

to be eligible to inherit the old man's fortune. This leads to a dual existence. At home with his two maiden aunts he remains the gentleman. Away from their supervision he raises some good natured hell with a local car club. When the kids needs money to build a newly designed hot rod for national competition, John disguises himself with a fake beard, calls himself "Big Daddy," and earns some cash as a rock singer. Meanwhile, some other members of the clan indulge in some quicker, illegal money raising activities and John becomes implicated in their crimes. John's dual existence is exposed and all seems lost. But, wait! John is cleared of the charges, freeing him to engage in a racing duel with the leader of the outlaw faction. He emerges victorious, gets the girl (Jody Fair), wins the acceptance of his aunts in spite of his unorthodox lifestyle, and the gang gets together for a rocking victory celebration at his mansion. The audience is left hoping that John will retire from the music scene after the fade out and leave the singing chores to Gene Vincent whose four songs were the only asset of this otherwise dismal entry. Actually, after one more bout with singing in *How to Make a Monster* that same year, Ashley voluntarily dropped out of the music biz. "There was a sequence in *Dragstrip Girl* in a pizza parlor," Ashley recalled with a smirk, "where I pick up a big pizza board that looks like a paddle and did what I thought at the time was a dynamite impersonation of Presley. Elvis and I laughed about it later."

Roger Corman was back at it with *Hot Car Girl* (1958), another Allied Artists picture. Richard Bakalyan was in the lead role as Duke. Together with his friend, Fred (John Brinkley), the two steal auto parts and sell them to a "fence" (Bruno Ve Soto). Duke's cleancut girlfriend, Peg (June Kenney) tries to get him to clean up his act but Duke isn't having any of that. He becomes irritated with Peg's incessant sermonizing and engages in a flirtatious hot rod race with Janice (the everample Jana Lund). A pursuing police officer gets his lunch when his motorcycle collides with the rear of Janice's car. Duke manages to escape but Janice is taken into custody. Duke fears she will spill the beans on him and kills her, then splits from town, taking Peg with him. Following a series of hold-ups, Duke realizes that it's just a matter of time before he's caught so he sends Peg packing. The showdown occurs at the overly familiar Bronson Canyon.* Duke is killed in the gun battle, leaving a note exonerating Peg of any guilt.

Site of hundreds of movies and TV shows, Bronson Canyon was originally a quarry, its minerals used for construction. Once it was abandoned in 1930 it became a convenient location for movies crews, serving as western, Roman or African setting, and even as alien planets.

To many adults, rock and roll and juvenile delinquency were irrevocably linked. Often rock and J.D. movies were played together, as in the 1957 double-bill, Carnival Rock and Teenage Thunder (both Howco-International).

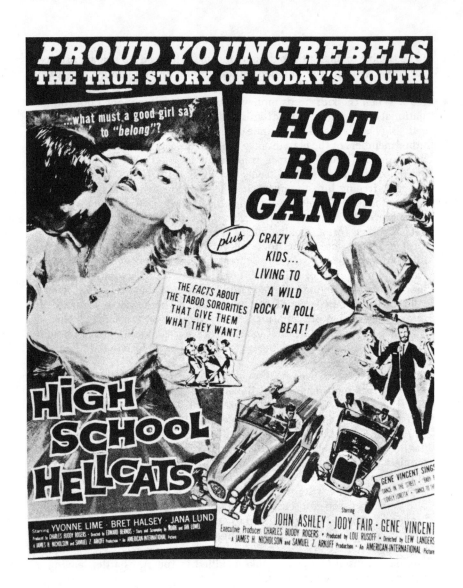

High school, hot-rods, and, of course, girls, were the appeal of this 1958 double feature from AIP, High School Hellcats and Hot Rod Gang.

It is time for June Kenney and Dick Bakalyan to part company: Hot Car Girl (AA 1958).

A "joy ride" in a stolen car escalated into murder in Republic's *Young and Wild* (1958). Rick Braden (Scott Marlowe) and two of his friends take off for a wild ride in a "hot" car. They sideswipe another vehicle driven by Jerry Coltrin (Robert Arthur), and then attack his girl-friend, Valerie (Carolyn Kearny). The couple is saved by some truck drivers. Rick and the gang speed away only to hit and run over a female pedestrian. They abandon the car which is discovered by the police. Rick threatens to kill Jerry and Valerie if they cooperate with the investigating

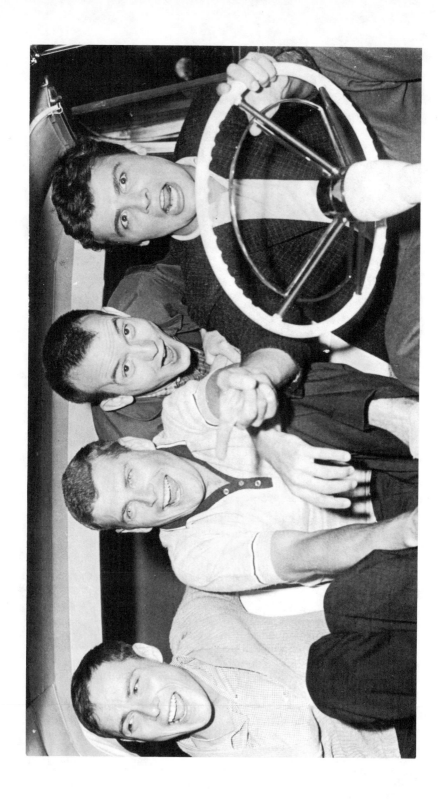

officer, Sgt. Janusz (Gene Evans). Valerie later intimates that she plans to inform on them and when Rick moves in to make good his threat, Janusz and Jerry are waiting.

As the decade progressed, hot rods lost some of their popularity to the new European sports cars. How the kids were expected to make the payments on these expensive imports is another problem. In *Speed Crazy* (1959), Brett Halsey makes ends meet by robbing a gas station. He is forced to kill the attendant and make his escape in his super sport to another town where a racing event is being held. During a series of romantic affairs, Brett becomes rivals with another driver, Charles Wilcox. Meanwhile, the police have traced Brett's special racing tires to the big event. Once the race is underway, Brett tries, unsuccessfully, to force Charlie off the track. At the conclusion of the race, Brett spots the police and tries to escape. Some well-aimed bullets puncture his tires and he careens off a cliff to his death.

The early Ford Thunderbirds may not have been sports cars but they looked sharp enough in *T-Bird Gang* (1959). The "T-Birds" were a gang of thieves headed by sadistic Ed Nelson. He's brought to his just end by a disillusioned member of the group but his days were numbered anyway. John Brinkley had infiltrated the group in co-operation with the police to get the evidence necessary to convict them for the murder of his father.

A unique deterrent for car thieves was demonstrated in *Joy Ride* (1958), shot in eight days for Allied Artists. With such a brief shooting schedule it was necessary for the studio to farm out the chase sequences to a nonunion second unit while director Edward Bernds was back at the studio busily completing the bulk of the film. The story concerned four youths who go to the trouble of breaking into Regis Toomey's home and beating his wife (Ann Doran) just to borrow his car. Obviously there's more at stake than a simple little joy ride. The car is symbolic of power. And when Toomey finally decides to deliver the car to them, the punks assume they have struck a blow for teenage supremacy. But Toomey turns the tables on them. At gunpoint he forces the group's leader (Rad Fulton) to drive the car at breakneck speed through a dangerous mountain road until the tough is reduced to tears. It was the visual realization of movie critic Gerald Weales' request for all delinquent boys to put down their switchblade knives "and come over here and tell Daddy what's the matter." The picture was definitely a fantasy for those indignant adults who had had enough of all this nonsense.

The final destination for such youthful criminals was either the cemetery or juvenile prison. But the sight of teenagers behind bars was a bit too sobering; a wet blanket on the fire of fantasy. So there wasn't a plethora of the type of film that had made the Dead End Kids such a hot item, but there were a few. *So Young, So Bad* (1950) had much in common with those old Warner Brothers' pictures — the sympathetic new

From left: Rad Fulton, Nicholas King, Robert Levin, and an unidentified actor, in Joy Ride (AA 1958).

The sympathetic administrator attempting to reform a reform school was an often used plot device before, and after, So Young, So Bad (UA 1950). Paul Henreid played the psychiatrist, Anne Francis and Rita Moreno were two of the inmates.

authority fighting the cruelty of the old regime — but, unlike its predecessors, took a look at the why and wherefore of juvenile delinquency by offering some background information on four of the wayward girls in the Elmview Corrective Home for Girls.

Paul Henreid played Dr. Jason, the psychiatrist at odds with Superintendent Riggs (Cecil Clovelly) and his brutal head Matron, Mrs. Beuhler (Grace Coppin), a sadistic woman who thinks nothing of using a high-pressure fire hose to discipline the inmates. Only by threatening to expose some of the rampant cruelty is Jason given a free hand to run the school. The psychiatrist takes a special interest in four girls: Loretta Wilson (Anne Francis), Jane Fleming (Enid Pulver), Jackie Boone (Anne Jackson), and Dolores Guerrero (Rosita Moreno — later Rita Moreno).

Loretta describes her childhood as one long struggle for survival. Her mother had always been too sick to care for her and died when she was seven. Her father was a drunkard. "Good thing I was old enough to use a can opener," she tells Jason, "or a lot of times I'd have starved." When her father died some few years after her mother, Loretta "just bummed around," finally marrying one young man who she describes as "a jerk." The marriage ended. Loretta abandoned their child and became a thief to support herself. She was sent to Elmview after being arrested for the attempted theft of a policeman's wallet.

Jane had been raised in a number of orphanages, never having known her parents. At fourteen she went to work on a farm where she was nearly raped by the farm's owner. The act was interrupted by Jackie who chased the farmer away with a pitchfork. The two became inseparable, a sort of mother-child relationship. Breaking into a market to steal some food was their ticket to Elmview.

Dolores was so ashamed of her immigrant parents that she rejected them. "People say we don't even look related," she anxiously confides to the doctor. "Sometimes I don't think they *are* my parents." Jason's efforts to help the girl gain the strength necessary to face the prejudice she had and will encounter prove unsuccessful. Mrs. Beuhler eventually drives the girl to suicide. Her death is then used to illustrate the ineffectiveness of Jason's methods. Fearing that Riggs will have his way again, Loretta and Jackie run away. They return to testify against Riggs and Beuhler when they read of a state investigation in the newspaper. The old administrators are given the axe and Jason is left in charge.

Before putting pen to paper to script *Reform School Girl*, Edward Bernds did a bit of research at a couple of reformatories. As a result, his picture was quite believable, surprisingly well mounted for such a low-budget effort and, in contrast to *Joy Ride*, was sympathetic to the teenagers.

Bernd's film has a slam-bang opening. In less than five minutes, Gloria Castello is nearly raped by her uncle and becomes involved in a hit and run accident. The driver of the car (which was stolen) was Edd Byrnes. He threatens to kill both Gloria and her uncle if either of them squeal on him. The uncle is sufficiently intimidated but Gloria's reasons for remaining silent offers some insight into her past. "You wouldn't believe anything I said anyway," she tells the judge who hustles her off to the Hastings School for Girls. "They're just youngsters here," the principal tells the new school psychiatrist. "Some of the things they've done would make your hair stand on end." It is in this unlikely environment that Gloria meets the first man she feels she can trust, a wholesome young fellow who converses with her through the wire fence that surrounds the school, a fence he later jumps in order to keep their nocturnal rendezvous. The second man to befriend her is the psychiatrist who keeps quiet about the young couple's secret meeting. Byrnes is eventually brought to justice and Gloria set free.

Untamed Youth (1957) was sort of a borderline J.D. prison picture. The restraining facility was not a reformatory but instead a cotton

plantation and besides a couple of the teenage characters looking as if they could use a bath, there were no delinquents in the crowd. It was the adults who ran afoul of the law. This fact did not bother Warner Brothers' publicity department, who exploited the film as if it were the wildest J.D. drama ever:

> Youth turned rock-n-roll 'wild' and the punishment farm that makes them wilder!
> Kids gone wrong — and the 'Farms' disgraceful penal abuse!
> Turns a searing spotlight on teen-age 'cons' in a House of Correction!

The plot, which would not be acceptable as even television drama today, goes something like this. Plantation owner John Russell devises a scheme to recruit cheap labor to pick his cotton. He marries Lurene Tuttle and gets her elected judge. Tuttle's desperate need for Russell forces her to rationalize that it is for the teenagers' own good that they serve a stint on Russell's farm, which she tells them will serve as a sort of rehabilitation program, a place where they can regain their "self respect." Nothing could be further from the truth. The kids live in shacks with inadequate toilet facilities, sleep on canvas cots, and eat dog food disguised as beef stew. And the little money that they earn is used for their clothing, food and medical expenses. When confronted with these facts by her son, together with the recent death of a pregnant girl who was never medically examined, Judge Tuttle can only sob, claiming that she "can't help" herself. She comes to her senses quickly when Lori Nelson makes an allusion to "the boss and the girls." Her Honor sets things right by ordering Russell's incarceration, freeing the kids, and resigning her office.

As stated before, *Untamed Youth* was not much of a J.D. film but as a lurid melodrama it ranks with the best of them. Les Baxter's score is appropriately sleazy and the love scenes between Russell and Tuttle are exquisitely ridiculous. Eddie Cochran sang "Cotton Picker" and superstar Mamie Van Doren supplied the rest of the film's five songs.

Riot in Juvenile Prison (1959) offered more of what the previously discussed film had promised. State psychiatrist Jerome Thor is appointed as the new supervisor to a juvenile hall, recently the site of a riot resulting from the death of two boys at the hands of some sadistic guards. Thor's coeducational rehabilitation program provokes the anger of Scott Marlowe, a young delinquent who resents any sort of help. But Marlowe comes to regret his mistreatment of Thor when another riot, coupled with a rape, forces the psychiatrist to resign, bringing about the return of the former tough regime. So Marlowe organizes a protest riot that continues until Thor is reinstated.

The film was produced by Robert E. Kent who once said that making movies was no different to him than selling shoes. His director was Edward L. Cahn: a perfect marriage of indifference and ineptitude.

Superstar Mamie Van Doren turns on the "hep cats" in this scene from Untamed Youth (Warner Brothers 1957).

High schools were a natural focal point for sordid teenage dramas, demonstrated quite well by *High School Big Shot* (1959). Tom Pittman was the student unpopular because of his high I.Q., in love with the most popular girl on campus, Virginia Aldrich. She plays up to him so that he will write her term paper. Tom's much sought after scholarship is withdrawn when he is caught helping Virginia cheat on her schoolwork. But by this time Tom is more interested in Virginia than he is his studies. He figures the only way to attract her away from her boyfriend is to make money so he applies his intellect towards masterminding a milion dollar robbery. He enlists the help of some professional criminals who are awed by his ingeniously plotted caper. Unfortunately, his plans are betrayed by Virginia to her boyfriend who is more than happy to fill the police in on the robbery.

Edward Bernds took one last crack at the J.D. genre with *High School Hellcats* (1958). Yvonne Lime, feeling alone and insecure, is more than happy to join the Hellcats. But her initiation into the club necessitates the theft of some jewelry. Being an honest girl, Yvonne figures out a way to please the Hellcats and herself. She pulls off the heist but, unbeknownst to the others, leaves the purchase price behind. Big trouble comes when the gang breaks into a deserted home and throws a little party. Suzanne Sidney takes this opportunity to bump off the club leader, Jana Lund, pushing her down a flight of steps so that her death will appear accidental. Fearing that Yvonne may have been a witness to the murder, Suzanne lures her into a movie theatre. She lunges at Yvonne with a knife, loses her balance, and falls to her deserved death over the balcony. This bit of unpleasantness is cushioned by the fact that a romance has been in the works between Yvonne and Brett Halsey.

Writing about the film in *The Hollywood Reporter*, Jack Moffit said: "Contrary to the current Hollywood dogma that young people demand a film diet of youthful criminal violence, I found this teenaged audience so enthusiastically and vociferously on the side of virtue that I left the theatre comfortably reassured concerning the next generation and more than a little inspired." Goodness!

On the subject of the three films he directed, Edward Bernds felt that they were pretty legitimate stories, in spite of the lurid titles and ad campaigns used to sell them. "I can't say I was aware of breaking any new ground. I merely tried to give a representation of what was going on at the time."

Like Bernds, Roger Corman was another director who divided his time between AIP and AA. It was Corman who had brought Nicholson and Arkoff their first release, *The Fast and the Furious* (1954). Republic had offered to purchase the film from Corman but he felt he could get a better deal from Jim and Sam. Which he did. The film was sold to various independent distributors with the stipulation that each would

Jana Lund (left) looks at her new recruit, Yvonne Lime in High School Hellcats (AIP 1958).

Opposite: Barboura Morris (black suit) and Dick Miller share concern over June
Kenney who has just tried to kill herself in this scene from Sorority Girl, Roger
Corman's female version of Calder Willingham's End As a Man (AIP 1957). Above:
Sex and violence were the mainstays of AIP's advertising campaigns, for instance:
the 1957 double-bill of Sorority Girl and Motorcycle Gang.

agree to buy the rights to five more films of similar quality, thereby earning Corman a profit while generating enough financing for new projects
as well.

One of Corman's favorite tricks was to lift the plot of a male oriented
film and switch it around to fit a female cast. He once took writer Charles
Griffith to a Randolph Scott western and the result was *Gunslinger* (1956)
with Beverly Garland filling in for the stalwart Scott. *Swamp Women*
(1956), *Oklahoma Woman* (1957), and *Viking Women and the Sea Ser-*
pent (1958) were all examples of this sort of role changing. Calder

Willingham's *End As a Man** provided the foundation for Leo Lieberman's screenplay, *Sorority Girl* (1957), which Corman produced and directed. In the film Susan Cabot must graduate from college to be eligible for the family fortune. Susan hates everyone at the small university, though she possesses an evil ability to dominate nearly all of the girls in her sorority. Above all she dislikes Barboura Morris, mostly because of the girl's popularity. Barboura really gets on Susan's bad side when she stops her from hazing one of the other students over some minor infraction. After that, Susan is determined to place Barboura under her control. She discovers a small box in Barboura's belongings that contains some letters written by her father in prison. Susan is then able to keep Barboura quiet about the hazing incident lest the word be spread about her "jailbird" daddy.

Things are going Susan's way until her mother decides to cut off her allowance just when she has incurred a number of debts. Susan figures to blackmail Barboura's boyfriend, Dick Miller, by forcing a pregnant girl, June Kenney, to name him as the father. Dick will not be railroaded and before he is through June admits the lie, then attempts to kill herself by leaping into the ocean from a high cliff. She is rescued by Dick.

This incident compels Barboura to risk her chances of being elected student body president in order to stop Susan from doing any further damage. She tells the other girls about the secret that Susan has been holding over her head. The girls confront Susan, strip her of her power and leave her to crawl back under the rock from which she came.

Popping over to Allied Artists, Corman produced *Cry Baby Killer* (1958), Jack Nicholson's first film. Corman had met Nicholson during his enrollment in an acting class which he hoped would broaden his working knowledge as a director. The two became friends which lead to Nicholson being cast in the picture. He starred as Jimmy, a quiet 17-year-old who is beaten up by three teenage punks because their leader has the hots for Jimmy's girl. When Jimmy challenges the leader of the gang to a fight at a hamburger joint, he is again attacked by the three toughs. Only this time one of the boys drops his gun and Jimmy gets a hold of it and shoots two of his assailants. Fearing he will be accused of murder, Jimmy races into a storage room and holds some bystanders hostage. The police, TV crews, vendors, and gawkers surround the joint and eventually tear gas is used to force Jimmy to surrender. By this time the authorities have learned that the shooting was in self-defense.

The difference between the class cultures was the underlying theme of Roger Corman's *Teenage Doll* (1957), another Allied Artists release. Charles Griffith's screenplay employs an unusual narrative structure,

---

**Columbia filmed it as* The Strange One *in 1957. In a southern military school, Jocko De Paris (Ben Gazzara) systematically tries to destroy the senior officer in charge. Through his malevolent domination of his classmates, he persuades several boys to force alcohol into the officer's son so the boy will be expelled in disgrace for being drunk. The boy dies and the other classmen rebel against Jocko's regime. Banding together they literally ride him out of town on the rail, Jocko screaming that he will be back.*

In the late 1950s, nonconformity among post-teenagers manifested itself in the "Beat Generation." The Rebel Set, a crime caper with beatniks, was cofeatured with a more traditional J.D. film, Speed Crazy (both Allied Artists 1959).

beginning in the middle of the story and reconstructing what has already transpired as the remainder of the plot continues.

The story takes place in real time during a single night in a lower class urban area. Nan Baker, an attractive teenage girl, lies dead in a deserted back alley. Fleeing from the scene is Barbara Bonney (June Kenney), a "nice" girl from the middle class section of town. Nan's body is discovered by the Black Widows, an all-girl street gang to which she belonged. Hel (Fay Spain), the leader of the Widows, surmises that Barbara murdered Nan and the gang sets out to get her. Barbara manages to make it home but the Widows track her down and she is again forced to escape into the night. She seeks sanctuary with the Vandals, another gang whose headquarters are hidden in an auto junkyard. Barbara confesses that she fought with Nan over the attention of Eddie (John Brinkley), the leader of the Vandals. During the fight, Barbara pushed Nan, accidentally sending her plummeting off a stairway. Eddie publicly derides her for her actions and for possibly leading the Widows to their hideout. Eddie mobilizes the Vandals for a showdown with the Widows and their male allies, the Tarantulas. The rival gangs raid the auto yard and a vicious rumble breaks out. The police, who have already traced Nan's death to Barbara, arrive and the gangs disperse. Hiding in a deserted warehouse, Eddie gives Barbara the option of giving herself up or escaping with him into a life of crime. Barbara chooses to surrender herself to the authorities.

Teenage Doll offers a bleak, uncompromising view of the underside of urban street life. Much of the film was shot on actual locations at night, giving the images a stark, desolate quality. June Kenney, as Barbara, is almost continually on the run throughout the picture, a fugitive from the gangs, the police, and her own feelings. The appeal of Eddie and what he represents is paralleled by a story told by Barbara's childlike mother (Dorothy Neuman). Like Barbara, her middleclass momma once had a brief, exciting affair with a notorious bootlegger before settling for a routine but secure husband. Eddie, despite his cynical exterior, understands Barbara's dilemma and the cultural differences which divide them. Eddie feels that Barbara has committed a greater crime than murder by stepping out of her class. During their momentary breather in the warehouse, he appraises her choices. She can be killed by the Widows, arrested for murder, or escape to Arizona and learn to scuffle like him. When Barbara recoils from her three options, Eddie retorts, "At least you have a choice." Barbara, true to her upbringing, places her fate in the hands of society. Eddie escapes to a life of crime and premature death, a fate shared by her mother's lover. Two members of the Widows, one of them the wayward daughter of a police detective assigned to the case, also surrenders to the authorities. Hel and the remaining Widows escape to their old haunts and decide to drink a few beers while they wait for the sun to rise.

Griffith's original script had each gang member returning to their respective homes to secure some kind of weapon before reuniting to kill Barbara. One of the weapons Griffith dreamed up was a little item he called a "potato grenade," which was a potato impaled on a peeler then riddled with razor blades. The idea was nixed by the Hays office. Instead the girls hire someone else to do the job. "That really ruined it," Griffith said. "We also had a very unsatisfactory ending because we couldn't figure out what the hell we could get away with."

One less than enthusiastic reviewer pointed out that while the picture seemed to be directed toward the fight against juvenile delinquency, the only real contribution it made in that direction was to keep its juvenile cast members off the streets by employing them.

Corey Allen, James Dean's rival in *Rebel Without a Cause*, put on his black leather jacket again (figuratively speaking) for *Juvenile Jungle*

(1958). He played a gang leader who masterminds a kidnapping scheme that falls apart when he falls in love with their female victim. Also featured in this minor epic was Richard Bakalyan who must certainly hold the record for performances as teenage hoods. Bakalyan's appearance forever cast him in black leather jackets and motorcycle boots. More often than not he was the brutish, inarticulate bad guy whose aura of almost psychotic menace made him more interesting than the comparitively bland heroes he supported. For a change of pace he was almost the hero of AIP's *The Cool and the Crazy* (1958), one of the first J.D. movies to tackle the subject of dope addiction.

According to Andrew Dowdy's *Movies Are Better Than Ever*, an independent outfit challenged the MPAA taboo against making films about drug addiction several years before Otto Preminger's now famous battle with his film *The Man with the Golden Arm* in 1955. Dowdy states that *Teenage Menace* (1953), released without a seal, played 41 states before New York's Board of Regents banned it as "the most dangerous of its kind," although no more information on this picture could be found.

It was not too surprising that most filmmakers were a little cautious about dealing with the subject even after the Code was revised in 1956. *Monkey on My Back* (1957) played it safe by being a biography (which were quite popular in the fifties), recounting the story of fighter Barney Ross and his bout with heroin addiction. *A Hatful of Rain*, released the same year, was based on a successful Broadway play. With those two nods to sincerity and respectibility out of the way, *Stakeout on Dope Street* (1958) told the story of three lowerclass teenagers who accidentally stumble upon a container full of heroin, abandoned by some criminals when things got too hot. One of the lads wants to turn the stuff over to the police but the other two see a potential profit to be made by selling it to the local pusher in small amounts. The boys soon learn the dispair and degradation connected with their potential money-making venture, caught in the middle with the police on one side of them and the criminals on the other.

AIP quickly moved in with *The Cool and the Crazy* that same year, a drama about "Seven Savage Punks on a Weekend Binge of Violence!"

Fresh out of reform school, Scott Marlowe (the lad who tried to rape Margaret Hayes in *Blackboard Jungle*) enrolls in a new school and immediately takes over a gang of toughs. On the advice of his pusher ("These kids ... they're ripe. They're looking for kicks"), Marlowe eases the gang into a life of drug addiction by first offering them marijuana cigarettes. They never graduate to heroin because in this film there is little difference between the two. In fact, the mentality of the picture was an unfortunate continuation of the ill-informed camp classics of the thirties, *Marijuana* and *Reefer Madness*. "I knew when we did *The Cool and the Crazy* that you don't smoke one joint and then try to bang your head on nails," confessed Dick Bakalyan. And if the actors knew better then, it is reasonably safe to assume that the writers, producers, and directors were also aware of the lie they were perpetuating. This knowledge belies any good intentions that the filmmakers professed, such as the disclaimer

at the end of this picture that the solutions to the problems of teenage dope addicts have been greatly simplified for story purposes. "However it is the sincere hope of the producers that this presentation will raise the guard of teenagers and their parents against the awful perils of narcotic addiction and dramatic license has been taken toward this end." It is obvious that the producers of this type of picture are merely trying to make a fast buck by playing on the public's ignorance and fear.

There is one especially fine moment in *The Cool and the Crazy* that shows Marlowe's connection complaining to his girlfriend about the young pusher. "These kids ... they're all the same. You pick 'em up, buy 'em a new suit.... You'd think they'd play it smart and stay off the stuff. A couple of weeks and he'll want the needle." His sleazy moll just shrugs her shoulders and remarks, "So? You gotta customer instead of a salesman."

As a matter of course with this type of film, the whole business ends in murder when Marlowe's contact will not give him a free shot. Marlowe then races to his own death when, in his drug induced state, he mistakes an automobile's headlights for two motorcycle policemen. By the time he realizes the lights belong to a car it's too late to avoid hitting them and make a safe turn at the same time. He plunges over the side of a cliff. "Take a good look," a policeman orders Bakalyan who has turned his head away from the spectacle of Marlowe's burning vehicle. "It could have been any one of you. Is this what you call kicks? If you don't wise up you're all going to wind up like this, one way or the other." Then, in the film's one brilliant moment, one of the teenagers throws away his regular cigarette in disgust as though the filmmakers had become confused as to what he was smoking. Unless, of course, they meant to also imply that smoking leads to marijuana as well. In all fairness, however, it should be noted that *The Cool and the Crazy* was fairly well directed and did contain some superior performances, especially by Bakalyan.

High School Confidential (1958) also spotlighted the evils of marijuana and heroin. It was the brainchild of producer Albert Zugsmith who once told a reporter from *Life* magazine that his films were moral essays. "I don't make movies without a moral, but you can't make a point for good unless you expose the evil." And his films took absolute delight in "exposing" sin and corruption wherever he found it. If necessary, he created it.

High School Confidential typified many of the current misconceptions about drug addiction, especially concerning marijuana. The "killer weed" is shown to be addictive. Diane Jergens plays one of the high school students "hooked" on reefers. Between "blasts" she exhibits many of the same symptoms of withdrawal normally associated with heroin addiction. The poor girl becomes so strung out that, at one point, she finks on her boyfriend in order to get her trembling hands on a "stick."

Richard Bakalyan (striped vest), Dick Jones (tie) and the boys get their first look at the new kid in school, Scott Marlowe. When Marlowe finishes with them, they'll all be The Cool and the Crazy, high from his reefers (AIP 1958).

Albert Zugsmith's *High School Confidential* (1958) typified many of the then current misconceptions about marijuana. Note that there are no references to drugs in the advertising, a common practice at the time.

Diane's redemption comes when, with the aid of an understanding teacher, she rips a joint apart and drops it on the floor in a frenzy of self disgust.

It stands to reason that if marijuana addiction is bad, then heroin must create a living hell. One female addict is continuously depicted undergoing the tortures of the damned. The audience is left wondering why anyone might find the drug appealing in the first place. The answer is, of course, that marijuana and heroin go together (to paraphrase a popular song) like a horse and carriage. The marijuana smoker continually needs bigger kicks, heroin being the inevitable outcome. The harm in this sort of propaganda lies in the possibility that once the kids realize that what they have been told about marijuana is false, they might be more inclined to believe that the scare tactics against the really dangerous drugs, like heroin, is just more of same.

Character actor Mel Welles, who appears in the film and is credited for providing "special material," told your authors that he not only wrote the "jive talk" dialogue for the film but acted as technical advisor by showing the actors how to roll a joint. An early beatnik himself, Welles had some knowledge about the effects of the drug but his firsthand experience was of no interest to those in charge of decision making. Perhaps it was felt that a more sensational melodrama would be more profitable. Whatever, more than ten years would pass before an objective treatment of the subject would appear on the motion picture screen.

To direct his marijuana exposé, Zugsmith chose Jack Arnold whom he had previously worked with on *The Tattered Dress, The Man in the Shadow,* and *The Incredible Shrinking Man* (all 1957) when both men had been under contract to Universal-International. Arnold's first feature had been a J.D. drama, *Girls in the Night* (1953), a variation on *City Across the River.* Arnold was not happy with the producer, calling him a man of "extreme bad taste," always "happiest when the films were the nastiest." One must confess that it is Zugsmith's lack of taste that sometimes makes his films more entertaining than many with loftier goals. And Zugsmith's casts were equally entertaining, employing as his regular stock company such unusual performers as Ray Anthony, Jackie Coogan, and, of course, Mamie Van Doren. Other stalwarts included Paul Anka, Billy Daniels, Steve Cochran, Elisha Cook, Jr., Margaret Hayes, Mickey Rooney, Fay Spain, Mel Torme, Conway Twitty, Vampira, and Walter Winchell. The producer was also fond of famous last names, frequently casting John Drew Barrymore, Charles Chaplin, Jr., Cathy Crosby, Harold Lloyd, Jr., and Jim Mitchum. It should be noted that he also kept one crewcut Neanderthal named Norman Grabowski (Woo Woo Grabowski or just plain Grabowski) out of the unemployment lines.

High School Confidential opens with the grim face of Dr. Stewart Knox, then chairman of the narcotics committee of the Los Angeles County Medical Association. After being introduced by an off-screen announcer, Dr. Knox asks the audience: "How many parents are awake to the temptations facing their children? I do not mean petty infringements.

I refer to the terribly dangerous traffic which this film exposes. The story takes place in America but could happen anywhere which is why police throughout the world have special divisions in close international cooperation to deal with this modern problem. *High School Confidential* will shock you and, I hope, alert you."

This pseudo-serious documentary tone is quickly dispelled by the enigmatic appearance of Jerry Lee Lewis, riding on the back of a truck, cruising past a high school, pounding away at his piano while he sings the film's title song, as though he was some kind of crazy pied piper. After his departure, Russ Tamblyn arrives on the scene and immediately causes trouble. He begins by bullying his way into one of the student's parking space. When the angry driver protests, Tamblyn cautions him. "You got thirty-two teeth, buster. You wanna try for none?" He then makes an obnoxious pass at the first cute girl he sees. "Hi ya, sexy. You look real cultured. Let's cut out to some drag 'n' eat pad." This proposition is also an insult to the girl's companion, John Drew Barrymore, the president of the Wheelers and Dealers. Later Tamblyn makes good his boast to one impressed student that, by the end of the day, the whole "crummy" school would know who he is. He accomplishes this by pulling a knife on three tough "cats" in the locker room, insulting his history teacher, and by propping his feet up on the principal's desk while he smokes a cigarette. A few loose remarks about his "looking to graze on some grass" nets Tamblyn his sought after drug connection who turns out to be Barrymore. Not realizing that Tamblyn is actually a narcotics agent, Barrymore unwittingly takes him to the top man, Mister A, played by Jackie Coogan. With the help of several "straight" teenagers, Tamblyn brings Coogan and his henchmen to justice.

Besides the script's being liberally peppered with jive talk, it contains equal amounts of sanctimonious preaching. When several dragsters are arrested and discovered to be in possession of marijuana, one outraged father threatens to sue the police. "[He's] no exception," the desk sergeant tells his subordinate. "The other parents will soon be here jumping all over us. 'Not my child! Oh! No! It's a horrible mistake!' They won't believe the truth because they don't want to, until it's too late. And then they'll call us bums because we didn't warn them in time."

Another sequence shows a police commissioner displaying a marijuana cigarette while he discusses the drug abuse problem with a group of skeptical teachers:

> *Miss Williams:* Commissioner, don't you think you're magnifying this issue?
> *Burroughs:* A marijuana cigarette was found on the floor of one of your classrooms. And another was found in the girl's gym.
> *Miss Williams:* And that's enough to start a big crusade in Santa Bella High?
> *Principal:* Mister Burroughs, please understand. Miss Williams, like many of us, believes in the progressive theory that there is no such thing as a bad boy or girl.
> *Burroughs:* Well, there's a high school in Indiana — I don't know

Top: Mamie Van Doren is looking to pitch a little woo with her nephew, Russ Tamblyn in High School Confidential (M-G-M 1958). Bottom: Ray Anthony (left) brings on the horse for Russ Tamblyn in High School Confidential. Jackie Coogan (middle) does not know it but Tamblyn is really a narcotics agent about to put him out of business (M-G-M 1958).

whether they followed your progressive theories or not—they had no problem three years ago. But out of a total enrollment of 1200 students, 285 were found to be using marijuana or heroin. And this dreadful condition was only uncovered through a horrible accident. One student, desperate for money to pay for his habit, sold bennies for quarters and dimes to kids in elementary school. It was the death of a thirteen year old who had been addicted to marijuana and then to heroine that exposed the ugly facts. But by that time it was too late for 41 teenagers who were addicted. *It can happen here!*

Burroughs' audience is notably shaken.

Within the context of a film which takes such delight in the antics of addicts, the pious diatribes against the evils of drugs seems as incongruous as a happy drunk giving a lecture on the "horrors" of alcoholism.

"I feel an obligation to give this new screen public what it wants," Zugsmith said. "*High School Confidential* was a true-to-life yarn and presented the dope problem in such a shocking fasion it scared the pants off those viewing it." The producer's obligation apparently didn't extend to 17-year-old Kathleen Briggs who instigated a law suit against Zugsmith to the tune of $9000. According to Miss Briggs, he had not paid her for material that she supplied for the script.

One of the film's many pleasantries is Mamie Van Doren in the role of Russ Tamblyn's aunt. That she is unaware of his being a federal agent is no more confusing than her constant attempts to seduce him. "I was always playing weird types in weird pictures," Miss Van Doren declared. And she played them to the hilt. More often than not her performance was the sole asset of the films in which she appeared. She paraded her pulchritude through a number of Zugsmith pictures—*The Big Operator*, *The Beat Generation* (both 1959), *Sex Kittens Go to College* and *The Private Lives of Adam and Eve* (both 1960).

Best of the lot was *Girls Town* (1959) which hilariously cast singer Mel Torme as a sports car enthusiast, Sheila Graham as a humorous nun, and Ray Anthony (Mamie's real-life husband) as a gumshoe. In this one Mamie is on probation for smacking one of her teachers. She is sent to Girls Town after being arrested as one of the participants in a fight at a beer bust. At Girls Town, Mamie finds a Father Flanagan counterpart in Margaret Hayes, the Mother Superior. In spite of her restrictive surroundings, Mamie manages to help love-starved Gigi Perreau hook up with Paul Anka and, with the help of Gloria Talbott, whip Mel Torme's ass with some well-applied judo. Mel was blackmailing Mamie's kid sister, Eleanor Donahue. She had accidentally pushed Harold Lloyd, Jr., over a cliff in self-defense and Mel saw the whole thing.

At the film's conclusion, Mamie turns religious. It proved to be too much for *Variety*: "At a time when Hollywood is facing a rising storm of opposition about films with adult themes and adult treatment, it cannot help but be ammunition for the opposition. In the case of 'Girls Town,' there is not a mitigating ounce of artistry or the pretense of it." Oh, well, what does *Variety* know anyway?

In terms of world cinema, it may have appeared that juvenile delinquency was exclusively an American phenomenon. If, as some unnamed M-G-M executive had once suggested, the problem was actually worse in the Soviet Union, it certainly was not displayed in their motion pictures. It remains one of the great strengths of our free enterprise system that governmental intervention in the arts is primarily a threat, seldom a reality. While the U.S. undoubtedly led the rest of the world in films about juvenile delinquency, a few other countries took a look at this sensitive issue with their own distinctive interpretations.

The influence of *Blackboard Jungle* and *Rebel Without a Cause* in West Germany prompted a homegrown product in 1956 titled *Die Halberstarken (The Half Strong Ones)*. The film was imported to England in 1957, dubbed, and retitled *Teenage Wolf Pack*. It proved popular enough for a minor U.S. distributor, D.C.A., to release it stateside. It hardly inspired a new vogue for German made J.D. films although its star, Horst Buchholz, enjoyed a modest success with American audiences a few years later in *Fanny* and *One Two Three* (both 1961).

Along with the obvious cultural differences, the members of the *Teenage Wolf Pack* did not ride hotrods or motorcycles. The postwar economy in Germany being what it was, the German J.D.'s had to be content to flaunt their defiance of society while riding bicycles. Buchholz and his gang attempt the robbery of a mail van and later a wealthy family and prove unsuccessful at both.

Great Britain had long since abandoned the concept that every motion picture should be acceptable for every family member, yet their censors were considerably stricter in spite of the fact that younger audiences were restricted from seeing a large portion of the films available, including those dealing with juvenile delinquency. In spite of this fact, the knife fights in both *Rebel Without a Cause* and *High School Confidential* were deleted in the British versions while *The Wild One* was banned altogether. The British-made juvenile delinquency films naturally reflected this more conservative attitude. *These Dangerous Years* (1957), released in the U.S. a year later under the more exploitive title, *Dangerous Youth*, was the motion picture debut of British star Frankie Vaughan as the tough leader of a dockside gang. Vaughan is on his way to becoming a star when he is drafted into the army. He initially rebels against military discipline but eventually "grows up," marries his singing partner (Carole Leslie), and becomes a military career man — which is far more of an adult fantasy than even the American made *Joy Ride* had been. The most noteworthy element in the film are the early sequences with Vaughan and his gang, roaming around the dreary seaport town of Liverpool, a locale later famous for spawning the Beatles.

In *Bad Girl*, another British entry (also known as *Teenage Bad Girl*), Sylvia Sims played a young lady who inadvertently wanders outside the law before returning, sadder but wiser, to the path of righteousness. Gillian Hills did a similar number in *Beat Girl* (1960), A.K.A. *Wild for Kicks*, in which she tries to dig up sordid information about her step-mother whom she hates.

It often happens that one genre will merge into another. The western began showing the influence of the J.D. dramas as early as 1957 when Robert Wagner appeared in *The True Story of Jesse James*. Director Nicholas Ray treated the legendary killer like a troubled adolescent. The same was true of *The Left-Handed Gun* (1958) in which Paul Newman portrayed Bill the Kid as if he had been James Dean. According to one critic, *Escape from Red Rock* (1958) would have been more aptly titled *I Was a Teenaged Desperado*. It was written and directed by Edward Bernds who frankly admitted that he had more or less transplanted *Rebel Without a Cause* to a western locale. Gary Murray was in the James Dean role, forced into hiding because of his peripheral involvement in a crime instigated by his older brother. Eilene Janssen was the Natalie Wood character, staying by Gary's side. Crunch, Goon and the gang became Murray's brother and his outlaw gang who know that Gary can identify them. Some Indians were thrown in for good measure.

The Plunderers (1960) in Allied Artists' western turned out to be four young saddle tramps — Ray Stricklyn, John Saxon, Roger Torrey, Dee Pollock — who ride into the town of Trail City, kill the cowardly sheriff (Jay C. Flippen) and take control of the place. (Once again the influence of *The Wild One* can be felt even in the 1860s.) But this time the hoods are not challenging the impotence of Wrightsville. They have Jeff Chandler to contend with and even with one arm paralyzed, he proves to be their match. Only Pollock is allowed to ride away alive once Chandler realizes he was simply the victim of bad company.

The most ingenious bit of genre mixing came from AIP and producer Herman Cohen with the release of *I Was a Teenage Werewolf*. The title, butt of countless jokes, seemed at first to reinforce adult fears that teenagers were nothing more than little monsters. The switch was that the villain of the piece was a psychiatrist whose evil influence over the youthful hero is responsible for making the boy a monster. "We did that purposely," confessed Cohen. He not only produced the picture but wrote it as well, with help from Aben Kandel, both using the single pseudonym, Ralph Thornton. "I felt this would appeal to a teenage audience ... which it did."

Michael Landon played the title character, a troubled youth in desperate need of guidance. His widowed father is well-meaning but his job keeps his away from the boy most of the time. After Landon engages in a series of nasty brawls, he is convinced to seek help from psychiatrist Whit Bissell. Alas, the doctor is quite mad. "Mankind is on the verge of destroying itself," Bissell tells his sniveling assistant. "The only hope for the human race is to hurl it back into its primitive dawn ... to start all over again." Bissell is positive that Landon's disturbed background makes him the ideal subject for his experiment in regression. Through hypnosis he takes the boy back to the time when he was a werewolf, something Darwin never told us about. Once Landon realizes what he has become

Michael Landon is the one under all that fur in one of his first film roles, I Was a
Teenage Werewolf (AIP 1957).

and that he is responsible for a number of brutal murders, he returns to
the doctor and begs him for help. Bissell responds by regressing him once
again so that he can photograph the metamorphosis. As the werewolf,
Landon kills both doctors just before the police conveniently burst in and
gun him down.

So successful was this hybrid of the J.D. and horror film that Cohen
quickly switched his male monster to a female, changed the werewolf to
a vampire and used the same plot for his *Blood of Dracula* (1957). The

only real difference between the two scenarios was the omission of the regression concept. Interest in regression had been sparked by a book called *The Search for Bridey Murphy* published by Doubleday in 1956. It was written by a young businessman named Morey Bernstein, recounting his experiments on Ruth Simmons who, in a trance, recalled events prior to her birth. When asked her name she replied "Bridey Murphy" and then proceeded to describe her life as a saucy-tongued girl in 1798 Ireland. The event, which took place in Pueblo, Colorado, in 1952, became table conversation for a short while. But interest soon waned. By the time Cohen was ready to make *Blood of Dracula*, scant months after *Teenage Werewolf*, the issue was already dead.

By combining the two genres, Cohen opened the door for other producers who were happy to follow suit. Cohen himself contributed *I Was a Teenage Frankenstein* (1957), *How to Make a Monster* (1958), and *The Headless Ghost* (1959), all combining teenagers and monsters. Howco-International quickly changed the name of their *Meteor Monster* to *Teenage Monster* (1958), AIP's *Prehistoric World* became *Teenage Caveman* (1958), and U-I's *Stranger in the Night* was retitled *Monster on the Campus* (1958). Since these yarns were primarily concerned with elements of horror rather than juvenile delinquency, we will leave the task of discussing them to some other film historian. However, *The Blob* (1958) contained many plot situations that paralleled *Rebel Without a Cause*. The film's star, Steve McQueen, affected many of Dean's mannerisms while wearing a red jacket. His efforts to warn the town about the giant gelatinous mass from space that is eating everyone in sight are misconstrued by the authority figures. To them McQueen is nothing but a trouble-making hoodlum with a penchant for drag racing on the city streets. Don Sullivan is viewed in a similar light until he sacrifices his prized hotrod, loaded with nitroglycerine, to kill *The Giant Gila Monster* (1959).

So desperate were the various studios to cash in on the new craze that Warner Brothers purchased a student film by Tom Graeff and released it as *Teenagers from Outer Space* (1959). As to be expected, considering its source, the film was pretty skimpy in production values and had little to recommend it in other departments as well. Basically it was another variation on "the new kid in school" theme, only this time the new kid was from another planet. The Amboy Dukes would have coveted the weapons used by the aliens, a gun which blasted the flesh off humans, certainly a major improvement over those metal shop zip guns.

There were one or two other combined genre films, *Teenage Zombies* (1960) being an example, but for all practical purposes Tom Graeff's film marked the end of an era. Teenagers were being filtered out of horror and science fiction films just as the juvenile delinquents began occupying less space in the newspapers. As the new decade approached the output of J.D. films decreased.

Chapter Four

Sex and Drugs
and Rock 'n' Roll

"The wrong people, the wrong drugs have taken
over. English majors (ugh), fraternity boys and the
down-and-outers who would have been bums anywhere are joining the culture. The aggressive
psychotic drunk has sprung up now in the drug
culture. Heroin and speed have replaced marijuana
and LSD. Hippie violence against hippie has
become commonplace. It is numbers: too many
hippies. We can only afford so many people alienated from society." — Charlie Whitman, 27 year old
hippie lawyer.

George Gobel was once asked if he thought the teenagers of the late
1950s would ever grow into responsible adults. "Frankly," replied Gobel,
"I don't think they'll live that long." His tongue-in-cheek remark was less
amusing than Jackie Gleason's earnest declaration that Elvis Presley
would be a short-lived novelty. Although both statements proved to be
equally false, for a brief period of time the two comedians appeared to be
prophetic.

After selling more than $120 million worth of RCA records, and at
the peak of his career, Elvis Presley left the spotlight for a tour of duty in
the Army. When he returned, rock 'n' roll had suffered a major setback,
partially due to his absence, but more as a result of the House of Representatives' probe into the music business. It was their desire to determine
if certain disc jockeys were taking bribes to play particular records. Alan
Freed, instrumental in bringing rock music to the public's attention, was
destroyed by what came to be known as the payola scandal.

To minimize further trouble, rock 'n' roll underwent a change in
image. New singing idols like Bobby Darin, Frankie Avalon, and Fabian
sported a much cleaner-cut appearance, their music less raunchy. Elvis
shaved his sideburns and discontinued the exaggerated pelvic thrusts that
had made him such a scandal. He began singing ballads in a series of
vacuous musical comedies that ruined any hope he had once had of being
a serious actor. *Blue Hawaii* (1961) became the prototype for Presley's
post-Army efforts, the recipe going something like this: take one listless

Elvis Presley, prisoner in another silly vehicle: Paradise, Hawaiian Style (Paramount 1965).

rock star (Elvis), place him in a scenic environment (Hawaii, Acapulco, Las Vegas, etc.), add a lot of attractive contract starlets, mix in enough musical numbers to fill a soundtrack album, just enough plot to bring everything together, and film it in color. Someone once noted that Presley's movies didn't need a title, just a number, and his fans would have flocked to see them regardless. But by the time he completed *The Trouble with Girls* (1969), not only had he worn out his welcome at the boxoffice, his singing career was in jeopardy as well.

But Elvis did not fade away as Gleason had predicted, nor did teenage America become extinct, although for a time, their rebellion did. Perhaps having succeeded in making their collective voices heard and their presence acknowledged, violent demonstrations of protest were no longer necessary. Youngsters were content to settle down to the business of fun and frolic, characterized by American-International's "Beach Party" series. Virtually unwatchable, and certainly incomprehensible, the films chronicled Frankie Avalon's endless efforts to free Annette Funicello of her virginity, more or less a teenage version of *Pillow Talk* (1959). Thrown in for good measure were plenty of bikini-clad girls, surfing shots, songs, and comedy bits that would have embarrassed the most hackneyed vaudevillian.

In retrospect, *Beach Party* (1963) was the culmination of a trend of communal confidence that America's young people were experiencing during this period. The wild motorcycle rebels of the fifties were now employed as comic foils for the surfing crowd. As the leader of some incompetent cycle bums, Harvey Lembeck's Eric Von Zipper was a merciless parody of Brando's character in *The Wild One*. Zipper constantly berated his companions ("You stupids!") for simply following his own inept instructions, a symbol of an outdated rebellion.

Frankie and Annette were healthy, wholesome adolescents who never questioned the "American Dream" the zenith of pre-Vietnam optimism. "When we did the beach pictures, AIP was more cognizant of an image," said John Ashley, a regular in the series. "It was a lot different from the old days. I can still remember going to sneak previews of those pictures like *Motorcycle Gang* and *Dragstrip Girl* and when the audience saw that damn AIP logo, they groaned. Of course, those pictures were made in ten days, sometimes less. But Bill Asher, the director of the beach pictures, wanted to maintain an image. We depicted the California surfing crowd as a bunch of fun-loving kids. Always cokes. No beers. Nobody smoked. They even asked us not to smoke between takes."

Director Asher was convinced that teenagers were bored with juvenile delinquency and welcomed clean sex. AIP's president, Jim Nicholson, saw the films as updated Mack Sennett bathing beauty silents while his partner, Sam Arkoff, believed that the films did not even have to make sense so long as they moved too fast to allow time for analysis. For that reason *Time* magazine had a devil of a time making heads or tails of *Beach Party*, calling it "an anthropological documentary with songs." The reviewer closed by branding it more "unoriginal than aboriginal" in its study of primitive behavior patterns. By the time *How to Stuff a Wild Bikini* (1965) came off the assembly line, *Time* nor anyone else even wanted to bother trying to make sense out of the pictures. Who cared? Certainly not Nicholson or Arkoff who were so happy about their successful series that they gave away "Bikini Stuffer" cards as a sort of thank-you to their enthusiastic patrons. The card is reprinted here for those who may not have received one and for the purpose of giving the reader some idea of the calibre of humor to be found in the pictures:

> The bearer is hereby assigned all rights and privileges as an accredited member of the "How to Stuff a Wild Bikini" Association of America and agrees to follow the laws of the organization.
>
> 1. How to .*. with dignity search for material that is proper BIKINI stuffin'.

Opposite: Candy Johnson rocks the surfing set in Beach Party (AIP 1963). Above: The sun soaked optimism of the early sixties was reflected in Beach Party. Frankie Avalon and Annette Funicello were the symbols of healthy, wholesome teenagers who didn't smoke, drink hard liquor, engage in premarital sex, or question the American dream.

2. How to ... properly react when sighting aforesaid material and blow official BIKINI stuffin' alert whistle.

3. How to ... with foresight review American-International Picture's "How to Stuff a Wild Bikini" and report reaction to club president.

Asher was correct in assuming his audience was bored with delinquency, evidenced by the fact that the most popular teen films of the late fifties and early sixties were less concerned with rebellion than with romance. Some of the more conservative studios had already attempted more "positive" youth films like *Rock Pretty Baby* (1956), *Summer Love* (1958), and *Going Steady* (1958). *Gidget* (a combination of "girl" plus "midget") was the nickname given to Sandra Dee in Columbia's 1959 romantic comedy of adolescent love. Gidget was the outcast of her boy-crazy girlfriends, unwilling to compete for the male population that hung around the beach. Before the summer is over, and without even trying, Gidget has made a conquest of Moondoggie (James Daren), the most desirable of the lot, and turned the head of the Big Kahoona (Cliff Robertson) as well, turning both of these beach bums into responsible citizens. It was definitely the forerunner of the "Beach Party" movies, the first to commercialize the lifestyle of the West Coast surf 'n' sand set. *Where the Boys Are* (1960) shifted the shenanigans to a Florida beach where thousands of collegians descended during Easter vacation. Although basically a frothy romantic frolic, the film features a gratuitously grim sequence following a gang bang on Yvette Mimieux, a punishment deemed suitable, in the early 1960's, for a liberal view of sex.

Heavier still, *Blue Denim*, *A Summer Place* (both 1959), and *Susan Slade* (1961) took an all too sobering look at what happens to young girls who let their boyfriends go "too far." *Blue Denim* did break new ground by at least admitting that normal, healthy young people did have sexual impulses. However, it was deemed acceptable for teenagers to engage in premarital sex *only* if everybody felt lousy about it afterwards. This epidemic of post-coital guilt was compounded if the girl got "in trouble," a delightfully antiquated euphemism for pregnancy. As part of the double standard, such a situation was usually the girl's problem, unless, as in the case of Brandon DeWilde in *Blue Denim*, the boy chose to share the responsibility. Even if a girl escaped having to get a rabbit test, a pre-marital affair was guaranteed to do irreparable damage to her reputation. Such an attitude may have been a reflection of the times but the producers of these films might have made some small effort to dispell that sort of thinking instead of wallowing in it, treating pregnant girls as though they had the bubonic plague. Compared with the sexual frankness and honesty of the more recent *Little Darlings* (1980), these movies seem as silly and dated as any of the less pretentious potboilers cranked out by Sam Katzman, and the mentality expressed seems like something from the Dark Ages.

Of course, leave it to AIP to produce the sleaziest motion picture about young lovers, *Diary of a High School Bride* (1959), which shamefully ignored all of the problems inherent in a teenage marriage by turning the whole affair into a killer-on-the-loose yarn.

Anita Sands played Judy Lewis, a 17-year-old student who elopes with Steve Redding (Ronald Foster), a poor but hard working law student. Judy's parents oppose the marriage, creating friction between the couple. Further complicating matters is Judy's jealous ex-boyfriend, Chuck (Chris Robinson), who makes Steve wonder if Judy has been entirely faithful. An argument sends Judy crying to mommy, which gives Chuck the opportunity to lure Judy to his father's studio late one night with promises of a reconciliation meeting with Steve. Chuck chases the girl all over the deserted studio, climbing atop a catwalk where a brush with a high voltage wire puts Chuck out of the running altogether. Judy and Steve are reunited in matrimonial bliss.

Besides being remiss in its handling of the subject matter, *Diary of a High School Bride* deserves some special award for its totally insensitive advertising campaign:

> "It's not true what they say ... we married for love!"
> "Does she get her lunch money from her husband or her daddy?"
> "I don't understand you. Why can't you control yourself? You're only seventeen?"
> "You can't live in two houses ... make up your mind ... books or babies!"

Another jealous ex-boyfriend popped up in *Date Bait* (1960). Gary Clarke and Marlo Ryan were the pair of young newlyweds, beset by a threatened annulment from Marlo's parents, and the bothersome antics of Richard Gerring, recently returned from a spell in the slammer. Richard tries to force himself on Marlo but is disuaded when Gary challenges him to a round of fisticuffs. Hopped up on heroin, Richard pulls a knife on Gary at a party, but he is eventually killed by his own knife. Marlo's folks finally admit their daughter could have done worse and the youngsters live happily ever after.

One of the most amusing entries was *Too Soon to Love* (1960). Jennifer West and Richard Evans were the lovers, kept apart by Jennifer's cruel and unreasonable father. He predicts that nothing but trouble can come of her relationship with young Evans, a stereotype reaction for parents in these pictures. Jennifer naturally ignores her daddy and ends up pregnant. Evans attempts to steal the money necessary for an abortion but is caught. He escapes, minus the badly needed $300. Dispondent, Jennifer tries to drown herself but she too is unsuccessful in her endeavor. The two decide to face the problem by getting married. The writer unwittingly made the wicked old father right after all.

Beautifully combining romance and rebellion was *West Side Story* (1961), adapted from a fall 1957 hit Broadway musical first presented at New York's Winter Garden Theatre. Envisioned as an updated musical version of *Romeo and Juliet*, it was written by Arthur Laurents, who later enjoyed success with another romantic drama, *The Way We Were* (1973). The music supplied by American conductor composer Leonard Bernstein, with lyrics by Stephen Sondheim, provided an ample number of memorable songs which included "Tonight," "Maria," and "Somewhere." Jerome Robbins choreographed the production and put his largely unknown young cast through a series of energetic dance numbers. The chemistry was just right. *West Side Story* became a smash success.

The Mirisch Company and Seven Arts Productions assigned producer-director Robert Wise to supervise the film version. Wise had an auspicious career directing such varied pictures as *Day the Earth Stood Still* (1951), *Helen of Troy* (1955), and *I Want to Live* (1958). He shared directing credit with Jerome Robbins. Natalie Wood, chosen for marquee value, replaced Carole Lawrence from the stage version as Maria. Richard Beymer, chosen for no discernible reason, replaced singer and former stunt man, Larry Kert, as Tony. Since neither Wood nor Beymer had the vocal range necessary for their roles, Marni Nixon and Jimmy Bryan provided the vocals. Fortunately, the secondary leads were chosen with far greater judgment. Russ Tamblyn, George Chakiris, and Rita Moreno brought conviction to their roles, along with the other members of the cast who were completely credible as both juvenile delinquents and singer-dancers.

The film opens with location footage shot in New York City before finally settling down in the studio-bound sets. The Jets, a lowerclass "American" street gang, are engaged in a dispute over their turf with the Sharks, a rival gang of Puerto Ricans. The leader of the Jets, Riff (Russ Tamblyn), is determined to have a rumble between the gangs. He prevails upon his friend and cofounder of the Jets, Tony (Richard Beymer), to accompany them to a dance where they will challenge the Sharks. Tony reluctantly agrees, although he has been moving away from the gang to the point of finding a steady job at the local soda fountain. Amid the friction at the dance Tony is immediately attracted to Maria (Natalie Wood), the sister of Bernardo (George Chakiris), the leader of the Sharks. Bernardo and Maria's jealous boyfriend, Chino (Joe De Vega), immediately move in to separate the two of them but an unspoken bond has already passed between the couple. Tony and Maria meet again and share their mutual love for one another. Maria begs Tony to stop the rumble between the two groups. Tony manages to turn the brawl from a gang war to a fistfight between the two group leaders but Maria wants no fighting whatsoever. Tony tries to comply with Maria's wishes by rushing to the scene of the fight. His appearance only serves to anger Bernardo who exchanges his fists for a knife. He inadvertently kills Riff. In a rage, Tony stabs Bernardo. The police arrive and the gangs disappear into the night, Tony staggering away, overcome with grief and guilt. He returns to Maria and explains what happened. Despite her own grief she agrees to go away with him. When she hears that Chino is searching for Tony, intent on shooting him, Maria sends Bernardo's widow (Rita Moreno) to warn Tony. Before she can deliver the message she is intercepted by the Jets who brutally degrade her. Bitter and angry, she tells them to inform Tony that Maria is dead, murdered by Chino. When Tony is told the lie he wanders the streets begging Chino to kill him too. In the distance, through his tear-filled eyes, he sees Maria. He calls to her and they rush toward each other. Just as they meet for an embrace,

Natalie Wood as Maria in West Side Story (United Artists 1961), searching the streets for her lover, Tony.

Chino appears and fires a fatal shot that sends Tony to the pavement. Tony dies in Maria's arms. She rises to her feet, yanks Chino's gun away from him and points it at the members of the two gangs which have gathered around her. She asks Chino how many bullets are left; how many others she can shoot and still have one bullet left for herself. She tells them it was their mutual ignorance and hatred that brought about Tony and Bernardo's death. Stunned by their shared loss, the two groups come together to carry Tony's body away.

As noted, *West Side Story* is not without its faults. Richard Beymer is utterly unbelievable as the cofounder and former leader of a street

Riff (Russ Tamblyn, arms in air) is stabbed by Bernardo (George Chakiris) in West Side Story (United Artists 1961).

gang and Natalie Wood fails to register the necessary Latin temperament for her role. Nevertheless, the dance numbers and songs are superb, the story is highly entertaining even to actual street gang members who, once they got over the fact that their onscreen counterparts were capable of bursting into song and dance at any given moment, enjoyed the picture.

West Side Story was voted best picture that year, with George Chakiris and Rita Moreno winning in the best supporting role category. Other Academy Awards went to the film's director, art director, cinematographer, costume designer, film editor, composer and sound electrician. The film was rereleased in 1968 with the ad line "Unlike other classics, 'West Side Story' grows younger." The fact that it has enjoyed repeated screenings in revival theatres seems to lend credence to the remark.

Sexual surveys like the Kinsey Report, coupled with the controversy surrounding sex education, inspired Albert Zugsmith's *College Confidential* (1960). Sociology professor Steve Allen initiates a survey of his students' sexual activities, the morality of the assignment questioned when one coed (Mamie Van Doren) indirectly blames Allen for her late night meeting with her boyfriend (Conway Twitty). An investigative reporter (Jayne Meadows) is invited to chaperone a student party where Allen plans to run some films he has taken of his students. The party turns out to be a disaster. Someone spikes the punch and Allen, a reformed alcoholic, watches helplessly as the students get out of control. Worse still, Steve finds that a "stag" film has been spliced on the end of his home movies. He is arrested for corrupting the morality of minors. This casts suspicion on his motives for initiating the sexual survey as well. The small town trial makes national headlines and none other than Walter Winchell leads the press corps covering the event. The culprit who inserted the pornographic film is discovered and Allen is let off the hook. He then uses the courtroom as a national podium to explain the social obligations inherent in his survey. The film unfortunately ignored the fact that sex education in college was another case of too little, too late.

The Explosive Generation (1961), deceptively titled, was another film about sex education in school, less sensational and far more noble in its aspirations than the previously discussed picture. William Shatner is a high school teacher suddenly faced with the dilemma of following the school curriculum or breaking the rules to meet the urgent needs of his students. Patty McCormack sets the wheels in motion by rising to her feet in the classroom and asking Shatner, "How far does a girl have to go to be popular?" Urged by his students, Shatner asks that each of them anonymously turn in essays about their sexual experiences. This unorthodox assignment attracts the wrath of the school board, the PTA, and various parents who, true to form, want to ignore anything too real. Shatner agrees to discontinue further sexual discussions but refuses to make the essays available to the parents. He is dismissed. The students stage a demonstration until he is reinstated, a foreshadowing of things to come later in the decade.

Amidst all of this sex and romance, there were a few throwbacks to the previous decade, but these remnants were the exception rather than

Surveys of Americans' sexual habits, such as the Kinsey report, and the controversy surrounding sex education in the schools, inspired Albert Zugsmith's College Confidential (U-I 1960).

the rule. As to be expected, most of these dilatory entries appeared during the period between 1960 and 1963.

The Wild Ride (1960) starred Jack Nicholson, angry at Georgianna Carter's clinging attentions toward Robert Bean. Jack wants her to stop monopolizing Robert's time so the two men can go back to having fun. Unfortunately, Jack's idea of fun is to try to kill policemen by running them off the road.

Undercover officers are assigned to enroll in a troubled inner city high school, believed to be the center for drug traffic in The Rebel Breed (1960). Infiltrating one of the school's many gangs, the cops get the goods on Richard Rust, a drug peddler and murderer. Rita Moreno appears as the pregnant girlfriend of a slain Mexican student and Diane (later Dyan) Cannon was featured as Rust's steady.

There was more high school trouble in Because They're Young (1960), based on the novel Harrison High by John Farris. Dick Clark, the likeable host of television's "American Bandstand," made his motion pic-

At a time when good girls supposedly did not do it, Tuesday Weld worried about her reputation in Because They're Young (Columbia 1960). Michael Callan portrayed a potential delinquent who is helped by an understanding teacher (Dick Clark).

ture debut playing a likeable high school teacher. Neil Hendry (Clark), new to Harrison High, feels a responsibility to his young charges outside as well as inside the classroom. Indeed, Hendry becomes so involved in the personal problems of his students one wonders how he found the time to teach. Among the youngsters in his class is Anne Gregor (Tuesday Weld), whom the pressbook synopsis describes as a girl "mature for her years," already scarred by an "experience." The second party to this "experience" (aren't euphemisms fun?) is Griff (Michael Callan), a tough transfer student from a lowerclass neighborhood. The kindness and consideration of his classmates thaws Griff's icy exterior and he slowly adjusts to his new environment. But Griff's past catches up to him and he is forced to participate in a crime with his old gang. With Hendry's help, Griff decides to cooperate with the police for which he only receives probation for his crimes. Griff and Anne reconcile their differences, Hendry learns to deal with his role as his eight-year-old nephew's guardian and even has a romantic resolution with the principal's secretary, Victoria Shaw. Musical interludes were provided by Duane Eddy and the Rebels, with James Darren singing the title song.

Filmgroup's *High School Caesar* (1960) featured John Ashley as Matt Stevens, a wealthy young boy who compensates for his lack of parental supervision by organizing his own little mafia. To the other students he sells test answers and protection. His position as a big wheel fails to impress Wanda (Judy Nugent), an attractive transfer student that Matt has fallen for. Wanda's boyfriend, Bob (Gary Vinson), joins Matt and some other kids for a drag race. Matt takes the opportunity to attempt to eliminate his rival but only succeeds in losing the race. In a rage he chases after the victor, a kid named Kelly, and forces his car over an embankment. When Wanda tells everyone what happened, the kids work Matt over and leave him ... along and desperate.

"It was probably the most violent of the ones that I did," John Ashley said. "I remember that Dale Ireland, the director, thought one scene that we did was really *cinema*. I was home in my room, talking to my father on the phone, hoping that he'd come home. When I hung up I started to cry. Dale panned from me to a pair of copper baby shoes. He felt we were really saying something but I think what we said was that we all got paid."

Platinum High School (1960) was Albert Zugsmith's version of *Bad Day at Black Rock* (1954), containing enough action and suspense to help the viewer ignore some of the sillier aspects of the story. Investigating the death of his estranged son at a remote island military school, Mickey

---

Left: John Ashley made a career of playing teenagers on both sides of the law. In High School Caesar (Filmgroup 1960), he was a spoiled rich kid involved in various illegal activities. Right: Albert Zugsmith's Platinum High School (M-G-M 1960) took place at an isolated military academy which was an exclusive playpen for the delinquent children of the very rich.

Rooney finds the place to be a haven for rich delinquents, Pinocchio's "Pleasure Island" for bad boys. He is given an unsatisfactory account of his son's "accident" by the school's owner, Dan Duryea, who seems unusually unsympathetic. When Mickey is nearly killed by a stray cannonball and, later, a falling boat, he becomes more than suspicious. His son's roommate, Warren Berlinger, the only nice kid on the whole island, confirms Mickey's worst fears. His son was beaten to death by Jimmy Boyd and Conway Twitty. Duryea cannot allow Mickey to leave the island and possibly destroy what has become a profitable enterprise, fearing such a scandal would close the school. He first sends two of his henchmen after Mickey and when that fails to work he uses Terry Moore to lure Mickey out into the ocean in a small rowboat. Duryea attempts to ram Mickey's craft using a larger boat. Mickey pours gasoline all over his own boat then swims clear as the boats collide which causes a fatal explosion, killing Duryea. Mickey returns to civilization with Berlinger, desiring to care for the boy in a way that he never did his own son.

The Choppers (1961) were a gang of thieves specializing in car stripping. Arch Hall, Jr., was their mastermind, patrolling the highways in his customized hotrod, searching for stalled or abandoned vehicles. He uses a walkie-talkie to alert his cohorts. They quickly arrive in an innocent looking truck, actually a mobile machine shop, and make quick use of the car. An insurance investigator, working in collaboration with the police, sets a trap for the boys who happily take the "bait." Before they can strip the deliberately abandoned car the police rush in. The Choppers barricade themselves in an auto junkyard belonging to their fence, Bruno Ve Sota. The police plow through in a bulldozer. One of the gang members is killed and the others surrender.

Statutory rape sends a youth to prison in *Jacktown* (1962), while on foreign soil, a Japanese *Bad Boy* (1960) learns quickly that reform school is no place for him. And in England, the "teddy boys" (a nickname for leather-jacketed British delinquents) were featured in two distinctively different entries, *The Damned* (1962) and *The Boys* (1963). The first, released in this country as *These Are the Damned*, begin with a display of motorcycle toughs operating around a seacoast village, then midway the story shifts to an enigmatic science-fiction yarn about a government installation isolating radioactive children.

The Boys was a courtroom drama with three teddy boys on trial for first degree murder and robbery. At first, prosecuting attorney Richard Todd believes the boys to be innocent, then tricks their leader into confessing.

The most critically acclaimed English made delinquency film of the period was Tony Richardson's *Loneliness of the Long Distance Runner* (1962), known also as *Rebel with a Cause*. This somewhat derivative alternative title is actually quite accurate. The young protagonist of the film manages, for reasons that he feels are justified, to deliver a devastating if self destructive blow against the system.

Tom Courtenay is sent to a reform school for a robbery. There he is placed in a routine assembly-line job in the school shop. By accident, he is discovered to be an extraordinary runner and is groomed by governor Michael Redgrave to win a foot race. Courtenay's victory would naturally reflect well on the reform school. During the race, a series of flashbacks reconstructs Courtenay's life. We see his father's death and his mother's wild spending spree when she inherits the insurance money; Courtenay's romance with a schoolgirl and the spur of the moment theft of a bakery that led to his incarceration. "I'll win in the end," Courtenay remarks, "even if I am in jail — because I'll have more fun and fire out of my life than ever that half dead gangrened governor. If he ran ten yards he'd drop dead. If he got ten yards into what goes on in my guts he'd drop dead as well — with surprise. Because I'm alive...." From the bits of Courtenay's life that we see, coupled with his philosophy, the audience can easily understand why, at the last moment, he throws the race. It is the ultimate expression of his contempt for the tradition and authority that the reform school official represents to him. He makes his own stand against the establishment but will pay for it dearly. The last scene of the film shows his return to the school shop.

Back on the home front, *Wild Youth* (1961) was a piece of muddled nonsense about a doll full of heroin that causes conflict among a cast that was neither youthful nor wild. Then there were the three punks in *Panic in Year Zero* (1962), Dick Bakalyan among them, but the movie was primarily about a family's struggle for survival following a nuclear attack on Los Angeles. As such a discussion of the particulars is best left to a book on science fiction films.

Similarly, *Village of the Giants* (1965) was a mixture of science fiction and juvenile delinquency, pitting normal-sized Tom Kirk against Beau Bridges and his gang of thirty-foot hoodlums. The whole business was the fault of Tom's kid brother, Ronnie Howard, who invented a spongy food called "Goo." When injested, the stuff causes abnormal growth. It was *The Amazing Colossal Man* (1957) gone groovy, supposedly based on H.G. Wells' *Food of the Gods*, though it is doubtful that the author would wish any credit.

The Young Savages (1961) was based on an Evan Hunter novel. Burt Lancaster was the prosecutor given the simple task of bringing in a "guilty" verdict against three members of an Italian juvenile gang accused of stabbing a blind Puerto Rican boy to death. But even with the governor's seat as a carrot, Lancaster has ambivalent feelings about the case. He too is of Italian origins and also a product of the slums. So when the evidence unravels and Lancaster discovers that the blind boy was actually the warlord of a gang, he begins to act more like a defense attorney than a prosecutor. He informs the court that the murdered youth, because of his blindness, was able to plan rumbles without incurring suspicion. And just in case there was any audience sympathy left, the kid also pimped for his 14-year-old sister. In a closing speech, Lancaster begs mercy for the three killers just as Humphrey Bogart had done for John Derek years earlier. The final verdict in, "not guilty," and with the governor's seat but a memory, Lancaster is approached by the dead boy's mother, hopelessly confused, wondering what happened to justice.

When she asks, "What about my boy?" Lancaster sanctimoniously replies, "A lot of people killed your son, Mrs. Escalante," as if that sort of grandiose philosophy would offer her some comfort at that point.

The ultra-liberal philosophy that permeates *The Young Savages* often clouds the fact that it is an extremely well-crafted motion picture. Actual street gang members were recruited to act in the film by 28-year-old Ben Moring, a hep New York minister who organized an amateur theatre group called "The Centurions." "While expressing their emotion in a legitimate way," Moring said, "the boys also soon noticed the girls were paying attention to them. Instead of showing off as troublemakers they were getting attention (and loving it) as actors." The thrill apparently was not enough for Ramón Ortíz who ended up in the City Prison on a homicide charge some months later.

In a further effort to give the film a more urgent feel, director John Frankenheimer got a permit from the New York City Police to film on the city streets. A block was roped off at 68th street and West End Avenue for the shooting of a gang fight. But the principal of a local high school caused such a stink that Frankenheimer and his crew had to pack up and film the sequence on Columbia's lot. It seemed that the beleaguered principal had for years begged the city to rope off that same block to use as a playground on various occasions and had been turned down cold. Adding injury to insult, the poor man believed that a mock rumble might set off a real one.

"Young people should see it," said Lancaster, referring to the film, "since it pertains to their age group and their innate hostilities. Older people — well, they're responsible, they should see it too." From this quote one can deduce that the actor endorsed the film's philosophy which is fine, to a point, but to totally exonerate a criminal from his actions is to suggest that he never had a choice in the matter. And in order to sway the audience to the film's point of view, events are often a little too pat to be real. It is true that parents can be blamed for making their children what they are, but it is the fault of the child if he or she remains that way.

The Hoodlum Priest (1961) was the biographical drama of Father Charles Dismas Clark, a latter day successor to Father Flanagan. Father Clark (Don Murray), devoted to the supervision and rehabilitation of delinquents and other criminals, offers support to Billy Jackson (Keir Dullea), a youngster with a bad police record. Billy gets a job, meets a nice girl, and seems on the verge of becoming a responsible citizen. But his past performance makes him a prime suspect when his employer is robbed. Billy is fired. Angry and discouraged, he decides to actually commit the crime for which he was blamed. His boss catches him in the act and Billy kills him in self-defense. Billy is arrested, convicted of first degree murder, and sentenced to death. Despite Father Clark's attempts for an appeal, Billy is looked upon as an incorrigible. On the way to his execution, Billy is accompanied by Father Clark who tells him the story of Dismas, the thief who died on the cross beside Jesus. Dismas was promised eternal life. Returning to his halfway house, Father Clark is chided by a drunken young delinquent for not being able to save Billy.

Helping the boy to fall asleep, the priest finds the courage and conviction to continue on.

Shirley Clarke's *The Cool World* (1964) provided an unrelentingly grim insight into the inner world of black ghettos. A largely amateur cast portrayed the members of the Royal Pythons, a black street gang involved in prostitution, heroin, and murder. Adding to the grim reality, it was filmed on location in Harlem in grainy black and white. Although screened at the Venice Film Festival, *The Cool World* proved to be too downbeat for mass consumption and received only a limited distribution.

By comparison, Universal's *Kitten with a Whip* (1964) was a smash success, although its appeal was probably due to the then current popularity of Ann-Margret. She played Jody, a delinquent teenager responsible for knifing a matron and setting fire to the detention home from which she escaped. She breaks into the suburban home of David Stratton (John Forsythe), an aspiring politician. Stratton's wife is conveniently out of town which makes it easier for Jody to take over the place, threatening to ruin Stratton's political career unless he agrees to give her free reign, which includes sheltering three of her delinquent boyfriends. When one of the boys is wounded by a knife during a drunken party, Stratton is forced to drive the creep to a doctor in Tijuana. There is an accident and Stratton awakens to find himself in a hospital. The three boys died instantly during the crash and Jody makes a deathbed statement clearing Stratton of any blame.

After stating emphatically that he would make no more films about teenage criminals, money got the better of Sam Katzman's morality and he went to work on a movie for television titled *52 Miles to Terror*. Since most of his theatrical features had the look of a television show anyway, there was no loss in "quality." Filmed at M-G-M for ABC-TV, the studio felt it had enough potential to hit the big screen. It became *Hot Rods to Hell* (1967). Robert E. Kent's screenplay was based on a story by Alex Gaby that had originally appeared in a 1956 issue of the *Saturday Evening Post*. Certainly the story was better suited to a 1950s project. By 1967 a film about drunken hotrodders terrorizing the highways had as much topicality as a Davy Crockett hat, a hula hoop, or Allied Artists' *Hot Rod Hullabaloo* (1966), a pointless repetition of films like *Dragstrip Riot*. It is only worth mentioning for Marsha Mason's appearance in it.

Considerably more effective, *The Incident* (1967) was a revamped version of *Ride with Terror*, broadcast on television in 1963. The story is strong stuff, the principal action taking place aboard a New York subway train car. Each passenger, like the jurors in *12 Angry Men*, exhibits a trait that makes delinquency possible. And when two psychotic teenagers— Tony Musante and Martin Sheen—board the car and systematically expose that trait, each individual is left defenseless and powerless to stand up to the bullies. Only a wounded soldier, played by Beau Bridges, cannot be degraded and Musante eventually resorts to picking on a small child in order to incite Bridges into a confrontation. Despite the odds— his arm is in a cast and Musante has a switchblade—Bridges kills the punk and knees Sheen in the balls.

Their credo is violence... Their God is hate... The most terrifying film of our time!

AMERICAN INTERNATIONAL PRESENTS

PETER FONDA · NANCY SINATRA

THE WILD ANGELS

PANAVISION and PATHECOLOR

BRUCE DERN and DIANE LADD · ROGER CORMAN · CHARLES GRIFFITH

MEMBERS OF HELL'S ANGELS OF VENICE, CALIFORNIA

JOINT... the fuzz-hater - show him a badge and he sees red!

BULL... swinging a cycle chain in each hand and lusting for "action"

DEAR JOHN... the "hog stomper" whose God is speed... he had a bath once but didn't like it.

THIS PICTURE IS RECOMMENDED FOR ADULTS

As good as the film was, many of the sleazier elements that endeared fans to even the most impoverished genre entries had been removed. Not that a healthy balance wasn't good, but with films like *West Side Story*, *The Hoodlum Priest*, *The Young Savages*, and *The Incident*, it looked as if the J.D. film was going to become more "adult," just as *Shane* (1953) and *High Noon* (1952) reshaped the shoot-'em-up oaters of the forties into the psychological western dramas of the fifties.

Then, the same company that produced the Beach Party flicks, American-International, released *The Wild Angels* (1966), a gritty, and far more unsavory lot of bikers than Brando and his boys had even thought of being. "The picture you are about to see will shock you, perhaps anger you!" cautioned the precredit opening. "Although the events and characters are fictitious, the story is a reflection of our times."

What were the times that they were talking about? Certainly not the same "times" that had created Gidget and turned Elvis into a Dan Dailey equivalent. No. A new sentiment had been carried on the wind that blew through the beginning of the sixties. The energy that had been previously channeled into rebellion had been used to shape the future of the country. A new President had been in office—the vigorous, charismatic, and young John F. Kennedy. His campaign speeches had not been the typical set of promises most likely unkept. Instead, Kennedy had presented the nation a set of challenges and an optimistic people had responded. Students took an active interest in civil rights, shaking the label of apathy and conformity that had stuck to them throughout the fifties. But the optimism was shortlived. In November 1963, Kennedy was shot dead in Dallas. By the time civil rights leader Martin Luther King and Robert Kennedy were similarly murdered, the nation had succumbed to a second wave of apathy. "To the rest of the world," wrote Art Buchwald, "the U.S. must look like a giant insane asylum where the inmates have taken over."

The war in Vietnam, our involvement escalated by President Lyndon Johnson in 1964, was another piece of insanity causing growing unrest. Escalating draft quotas, which had risen 5,000 per month from 1965 to 1966, were being met by reclassifying student deferments. Draft dodging became a new way of life and Canada seemed far more desirable than the jungles of Asia. Small wonder that the nihilistic and totally unsympathetic James Bond would emerge in this atmosphere of rampant pessimism as the movie hero of the decade. In the person of Sean Connery, Ian Fleming's superspy 007 was a far cry from the days when Errol Flynn and Gary Cooper would give even the chief villain a square deal. Double-oh-seven shot his rivals in the back. So when establishment hating Peter Fonda came roaring onto the screen with Nancy Sinatra holding on behind him, demanding freedom to "do their own thing," they found a ready audience.

A new trend in J.D. films was kicked off by Roger Corman's The Wild Angels (AIP 1966). The Angels' rebellion against the law and convention touched a nerve in young audiences.

During the early part of the summer, the industry trade magazines listed a new AIP film, *All the Fallen Angels,* currently in production at various locations around southern California. Producer-director Roger Corman, recently involved in a series of highly commercial movie adaptations of Edgar Allan Poe stories with Vincent Price, had been requested by AIP to make a contemporary (i.e., youth film) project. Corman remembered a photograph he had seen in a *Life* magazine of a biker funeral. The Hell's Angels, the most infamous motorcycle gang in California, had become a popular subject in the news media. Corman assigned screenwriter Charles Griffith to fashion a script around the gang's exploits within the framework of the biker's funeral which had initially inspired the project.

"I did *The Wild Angels* as a silent movie almost," said Griffith. His original script contained little more than 120 lines of dialogue. "My story constantly paralleled the police motorcycle cop and the scungey bikers, showing they were both motivated by the same impulses." Corman did not want a movie about cops so Griffith wrote a second version which focussed on the idea that the bikers believed they had "the power" without having any awareness of their limited position in life. The script was then altered by Corman and his new assistant, Peter Bogdanovich who (in Griffith's words) "turned it into that very cornball prototype of all the motorcycle movies."

To research the picture, Griffith persuaded a Hell's Angel friend of his to introduce him and Corman to some of the other members of the gang. Griffith spent some time hanging around a place called the Gunk Shop in Venice. "Roger went down there once and he sat with a grin from ear to ear the whole evening. They were all so funky—putting us on. I recorded a lot of the speech. It was pretty obvious what sort of people they were but it was what they *believed* they were that was interesting." It was Griffith's belief that had *The Wild One* been photographed in color, with the gang riding choppers instead of Triumphs, it might have set the trend off back in 1954.

Corman cast many of the Hell's Angels in the film, which proved to be quite a problem. When enough extras weren't available for the climactic brawl, Bogdanovich was ordered to participate as one of the townspeople at odds with the bikers. Unfortunately for Bogdanovich, the bikers, by this time, were at odds with Corman and took out their aggressions against the director by physically assaulting Bogdanovich.

While Corman did want professional actors in the lead roles, he did insist that every actor playing an Angel be able to ride his own motorcycle. This led to problems when George Chakiris requested a stunt-double for his riding scenes. The actor was nixed and Peter Fonda, originally slated as the second male lead, became the star and Bruce Dern stepped into his supporting role.

The final film emerged as more of a series of anecdotes than a cohesive story, largely because of its sequential structure. Blues (Fonda), heads an outlaw motorcycle gang residing in the beach town of Venice, California. One of its members, Loser (Dern), is angry over the loss of his motorcycle, stolen by a rival Mexican gang. The bikers invade the desert town of Mecca. They find Loser's bike and the thieves. They start a fight which attracts the police. Then Loser swipes a patrolman's motorcycle and rides off through a mountain terrain. The cops catch up and shoot him. The bikers engineer a plot to abduct Loser from the hospital in spite of his critical condition, knowing he'll be sent to prison the minute he recovers. Without medical attention Loser dies. A ceremonial burial is planned in the Loser's hometown and Blues leads the gang up to the isolated mountain community. During the funeral services, the minister pauses in his eulogy to challenge the philosophy of the bikers. Blues attempts to defend their creed, but in his inarticulate frustration, he instead proposes that the services should be turned into a party. The minister is bound and gagged (enough of his ridiculous questions) while the Angels engage in a drunken orgy. The Loser's corpse is propped up in a position of honor while his "old lady" is gang raped by several of his friends. Blues comes to understand the futility of their lifestyle, but still leads the procession to the graveyard. At the graveside, a group of irate locals taunt the Angels into a fight. Approaching police sirens dispells the group except for Blues. He realizes "there is nowhere to go" and stays to bury his friend.

Before release, the title was changed to *The Wild Angels* and the advertising promoted it as "the most terrifying film of our time." It proved terrifying enough to a great number of people, creating a storm of controversy unequaled in the genre since the days of *Blackboard Jungle*. The motion picture was first shown, by invitation, at the 27th Venice International Film Festival, causing consternation among some of the American representatives. Corman defended the festival invitation, contending that the film supplied proof that, in a democracy, artists have the freedom to show the darker side of our way of life. It won an award and was later shown at the Cannes festival. The European critics, some of whom were Corman cultists, were generally more generous with the film than their outraged American counterparts. Bosley Crowther, in the *New York Times*, called it a "brutal little picture" and "an embarrassment." *Newsweek* was even less kind, referring to it as an "ugly piece of trash" that revelled "in the shock value of murder, mob violence, gratuitous brutality and a squalid rape in a chapel during a funeral." Most critics attacked the film for its excessive violence and sex, although the industry trade papers proposed that precisely these elements would insure its acceptance among youth audiences. *Variety* warned that the film "carries shock impact of the sort that occasionally stuns," however they projected a "lush take" nonetheless. *The Hollywood Reporter* announced the movie had strong exploitation attractions "as well as pretensions to art" and that whatever the final judgment on its intrinsic values, it would make "a lot of money." *The Hollywood Reporter* was right, the movie was AIP's most profitable release up to that time. According to the company, kids would return to see the picture again and again, often sitting through more than one performance a day. Hardly anyone paid attention to the $4 million lawsuit that was filed against AIP by the Hell's Angels who claimed that the film presented them in a "false and

VIOLENCE IS THEIR GOD!

and they hunt in a pack like rabid dogs!

MAMA ...she was the property of all... but God help an outsider.

GROG ...the fuzz hater- show him a badge and he'll show you the busi- ness end of a tire iron...

ROBOT ...he can't walk straight, but he'll drive his chopper thru the gates of Hell.

FUNKY ...all he wants is a pint in his pocket – and a pig....when he wants to play around.

...from the Producers of 'THE WILD ANGELS'

ROGER CORMAN PRESENTS

DEVIL'S ANGELS

AN AMERICAN INTERNATIONAL PICTURE

IN PANAVISION AND COLOR

WRITTEN BY CHARLES GRIFFITH · DIRECTED BY DANIEL HALLER · PRODUCED BY BURT TOPPER

RECOMMENDED FOR MATURE AUDIENCES

STARRING JOHN CASSAVETES · BEVERLY ADAMS · MIMSY FARMER

derogatory manner," making it virtually impossible for them to appear unharmed in public. This is especially amusing in light of the fact that Corman was later subpoenaed to appear before U.S. Senator Thomas Dodd's committee investigating the root causes of juvenile delinquency. That was sort of like asking Raymond Burr for legal advice simply because he played Perry Mason on television for so many years.

The jingle of coins at *The Wild Angels'* boxoffices rang out through the Hollywood community louder than Quasimodo's Notre Dame bells, calling other producers to hop on their own choppers. The year following the release of Corman's picture, 1967, proved to be a red letter year for biker dramas. There was *Rebel Rousers, Hell's Angels on Wheels, Wild Rebels, Born Losers,* and, of course, *Devil's Angels* from AIP.

Never a company to make a successful film just once, AIP asked Corman to prepare a follow up to *The Wild Angels.* Since he and Fonda were already busy at work on *The Trip* (1967), Corman supervised the production of *Devil's Angels* (1967), another Charles Griffith script. It was Griffith's intention to make the bikers in this film the sons of "the Oakies," with the same sort of mentality but technologically inclined. This was to be his last bike picture because he didn't like the genre.

Some of the supporting actors from *The Wild Angels* were back again, with John Cassavetes as Cody, their leader. He may have seemed an odd choice, lacking the youth of Fonda, but he was actually closer in age to his real life counterparts. Cassavetes emerged as an ideal bit of casting, his age giving an added poignancy to the eventual alienation from his younger, more rebellious cohorts. The Skulls were a little softer than their predecessors. The mindless brutality of the previous picture was replaced by a more reasonable group of overaged pranksters.

The focus of the drama is on Cody and Sheriff Henderson (Leo Gordon). Henderson wants no trouble in his small town and neither does Cody, although the people that they each represent do. While Cody and Henderson are able to relate to each other, the fear, suspicion, and hate between the citizens and the bikers escalates into something which the two of them can no longer control. Henderson becomes the victim of the violent confrontation he sought to ward off which causes Cody to drive away alone, sickened by the senseless destruction of his former lifestyle.

The events begin when a member of the Skulls accidentally kills a pedestrian in their hometown. Cody leads the gang out of town before the police can apprehend them. Cody's second-in-command, Joel, tells him about "Hole-in-the-wall," the legendary sanctuary for western outlaws where they can be free to live without hassles once and for all. On their way to freedom, the gang makes a stopover in the small town of Brookville. The local citizens are upset by their appearance. The sheriff

---

Never ones to make a successful movie once, if they could make it twice, AIP brought out The Devil's Angels (1967), one of the first of over thirty motorcycle films following the success of The Wild Angels.

wants to avoid a confrontation so he agrees to let the bikers camp overnight on a nearby beach, provided they stay out of town, out of trouble, and leave the next morning. That night, one of the local girls, Marriane (Mimsy Farmer), joins the Skulls who are having a party. When she feels abused, she runs back to town and a couple of the leading citizens, despite her denial, believe that she has been raped. Henderson arrests Cody and runs the others out of town. This compromise neither pleases the Skulls, who feel they have been wrongly accused, nor the townspeople who want to see the whole group behind bars.

On the road, the Skulls meet with another gang of bikers, the Stompers. With their combined strength, the two gangs invade the town, free Cody, and proceed on a destructive rampage. Disillusioned, Cody learns that "Hole-in-the-wall" was just a story and that he was the only one who needed to believe in it.

Crying, and looking every year of his age, Cassavetes' face in the last scene speaks far more eloquently than any of his dialogue. At the time, he was appearing as an actor in films to earn the money necessary to finance his own low-budget, personal dramas like *Faces* (1968) which he directed in a loose, improvisational style. A few of the scenes in *Devil's Angels* seem to indicate that Cassavetes may have directed parts of the picture, confirmed by the actor, though Daniel Haller undoubtedly was responsible for the bulk of the picture.

Either way, despite being held for prime summer release, *The Devil's Angels* failed to score at the box office as well as its predecessor. This, however, did not prevent a whole bumper crop of other biker films from hitting the screen.

One of the first to tap this new market was Joe Solomon, a producer who gambled all of his assets and credit on *Hell's Angels on Wheels* (1967). The movie was brought in for approximately $200,000 and ultimately grossed ten times that amount. Solomon parlayed his profits into another bike film, then another, until he built his own releasing firm, Fanfare pictures.

Richard Rush, who later directed *Getting Straight* (1970), *Freebie and the Bean* (1974), and *The Stunt Man* (1980), got his start on *Hell's Angels on Wheels*. Laslo Kovacs was the director of photography. Jack Nicholson, whose career had been in a slump since his early Corman days, was given the lead role originally intended for John Ashley. He costarred with Adam Roarke, a diminutive actor who built a career playing hard-assed bikers. Various chapters of the Hell's Angels from Northern California were employed for a spectacular sequence of 155 motorcyclists on the Golden Gate Bridge. Sonny Barger, the notorious leader of the Oakland Hell's Angels, blessed the film with a brief appearance, playing himself.

Attempting to bridge the gap between commercialism and art, director Richard Rush tried to inject more than the standard violence into his film. He told Solomon he would include all the "razzle-dazzle fights and action" expected, just as long as the producer would let him "play a little bit" with what he wanted to do. Exactly what Rush wanted to do is difficult to ascertain, although the film has an indefinable elusive quality which sets it apart from others of its type. Like most motorcycle films, it sacrifices a cohesive narrative structure in favor of a sequential, semi-documentary approach. In these films, it is not uncommon for whatever is happening to stand still for an elongated party sequence or a demonstration of motorcycle dexterity. While Rush's film shares these faults, its strength lies in its quieter moments when the film manages to be a convincing portrait of the way these people actually live, whether or not such is actually the case.

Buddy (Adam Roarke) and his gang travel through the small towns north of San Francisco, encountering Poet (Jack Nicholson), a disenchanted gas station attendant, attracted to the bikers' freewheeling lifestyle. He joins the gang in a couple of fights and is invited to become a member. Poet becomes involved with Shill (Sabrina Scarf), Buddy's "old lady," believing she also loves him. He will not commit himself to her yet refuses to let her go. At a party in some deserted ruins, Poet confronts Buddy with the hypocrisy of the biker's lifestyle, which leads to a fight. At a crucial moment, Shill sides with Buddy. Disgruntled, Poet starts to leave. Buddy tries to run him down but crashes his bike through a window instead. He dies, his cycle bursting into flames. Poet and Shill reach out for each other, but the distance between them is too great.

One critic, who felt the film was extremely hostile, took delight in pointing out that it was far more damaging to the image of the Hell's Angels than Corman's film had been, yet was made with the full approval of Angel leader Sonny Barger. In fact, Barger reportedly saw it ten times and enjoyed it so much that he volunteered to make personal appearances in connection with the film's playdates.

Jack Nicholson played yet another role on two wheels in *Rebel Rousers*, taking fourth billing to Cameron Mitchell and two *The Wild Angels* alumni, Bruce Dern and Diane Ladd. Mitchell was a sedate architect and Ladd his pregnant girlfriend. She is abducted by a motorcycle gang, their leader none other than an old high school chum of Mitchell's, Bruce Dern. For old times' sake Dern tries to keep the girl from being molested but when Nicholson wins her in a bike race he wants to take posession of his property. A neighboring Mexican family agrees to assist Mitchell and, armed with pitchforks, drive the outlaws away. The film was noted mainly for Nicholson's ridiculous striped pants and is best described by its producer who said it was "the worst thing I ever did."

Born Losers marked the first screen appearance of Billy Jack, a character that became wildly successful several years later when Tom Laughlin would take the role again for *Billy Jack* (1972), the half Indian ex-Marine karate expert who magically appears at crucial moments to help the picked-on flower children at a free school. AIP was naturally delighted when Laughlin's later effort became so popular, enabling them to reissue *Born Losers* as "the original Billy Jack" and make an additional profit. Laughlin demanded $5 million in damages.

Instead of the rich town bully, and his worthless cowardly son in the later film, in *Born Losers* Billy is pitted against an outlaw motorcycle

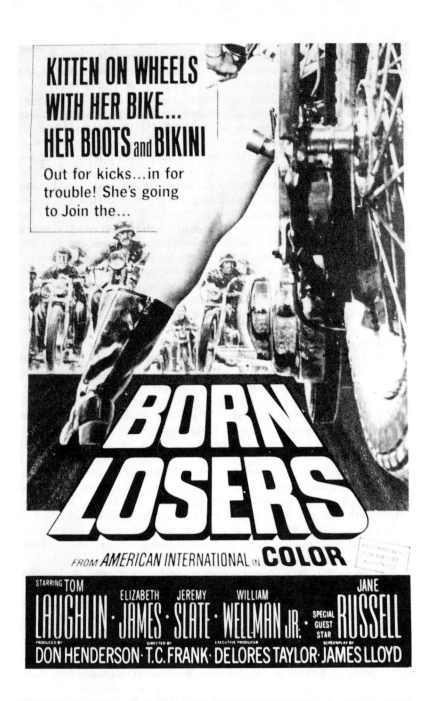

KITTEN ON WHEELS
WITH HER BIKE...
HER BOOTS and BIKINI

Out for kicks...in for
trouble! She's going
to Join the...

BORN LOSERS

FROM *AMERICAN* INTERNATIONAL IN **COLOR**

STARRING TOM LAUGHLIN · ELIZABETH JAMES · JEREMY SLATE · WILLIAM WELLMAN JR. · SPECIAL GUEST STAR JANE RUSSELL

PRODUCED BY DON HENDERSON · DIRECTED BY T.C. FRANK · EXECUTIVE PRODUCER DELORES TAYLOR · SCREENPLAY BY JAMES LLOYD

Like a modern day western hero, Tom Laughlin as Billy Jack rode into town to set things right in Born Losers (1967).

gang headed by Jeremy Slate. Slate and his mob overrun a small mountain community. The only ones to stand up to the ruffians are Billy and his friends. For their trouble they are fined and tossed in jail. But even after being set free, Billy cannot seem to hold onto his lady love (Elizabeth James), who is kidnapped and abused so often it becomes laughable. It is the police who finally restore order, accidentally shooting butter-fingers Billy in the process.

Laughlin directed the film under his pseudonym, T.C. Frank, the story based on two rather appalling real life incidents. The first was poor Kitty Genovese, the girl repeatedly stabbed with dozens of people in earshot, none summoning aid. The other was the ex-Marine from Pittsburgh who, upon seeing some hoodlums molesting three girls, first phoned the police then rushed to the defense of the girls, ending with two of the boys being wounded. The ex-Marine was fined $1400 and sentenced to 180 days in jail. The two assailants escaped with mere $50 fines.

Wild Rebels (1967) had Steve Alaimo as a stock car driver, going undercover to help the police get a conviction on the Satan's Slaves, a rather paltry motorcycle club with only four members. One particularly tasteless sequence showed one of the four holding some poor fool's head while another kicked it like a football.

As Robert Ebert pointed out in his *Esquire* article on Joe Solomon and *Hell's Angels on Wheels*, such films have little to do with good taste, but can also be set apart from the entire class of "inspired dreck" that comes to rest and take root where the American exploitation film "bottoms out." From 1967 to 1972 there were probably two dozen motorcycle epics, at least, most of them from American-International, some from Joe Solomon, the majority of which were repetitions of what had gone before. The biker films never did very well in the big cities. Their market was driveins in the Midwest, the South, and smaller towns, areas that had traditionally been the prime target for westerns. It is not odd then that many of the motorcycle pictures came more and more to resemble westerns, good guys against bad guys, damsels in distress, the action taking place in some surreal isolated small town or the vast expanses of the southwest. It was a simple matter to replace the horses with motorcycles. Almost any western cliché could be updated for contemporary use. The rest was simple.

Screenwriter James Gordon White frankly admitted to lifting plots for his biker dramas from the old westerns he watched on television. His script for *Hell's Belles* (1969) was *Winchester '73* (1950) revamped. In that film, James Stewart wins a rifle in a shooting contest. It is stolen by his brother and Stewart spends nearly 70 minutes tracking down both his brother and the rifle. Jeremy Slate subbed for Stewart and the gun became a motorcycle.

The Mini-Skirt Mob (1968), despite a vaguely feminist title, was basically another western on wheels. This time Diane McBain, as a woman scorned, unleashes a reign of terror against her former fiancé and his new bride. She locates the newlyweds at a house trailer in the desert and, with the help of some friends, terrorizes the couple. In the end, the

MEET THE
DEBUTANTE IN A
LEATHER SKIRT

Too Young...Too Tough
...Too itching for Action
to Look for it--
She'll make it
Where she is!

"HELL'S BELLES"
COLOR — BERKEY PATHE

M Suggested for MATURE audiences
(parental discretion advised)

STARRING
JEREMY SLATE · ADAM ROARKE · JOCELYN LANE
WRITTEN BY JAMES GORDON WHITE AND R. G. McMULLEN · PRODUCED & DIRECTED BY MAURY DEXTER
A MAURY DEXTER PRODUCTION · AN AMERICAN INTERNATIONAL PICTURE

Another western on wheels, Hell's Belles (AI 1969) had Jeremy Slate tracking
down a pack of motorcycle rustlers.

new bride, Sherry Jackson, finds herself in a position where McBain's life is totally dependent on her desire to save her. Proving that the James Bond philosophy is alive and well in biker films, Sherry allows the villainess to fall to her death without so much as a second thought. Such is hardly the stuff of which our virtuous heroines are supposed to be made.

The revenge theme, a western favorite, could always carry 80 or 90 minutes. In *The Glory Stompers* (1968), Dennis Hopper heads a nasty bunch of scumbags who kidnap Chris Noel with plans to sell her to some Mexican flesh peddlers for $1000. Her boyfriend, Jody McCrea, beaten and left for dead, joins forces with lone biker Jock Mahoney to get the girl back. Mahoney, once *The Range Rider* on television, as well as a face in a number of UI oaters, provided another connection to the old west.

Bury Me an Angel (1971) was an unwatchable New World picture about Dixie Peabody's obsession to kill the biker that gunned down her brother. The search for revenge becomes a descent into madness until the crazed girl believes that only the death of her brother's killer will free her mind of its tortured visions.

William Smith, a veteran of the cycle films, played a desperate biker who sells information to a magazine for $10,000. *Run Angel, Run* (1969) is exactly what he does, trying to get to the San Francisco bank where the money is deposited before his fellow bikers, who feel betrayed, get to him.

It was outlaws against the townfolk in *Angels Die Hard* (1971). The sentiment expressed in the title, like *Frankenstein Must Be Destroyed* (1970), must have been obvious to the beleagured moviegoer. Another biker is arrested for causing trouble and the sheriff agrees to release him if he and his gang will clear out. Then the biker is killed by some unknown assailant and the gang swears vengeance. A bloody battle breaks out. The phantom killer turns out to be the sheriff. He is eventually put to rest by his own deputy.

The Dirt Gang (1972) contained a modern-day Ahab-like cyclist searching for the man responsible for putting out his eye. And like Captain Ahab when he finally caught up to Moby Dick, the confrontation results in his death.

While all of this imaginary brutality continued to fill movie screens, the all too real violence half a world away in Vietnam continued. The undeclared war was at its height during the same period that the motorcycle films achieved unparalleled popularity. Just how much of America's preoccupation with war during that period was reflected in the motorcycle films is difficult to ascertain. It is clear, however, that from the beginning, these films acknowledged that the Vietnam war was somehow integrated into the actions of their protagonists. As Blues and Mike prepare for their last "run" in *The Wild Angels*, a radio in the background briefly broadcasts a news item recounting the latest casualties from the war. The radio is quickly shut off. What is going on here is just a dress rehearsal for the wholesale slaughter over there. Blues and his outlaws were small time operators compared to the clean-cut kids

THEY LIVE HARD...THEY LOVE HARD...
"ANGELS DIE HARD!"

CHOPPER OUTLAWS!..
riding their hot
throbbing machines
to a brutal climax
of violence!

IN COLOR

THEIR BATTLE CRY-
"KILL THE PIGS!"

ORIGINAL
SOUNDTRACK
ALBUM
NOW ON
UNI RECORDS!

Angels Die Hard (1971), another variation on outlaws against townsfolk, was released near the end of the cycle.

dropping napalm on entire villages. With television bringing the war right into people's homes during the evening news, it was hardly a popular subject for motion pictures at the time. Only John Wayne with *The Green Berets* (1968) attempted to take audiences to the front. But Wayne's well-meaning attempt to "back our boys" was a distorted, unrealistic view of the situation and was ultimately nothing but a horrible parody of World War II clichés, chillingly out of step. Yet, no better character could be found for study than the young man who had been to hell and back, fighting a war for which he would receive no glory.

In *Angels from Hell* (1969), Tom Stern portrayed a Vietnam veteran who returns home with the fever of battle still inside him. He uses his military training to build an army of outlaw bikers, hoping to bring every gang in the state under his leadership for an ultimate showdown against the police. Eventually the authorities close in on his stronghold and, rather than surrender, Tom is brought down by the establishment he fought for in Nam.

While the psychotic war veteran became a staple of television dramas in the next decade, the motorcycle films primarily used them as reluctant heroes in "another kind of war." Robert Fuller was a discharged veteran who takes *The Hard Ride* (1971). As Phil, he returns home with the casket containing Lenny, his black Marine buddy killed during the war. Phil is bequeathed his pal's motorcycle, a highly modified chopper, and a letter from Lenny requesting that all of his friends from the local cycle gangs attend his funeral. Phil meets with Lenny's former girlfriend (Sherry Bain) and together they set out on a quest for the funeral party. Some rival bikers kidnap Phil and his motorcycle. Lenny's friends show up and in the resulting conflict, Phil is shot and killed. The next day there is a double funeral as the two dead friends are laid to rest.

The Green Berets proved more effective against their new enemies in *Chrome and Hot Leather* (1971). Tony Young swears vengeance against the Wizards, a motorcycle gang that murdered his girlfriend after she accidentally knocked one of them off his bike while riding in her car. Enlisting the aid of three of his war buddies, Young corners the Wizards in a box canyon and, using tear gas and mortar rounds, wipes them out. The whole business proved to be little more than a waste of a good, kinky title.

The Hell's Angels reportedly volunteered, at one point, to go over to Vietnam as a unit to clean things up. The idea was appealing, in much the same way as the buttons that read "Send John Wayne to Vietnam." But all we got from both suggestions was two bad movies.

The Losers (1972), about a handful of cycle bums recruited to rescue a presidential advisor held captive in Cambodia, was so similar to *The Dirty Dozen* (1967) that one reviewer suggested calling it "The Filthy Five." It opened promisingly enough with a troop truck moving through the jungles of Vietnam. The transport is attacked and a violent skirmish follows as the Army escort fights to protect its precious cargo. The enemy is slaughtered and the truck continues to its destination, a command post near the Cambodian border. The canvas is lifted off the back of the truck and, to the astonishment of a group of officers, the "cargo" emerges ... five motorcycle outlaws in full "colors"! The film goes downhill from there.

On the opposite end of the spectrum from the violent bikers were the drug-ingesting pacifists known at the time as "hippies." As we shall later see, this counter-culture had their own films, but occasionally they would pop up in cycle dramas, and vice versa. *Angels Hard As They Come* (1972) used a confrontation between two bike gangs — one a fascist group, the other isolationists — and a group of peace-loving hippies to illustrate the weaknesses of all three. A reformed biker settles into a hippie commune in *Angel Unchained* (1970) but must return to his old ways when the commune is about to be ravaged by some local dune buggy riders. And the leader of a hippie commune must finally resort to violence in *The Peace Killers* (1971) to save a motorcycle mama seeking refuge from the gang who wants her back. This dualistic attitude towards violence and nonviolence finally reached its illogical conclusion in *Billy*

Jack in which Delores Taylor went about preaching peace while Tom Laughlin kicked the ass of anyone she could not convert.

While a number of bike films featured all-girl gangs, few were as decidedly antimale as the *She-Devils on Wheels* (1968). The "Man-Eaters," as they were called, took some sort of perverse delight in choosing their sexual playthings from a "stud line" and later tying the discarded lover to the back of a motorcycle, dragging him to his death. There are numerous other violent pasttimes, such as decapitation, which is hardly surprising since the film was produced and directed by Herschell Gordon Lewis, the entrepreneur responsible for mindless carnage pieces like *Blood Feast* (1963), *Two-Thousand Maniacs* (1964), and *The Gore-Gore Girls* (1972). His sordid combination of sex and sadism was a solid indicator that the genre was rapidly reaching the bottom of the barrel.

In desperation, producers attempted almost anything to pump new blood into an ailing subject. Football star Joe Namath hopped aboard a chopper in *C.C. and Company* (1970) with Ann-Margret as a fashion photographer along for the ride. The trend in black exploitation films resulted in *Black Angels* (1970) which had the police standing idly by while two rival gangs massacred each other, a chilling comment on the times no matter which way you viewed it. Bruce Dern was back, tracking down an artist who had been drawing pictures of his illegal activities in *Cycle Savages* (1970). *The Savage Seven* (1968) threw some Indians into the pot while James MacArthur discovered a wilder crowd than the bikers in "way out" Hollywood in *The Angry Breed* (1969). And once again the horror and J.D. dramas converged when Joe Solomon produced a movie in which a biker gang tangles with a coven of witches who transform them into *Werewolves on Wheels* (1971). It was a suitable feature to couple with *Death Wheelers* (1973), known also as *Psychomania*, in which members of a cycle gang kill themselves in order to return from the grave indestructible.

Sonny Barger and the boys even got a chance to play Las Vegas in *Hell's Angels '69* (1969), dupes of two wealthy brothers (Tom Stern and Jeremy Slate) who used the group to divert attention away from their robbery of Caesar's Palace.

Motorcycle gangs continued to appear infrequently as supporting villains in films like *The Gauntlet* (1977), *Every Which Way but Loose* (1978), and *Ninth Configuration* (1980) but, like the Dead End Kids, the fight had been knocked out of them. And although scarcely any of the films mentioned could claim a place in cinematic art, a few last as reminders of where audiences' heads were at at the time.

What killed the motorcycle movie? Overexposure is the easiest answer, but hardly the most satisfying. The problem may have been intrinsic in the subject matter. No matter how much Hollywood may have glamorized them, the Hell's Angels and their ilk represented an extreme to which most people were opposed. No further proof of this fact need be looked for after the documentary film of the Rolling Stones' 1969 tour of America, *Gimme Shelter* (1970). As a finale for their triumphant comeback, the Stones mounted a massive free concert at the Altamont Speedway in northern California. As part of the currently hip attitude, the singers had a disdain for professional security guards, too closely resembling the police. The Grateful Dead had previously employed the Hell's Angels in that capacity at their free concerts and suggested the Stones do the same. A free concert with the Rolling Stones, however, was a major event and the increased politics, pressure, and participants would adversely affect everyone involved. Someone should have also noted the inherent hypocrisy of hiring an outlaw motorcycle gang to keep the peace, but everyone was too strung out promoting "Woodstock West."

Bad vibes, bad acid, and bad planning marred the event from the beginning. As the massive audience pushed closer to the stage, the Angels inflicted random violence on anyone in their way. During an early set by the Jefferson Airplane, singer Marty Balin protested the Angels' manhandling of the audience. For his trouble, he promptly got punched in the mouth. The Angels commandeered the stage and, from that point on, the inmates were in charge of the asylum. By nightfall, when the Stones finally came on to perform, the scene had taken on an apocalyptic image. The Stones were repeatedly interrupted by violent outbursts. Mick Jagger vainly attempted to cool everybody down, but the situation had escalated beyond anyone's control. During one scuffle in the audience, a black man pulled a gun (unloaded, as it would later be discovered) from inside his jacket. Within seconds the Angels were on him, stabbing him to death. Ending amid chaos and violence, Altamont marked the end of the "Woodstock" dream. What was meant to symbolize a reaffirmation of the counter-culture emerged instead as its downfall.

The cameras of the Maysles brothers had captured every horrifying second. Frame by frame the audience saw the black man reach for his gun. Frame by frame the Angels descended upon him. We could accept make-believe Angels committing make-believe violence, but we were not prepared for the reality of it. The motion picture audience saw the Angels as they actually were, no longer romantic rebels, but vicious, violent animals. Fantasy had collided head on with reality, and few could ever accept the myth again.

That same year, another event brought the motorcycle mania a step closer to its finish. Two veterans of the genre, Peter Fonda and Dennis Hopper, produced, directed, and coauthored the ultimate biker film, *Easy Rider*.

Samuel Z. Arkoff blew American-International's one opportunity to participate in what would become a classic biker drama. In order to get AIP to finance *Easy Rider*, Arkoff wanted the right to replace Dennis Hopper as director if he fell behind schedule. Hopper and Fonda took their project to Columbia where producers Bert Schneider and Bob Rafelson delivered the necessary financing. And by letting this classic slip through his hands, Arkoff had inadvertently put the nix on what would have been the company's greatest financial success, a fact that probably upset the mogul a lot more than passing on a piece of art.

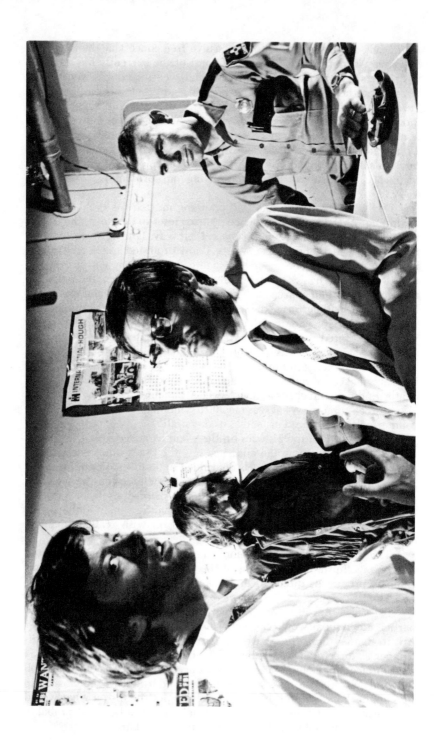

From the outset, Columbia wanted to distinguish the film from AIP's offerings. The advertisements were extremely low key: "A man went looking for America. And couldn't find it anywhere." This was decidedly more cerebral than "hot steel between their legs" or "hog straddling female animals on the prowl!"

Fonda and Hopper's film was entered in the Cannes Film Festival and won an award for "Best Film by a New Director." Accompanied by full page ads and critical raves, the film opened in New York and Los Angeles where patrons waited for hours in lines to see it. Within weeks it became "the" movie of the summer and the rallying point for an entire generation.

For a change, Fonda and Hopper were not playing members of an outlaw gang, although their cross country odyssey in the movie is financed by an illegal cocaine transaction before the opening credits. Throwing away their wristwatches (symbols of responsibility), Wyatt (Fonda) and Billy (Hopper) leave California and head for New Orleans and the Mardi Gras. On their way they encounter a self-sufficient rancher, a hitchhiker who takes them to a commune, and an alcoholic lawyer. When they reach New Orleans they drop acid with two prostitutes and freak out through the entire Mardi Gras celebration. On their way home, Wyatt and Billy are killed by shotgun blasts fired by two rednecks in a pickup truck.

The strength of *Easy Rider* is certainly not in the cohesive narrative structure of the story which is all but absent, but rather its evocation of the current polarization between the generations. In effect, it is a freak's tour of America, a tripping travelog which begins with optimism and ends in disillusionment. Perhaps Fonda and Hopper represent the freedom America is supposed to stand for and, like the two Kennedys, must die because they pose a threat to conformity. Their interlude with the rancher expresses their own aspirations—"You do your own thing in your own time. You should be proud." Even in the commune where ill-prepared city kids attempt to work dry land, Wyatt can still reflect their idealism. "They're gonna make it." But after being exposed to fear and intolerance, their doubts are expressed by George Hanson (Jack Nicholson), a misfit and drunken lawyer. "You know," Hanson remarks, "this used to be a helluva good country." After their "bummer" in New Orleans, Wyatt becomes aware that they, like everyone else in the country, "blew it." They sought the American dream (money, freedom) and found only futility. The movie was, literally, a "bad trip," offering no hope for the future, reflecting the growing pessimism of the audiences who embraced it. *Easy Rider* served as an exclamation point at the end of a decade in which American ideals were being blasted apart in the jungles of Vietnam and burned to the ground in the black ghettos of Los Angeles, Cleveland, and Chicago. Dr. Martin Luther King, Jr., an Alabama

Peter Fonda (as Wyatt, left) and Dennis Hopper (as Billy) talk to their new friend and lawyer Jack Nicholson (as George) in Easy Rider (Columbia 1969).

VICE SQUAD
admits there is no way to cope with these...
SHAMELESS SCANDALS
where teen-agers and college students become Beatniks, Sickniks and Acid-Heads, 'experimenting' in the name of science...They enter a wanton world of Psychedelic ecstasy.
BIZARRE - WEIRD - WILD
FOR THE ADULT MINDED
The revealing story of today's...
HALLUCINATION GENERATION
GEORGE MONTGOMERY · DANNY STONE
NIGEL COX · EDWARD MANN · A TRANS AMERICAN RELEASE

preacher, had hoped to lead the black people of the country in a peaceful movement toward civil rights but he had been shot by a white exconvict and now people like Malcolm X and Elijah Muhammad were advocating a "bullet or ballot" philosophy. "Plastic" became a word used to describe the hypocritical dishonesty of a country which no longer upheld its standards of equal opportunity and justice for all. Many young people turned to drugs as the answer, dropped out of society and became "hippies." They wore long hair, Mexican sarapes, Navajo headbands, love beads, and ragged denim pants and often lived in communes. "Make love, not war," became their slogan and if they often appeared to be more interested in irresponsibility than in their devotion to love and peace, playwright Lillian Hellman found some comfort in their movement. "God knows many of them are fools, and most of them will be sellouts," she said, "but they're a better generation than we were."

Easy Rider is filled with scenes of the principals sitting around campfires at night, smoking marijuana. Hopper admitted to smoking the real thing in these sequences, which filled their seemingly improvised dialogue with stoned humor and drug induced revelations.

> *Billy:* Yeah man—you're pulling inside, man. You're getting a little distance tonight.
> *Wyatt:* Yeah, well, I'm just getting my thing together.

> *Wyatt:* You ever want to be someone else?
> *Stranger:* (after some deliberation) I'd like to try Porky Pig.

> *Stranger:* You know, this could be the right place. Time is running out.
> *Wyatt:* Yeah. I'm hip about time.

The film can be faulted on several counts and, indeed, has been. Many viewers did not appreciate the fact that its two heroes were inarticulate cocaine dealers, described by Vincent Canby as "lumps of gentle clay; vacuous, romantic symbols, dressed in cycle drag." One might suffer also through the dialogue, which is anything but eloquent. But the unalterable fact is that it managed to transcend all of its shortcomings and become an emotional experience, possibly the sixties' only real depiction of the youth culture. America was, after all, shaped by nonconformists and even if the two lead characters are not particularly desirable nonconformists, that in no way negates what they are trying to say.

Other late sixties films to deal with the youth culture and drugs were more on the side of the establishment than *Easy Rider* had been. George Montgomery's Timothy Leary* type character in *Hallucination*

Dr. Leary was the dropout Harvard professor who believed that LSD was a sort of Western yoga; his slogan was "Turn on, tune in, and drop out," and he was firmly convinced that the drug could expand the consciousness of the user, enabling that person to find "ecstasy and revelation within."

The controversy surrounding campus experimentation with LSD provided the subject matter for The Hallucination Generation (Trans American 1966). The movie was filmed in black and white with the LSD sequence in "psychedelic" color.

Generation (1966) was hardly sympathetic, experimenting on young dropouts on his island off the coast of Spain. He even incites Danny Stone and Tom Baker to rob an antique dealer. Reluctant at first, Danny is set right by a little LSD.* He agrees to the plan. During the robbery the owner is killed by Baker who places the gun in Stone's hand and convinces the higher-than-a-kite youth that it was he who committed the crime. The police catch up to Baker, Montgomery and the others while Stone escapes to a monastery above Barcelona where he confesses to a group of monks, seeking their assistance to solve his problem.

Richard Todd portrayed a somewhat more charismatic variation of Leary in Sam Katzman's *The Love-Ins* (1967). The famous slogan was altered to "Be more, sense more, love more." Otherwise, Dr. Jonathan Barnett (Todd) was another thinly disguised version of the LSD guru.

A student protest surrounding an off-campus newspaper propels Professor Barnett into the national spotlight. On the Joe Pyne television show, he stirs up another controversy by advocating the use of LSD. An enterprising entrepreneur, Elliot (Mark Goddard), successfully promotes Barnett as a hippie messiah for San Francisco's Haight-Ashbury district (the real-life epicenter of city hippies). Two of the professor's former students, Larry (James MacArthur) and Pat (Susan Oliver), develop mixed feelings about Barnett's powerful influence. Pat moves in with him and becomes pregnant. Barnett feels a child would be bad for his image and orders the girl to have an abortion. Larry intervenes when Pat attempts suicide and, for the first time, fully realizes the danger of the professor's irresponsible preachings. At a massive "happening" in Golden Gate Park, Larry approaches Barnett while he is addressing the crowd and murders him. When another hippie is able to pacify the hostile crowd, the opportunistic Elliot realizes he has an instant replacement for the slain guru.

San Francisco's Haight-Ashbury section became the setting for another, more objective study of the drug culture, *Psych-Out* (1968). The principal character was Stoney (Jack Nicholson), the leader of some "acid rock" musicians living in a communal home. Stoney and the group befriends Jenny (Susan Strasberg), a deaf runaway searching for her missing brother, Steve (Bruce Dern). Stoney takes the girl to see Steve

---

LSD (lysergic acid diethylamide), or just plain "acid," was a hallucinogenic drug previously used in medical research of mental disorders, the subject for an early Science Fiction Theatre television episode with MacDonald Carey. A silly horror film called The Tingler (1959) contained a sequence in which Vincent Price was supposedly reacting to the affects of the drug. When it was discovered that it could be manufactured in almost any chemistry lab, LSD use spread like wild fire, providing eight to ten hour "trips" which could be heaven or hell (or both) depending upon the quality of the drug and the mental attitude of its user.

Richard Todd portrayed a college professor resembling LSD advocate Timothy Leary, in Sam Katzman's The Love-Ins (Columbia 1967). James MacArthur and Susan Oliver were two of his disenchanted followers.

TASTE A MOMENT OF MADNESS...LISTEN TO THE SOUND OF PURPLE

come where the PLEASURE LOVERS are

SUSAN STRASBERG
DEAN STOCKWELL

STARRING IN

PSYCH-OUT IN PATHÉCOLOR

AN AMERICAN INTERNATIONAL RELEASE

FEATURING MAX

ALSO STARRING JACK BRUCE ADAM

NICHOLSON · DERN · ROARKE · JULIEN AND ALARM CLOCK AND SEEDS

THE STRAWBERRY

THE

Dick CLARK Richard RUSH E Hunter WILLETT · Betty ULIUS E Hunter WILLETT

Heart Incense & Peppermints by the Strawberry Alarm Clock

RECOMMENDED FOR MATURE AUDIENCES

(Dean Stockwell), an acid freak known as the Seeker. He attempts to calm Jenny with a dose of STP, a highly concentrated psychedelic. Under the drug's influence, Jenny wanders away from the two and finds her brother incinerating himself. When she finally returns to reality, Jenny has stranded herself on a center divider on the Bay Bridge. Stoney and Dave make their way through some heavy traffic to rescue her and on the way back, Dave is struck and killed by one of the passing automobiles. Stoney accepts the responsibility he has so long avoided by admitting the feelings he has for Jenny.

Since the effects of drugs like marijuana, LSD, and STP are primarily an internal experience, impossible to render cinematically, it would have been better if the films dealing with the subject restricted their observations to the users, but, unfortunately, this was not the case. In *Hallucination Generation*, a black and white film, color footage was inserted for an LSD sequence. *The Love-Ins* built an embarrassing production number around the theme of *Alice in Wonderland* for Susan Oliver's "trip." *Psyche-Out* fared slightly better with Susan Strasberg seemingly trapped inside a drug induced inferno. None of these films, however, could convey the actual feelings. Even the talented Ken Russell failed to simulate anything more than the most superficial elements in his recent film, *Altered States* (1980).

In *The Trip* (1967), with only three weeks and $100,000, Roger Corman attempted to build an entire motion picture depicting an "acid trip." To research the project, the director actually took some LSD, for which he deserves a round of applause in the "above and beyond the call of duty" department. But the resulting film imagery, though occasionally imaginative, ultimately resembled outtakes from Corman's own Edgar Allan Poe productions. So it fails to be a vicarious means of experiencing LSD although it does succeed in evoking a feeling of being *with* someone on the drug. At one point, Bruce Dern suggests to Peter Fonda, who is experiencing a trip, that the two of them go into the living room. "Yeah," says Fonda, "the *living* room." Almost anyone who ever dropped acid knew what Fonda was talking about. Unlike most of the drug-based films during the period, Corman, Fonda, and Jack Nicholson, author of the script, brought firsthand experience to the subject.

In *The Trip*, Fonda plays a successful young director of television commercials, undergoing a crisis with his wife (Susan Strasberg). Frustrated by the emptiness of both his marriage and career, he hopes to find some meaning for his life by dropping acid. During his hallucinations, Fonda imagines that he has killed his friend and "guide," Bruce Dern. He then escapes to the Sunset Strip and after several paranoia producing encounters, is picked up by Salli Sachse. Further

---

San Francisco's Haight-Ashbury district provided the backdrop for a more objective treatment of the emerging drug culture in Psych-Out (AIP 1968). Jack Nicholson portrayed a hippie who eventually assumes responsibility for his feelings towards Susan Strasberg.

Five kids smoked this

…the shocking facts behind the marijuana controversy!

Two are in the hospital, One in jail— and the others have blown their minds!

AMERICAN INTERNATIONAL presents

"MARY JANE"

IN PATHECOLOR

STARRING

FABIAN · DIANE McBAIN · Michael MARGOTTA

KEVIN COUGHLIN · PATTY McCORMACK

Written by DICK GAUTIER & PETER L. MARSHALL · A MAURY DEXTER PRODUCTION

Produced and Directed by MAURY DEXTER

hallucinations clue Fonda into the fact that many of his problems are sexual — the hooded figures that stalk him on horseback are discovered to be Miss Strasberg and Miss Sachse. Fonda finally comes "down" the next morning, wondering what to do next.

Although Corman tried, more than any other filmmaker, to present an objective treatment of LSD, American-International got an attack of cold feet when it came time to release the film. A foreword was added which warned the audience that drug experimentation was not a good thing. According to the director, AIP further excised some scenes that altered the film. Finally, where Corman's version was intended to be open-ended, AIP optically inserted a cracked glass over Fonda's face, indicating that somehow the experience had irreparably shattered his life. Even with these concessions to social obligation several critics took issue with the film. On NBC's *Today* show, Judith Crist blasted the film as "an hour and a half commercial for LSD." The critic labelled it nauseating both intellectually and physically, then superfluously added: "This is one to skip."

While LSD experimentation was relatively isolated, another milder hallucinogen, marijuana, was gaining in popularity among college and high school students. Rather than attempt any sort of enlightened treatment of that issue, AIP opted to return to the dark ages with *Maryjane* (1968), the most inane thesis since *High School Confidential* nine years earlier. Producer-director Maury Dexter went no further in his research than to hire Peter Marshall, the affable host of television's *Hollywood Squares*, to coauthor the script. A plot device even had the kids who smoked grass carry little plastic emblems inscribed with the words "Mary Jane" for easy identification. By 1968 this sort of nonsense was instantly laughed off the screen.

At one point early in the film, a police officer lectures a roomful of teachers about the potential threat of the drug. "It spreads, like cancer," he says in a sober, ominous tone. "First it's marijuana, then LSD and STP, then it's heroin and cocaine." One suspicious teacher asks: "Are you saying that marijuana leads to the hard stuff?" The cop has to admit that "big-time scientists" say "no" but that his own statistics prove that *every* hardcore addict started with marijuana. To mention that they also, in all probability, started with mother's milk would probably not have altered the outcome of the sequence nor the film's conclusion. It was, for all practical purposes, an updated version of *Reefer Madness*, though for just one brief moment, when Fabian admits that he has smoked marijuana once and it had no ill effects on him, it looked as if the film might be taking a more objective stand. But after Fabian is witness to a suicide caused by marijuana, and learns that a fellow teacher (Diane McBain) not only graduated from grass to heroin but is supplying the

---

In 1968, marijuana was becoming increasingly popular with high school and college students. AIP went back to the dark ages with "Mary Jane," the most inane thesis on the subject since High School Confidential.

other students, he has a change of heart. As does Michael Margotta who wanted desperately to belong to Kevin Coughlin's Mary Jane group. After being set up for the fall guy in Coughlin's scheme to foist some phoney grass on a group of toughs, Margotta, cradled in Fabian's arms, throws his "Mary Jane" emblem to the ground in disgust.

It seems only fair to add at this point that the film is not without entertainment value, if one can ignore its gross misrepresentation. The plot moves along at a rapid pace and Fabian turns in a surprisingly good performance. And there is the simply hilarious moment when it is discovered that the ice cream man is a pusher.

Sidney Poitier has less trouble with his students in *To Sir, with Love* (1967). Reversing his *Blackboard Jungle* role, Poitier takes a job as a teacher while he waits to secure a position as an architect. He is assigned to a rough East End London school and, at first, finds it impossible to teach his belligerent and ignorant students anything. After a time, he realizes that they are not children but adults and must face the outside world, ill prepared, at the semester's end. Poitier collects all of their textbooks and deposits them into the trash. From that point on he and the students will discuss whatever topics they desire, so long as they bathe regularly, dress appropriately, and treat each other in a respectful manner. He shows them how to make good, healthful meals on a tight budget, how to look for jobs, what to look for in a mate, etc. A field trip to a museum helps them relate the past to the present. In the end, Poitier has succeeded in making the whole class into responsible, thoughtful adults. Realizing the importance of his accomplishment, Poitier decides against accepting his architect's position and decides to build stronger generations of students instead. Warm and real, *To Sir, with Love* suggested an alternative method of teaching that might one day prove most beneficial.

The integration of public schools became the subject of two films, *Born Wild* (1968) and *Halls of Anger* (1970). In the mid fifties the Supreme Court had ordered that school integration proceed with "deliberate speed" but by 1970 over 2000 school districts in the U.S. had still failed to comply. And even when they did, there was certainly no guarantee of smooth sailing.

Racial tensions between the white and Mexican-American students bubbles over in a small border town high school in AIP's *Born Wild* (also released as *The Young Animals*). Tom Nardini, a newcomer to the school, is quickly made aware of the prevailing prejudice attitude toward the Mexicans by both the students and the faculty. He joins forces with a liberal student activist, Patty McCormack, to organize a grievance committee. Patty's exboyfriend, David Macklin, launches a terrorist campaign against the Mexican-Americans and when one of their women is raped, there is a unanimous decision that the "Gringos" need a lesson. But the racial riots are not enough for Macklin. He goes berserk and begins chasing Tom and Patty around an old junkyard, stalking them with a steel wrecking machine. Macklin is finally arrested, things at the school quiet down, and Patty and Tom lead the entire student body in a mass demonstration for racial unity. Having previously turned a deaf ear, the principal agrees to their demands for equality in school affairs.

Writer Budd Schulberg found more tension *behind* rather than in *front* of the camera during the filming of *Halls of Anger*. Director Paul Bogart was angry with his star, Calvin Lockhart, who, he claimed, took two-hour lunches from which he returned not knowing his lines. The black actors complained that the script, authored by a white writer, inaccurately depicted the way blacks thought, felt, and talked. Actress Ta-Tanisha was especially unhappy about a sequence showing a white girl stripped by a group of blacks. "I couldn't believe that line we had to say," she remarked. The line in question expressed a curiosity as to whether or not the girl was "blonde all over."

In the film, Lockhart is taken away from his comfortable job as an English teacher in a white suburban school and reassigned to a ghetto school as a vice principal. The white principal there is more interested in keeping the kids in line than he is in their learning anything and runs the place like a minimum security prison. Two busloads of middleclass white students come rolling in and are naturally mistreated. One boy is given a sound thrashing just for trying to join the basketball team while one demure young lady finds herself buck naked in the locker room, victim of harassment by a group of black girls. When the whole business proves too much for Jeff Bridges, Lockhart stops him from leaving the school, reminding the boy that he has suffered but a small taste of what the blacks have been facing for years. Lockhart tells Jeff that the only way he can win the respect of the black students is to have the courage to return to the battlefield.

The picture was not particularly well received. Several critics were not convinced that the best way to induce illiterate, disinterested students to read was to hand them pornographic novels.

The invasion by hippies into certain locales was likely to cause adverse reactions, as it did in the Los Angeles area, in particular, the Sunset Strip. In the mid-to-late sixties it became a place where thousands of teenagers congregated every weekend, paralyzing the street with bodies and traffic. This influx of teenagers was welcomed by the businesses that catered to them, but other establishments discovered that their regular customers were unwilling, or unable, to bridge the mass of humanity and for them the situation was economic disaster. A misguided attempt to disperse the crowds and return the Strip to some order in 1967 resulted in one horrible weekend of violence and police brutality. And before you could say "Starts Wednesday at a theatre or drive-in near you," producer Sam Katzman had completed a film about the event, appropriately titled *Riot on Sunset Strip* (1967). Well, sort of appropriate. Actually, Katzman's film had very little to do with the Sunset Strip riot which is only shown briefly, almost as an adjunct to the conclusion of the story, suggesting the possibility that the script had been a preexisting property.

Although the feature was made for M-G-M, the studio was not geared to dispatch the picture with the speed necessary to have it theatres while it was still topical. Katzman took it to AIP and it was meeting play-dates within months of the actual event.

The story periodically shifts from police detective Aldo Ray and his attempts to keep things quiet on the Sunset Strip to his estranged daughter, Mimsy Farmer. Besides having to deal with the absence of her father, Mimsy must contend with an alcoholic mother. Her search for security takes her to a wild party held in a deserted mansion. One of her drinks is spiked with LSD and while under the drug's influence, Mimsy is coerced upstairs where three boys rape her. Noise from the house attracts the attention of some neighbors who phone the police. Mimsy is found and taken to a hospital. The sight of his brutalized daughter sends the nonviolent Ray into a rage. He finds the boys responsible and severely beats them. He is able to calm himself enough to prevent the police from cracking a few heads during the riot which breaks out on the Strip.

Several factors may have contributed to the film's boxoffice failure. For one thing the riot lasts only a few minutes and is a pretty lackluster affair at that. The sequence was not even shot on location, a few scant miles from M-G-M's Culver City Studio, but instead on the studio's backlot "New York" street, which bore no resemblance to the Strip. Grainy newsreel footage was badly intercut with director Arthur Dreifuss' sequences in which a few dozen teenagers substituted for a supposed crowd of thousands. And if these aesthetic reasons were not responsible for the film's lukewarm reception, perhaps it was the theme of the story, which may have been too localized.

Undaunted, Katzman, Dreifuss, and writer Orville Hampton took another shot with *The Young Runaways* (1968). Chicago was the destination for three Midwestern youths: Brook Bundy, rejected by her father; Kevin Coughlin, unable to tell his father about his pregnant girl-friend; Patty McCormack; driven from her home by a distrustful mother. In the big city the three become involved with an assortment of seedy characters — prostitutes, thieves, murderers — to include Richard Dreyfuss, several years before he would achieve stardom in films like *American Graffiti* (1973), *Jaws* (1975), and *The Goodbye Girl* (1977). One of the three ends up in the morgue. The other two return to their remorseful parents. The original title was *Where Are Our Children?* which was changed probably because no one involved wanted to hear the answer.

Perhaps in no year before or since did the generation gap appear as wide as it did in 1968. The postwar "boom" babies, raised on James Dean and Bob Dylan, watched with confusion as their parents gulped martinis to down tranquilizers while, at the same time, police were enforcing laws against the possession of marijuana. They saw racism unofficially condoned and found themselves sacrificial pawns in a futile foreign conflict. They realized the insanity of being old enough to die for their country and simultaneously too young to vote. Yet they were supposed to support the government in which they could play no part. So they protested, loudly, and in large numbers.

The unrest of the nation's young reached its peak in August of 1968 at the Democratic National Convention in Chicago. The optimism of the early sixties was briefly reborn when Bobby Kennedy seemed certain to win in the primaries, and, in November, win the election. Young Bobby gave the impression he was willing to listen — that he cared and for the first time, many people voted. Hours later, their votes and dreams were cancelled by an assassin's bullet. Bobby Kennedy was dead. Eugene Mc-Carthy, a candidate strongly opposed to the war appeared to be an obvious second choice, but old line Democratic party bosses wanted Hubert Humphrey, a man irrevocably linked with the Johnson administration that had escalated the war. Thousands of young people came to Chicago to protest what they felt to be a miscarriage of the democratic process. Mayor Daley, himself an old line party boss, wanted to deny their right to protest. And when he did, the city's police began bashing in skulls. A few innocent bystanders got a dose of the same and the whole violent scene was telecast to homes across the nation by all three networks.

The release of *Wild in the Streets* (1968) could not have been better timed. After losing the battle of Chicago, a movie about a 24-year-old president who sends everyone over thirty-five to concentration camps was just what the doctor ordered. It did not matter that, in the film, Lyndon Johnson is the Democratic candidate, his withdrawal from the race something the writers had not predicted. Nor did it matter that the film's 24-year-old president was nominated by the Republicans, when it was common knowledge that Richard Nixon had that party tied up. It did not matter even that it was not a good movie. Young people wanted a chance to see just what would happen when the "youth revolution" reached its logical, or illogical conclusion, and that is *all* that mattered.

The story began as a novella published in *Esquire* entitled "The Day It All Happened, Baby." For a while, Paramount and M-G-M expressed some interest in the property but nothing came of it. American-International bought the story and hired its writer, Robert Thom, to author the screenplay. Since the company had previously designed posters and ad art for a cancelled project they intended to call *Wild in the Streets*, that became the film's title.

Christopher Jones (bearing a striking resemblance to James Dean) played a multimillionaire rock star, Max Frost. When his appearances at a liberal congressman's campaign rallies nets the man a landslide victory, primarily due to the youth vote, Frost realizes his own potential as a political force. Frost uses the passing of an 84-year-old congressman to mount a campaign to elect his accompanist, Sally Leroy (Diane Varsi). Then Frost and his group pollute the Washington water supply with LSD. While the legislators are "tripping," Sally persuades them to pass an amendment which lowers the voting age to 14. That done, and with 52 per cent of America under the age of 25, Max Frost is swiftly nominated, then elected President. One of his first acts is to lower the retirement age to 30. Anyone over 35 is isolated in a concentration camp and kept sedated with LSD. Johnny Ferguson (Hal Holbrook), the congressman who convinced Frost to support him, realizes that he is partially responsible for the political monster and makes an unsuccessful attempt to assassinate Frost. Ferguson is captured and shut away in one of the concentration camps, where he hangs himself. Later, playing with his child, Frost casually mentions his own age. "That's old," the child says.

According to director Barry Shear, the film was originally to conclude with Max Frost's mother (Shelley Winters) clinging to the barbed wire surrounding one of the concentration camps, singing "The Battle Hymn of the Republic." Instead, AIP inserted a superfluous epilog in which Max Frost bullies a small child who turns to the camera and says: "Everybody over ten ought to be put out of business."

The film was completed in twenty days for a cost of $700,000. It opened in Chicago in the Spring of 1968, a few months prior to the Democratic Convention. During a televised appearance, Mayor Daley expressed his concern over the possible repercussions *Wild in the Streets* might inspire and ordered a barbed wire fence and 24-hour guards placed around Chicago's reservoirs. He did nothing about the "Max Frost for President" signs in the convention hall. Perhaps he did not see them.

One year earlier, Peter Watkins had attempted to mix pop and politics in the British made *Privilege* (1967). Paul Jones (of the Manfred Mann group) starred as Steven Shorter, a popular rock singer molded by the government into a political force. He is then manipulated by the powers to control the masses. It proved too downbeat for American audiences and received a limited release.

Where *Wild in the Streets* segregated everyone over 30, Roger Corman's *Gas-s-s-s* (1970) managed to eliminate them entirely. The premise of the film has a mysterious gas accidentally released from a defense research base in Alaska. It spreads across the continent, accelerating the aging process of everyone over 25. The older generation quickly becomes extinct, leaving the world to the young. Running from the anarchy, Coel (Robert Corff) and Cilla (Elaine Giftos) begin a trek toward an isolated desert commune in New Mexico. Their quest leads them into several encounters with groups of youngsters, all falling into the same sort of destructive patterns as their elders. One such group, the Nomads, is a fascist society on dune buggies, purging the countryside of anyone who will not join them. In the end, Coel and Cilla reach their destination and establish a peaceful existence.

Once again, AIP was unsure of the finished film and recut it, eliminating anything controversial and altering the original ending. In its truncated version, *Gas-s-s-s* bombed, despite the fact that a number of supporting players — Ben Vereen, Cindy Williams, Bud Cort, Talia Shire — achieved later stardom. The picture marked the final break between AIP and Corman after an association of over fifteen mutually profitable years. Roger Corman would continue as a producer with his own distribution company, New World Films. After the loss of Corman, and cofounder James Nicholson,* AIP would flounder for the next decade before being absorbed by Filmways.

*Nicholson left AIP, refusing to say why, and formed his own production company, his first and only effort being The Legend of Hell-House (1973). He died of a brain tumor before the film was released.

Why should
Bogart Peter Stuyvesant
go to war
and kill strangers,

when the pickings are
better in his own
bedroom?

JAMES H. NICHOLSON & SAMUEL Z. ARKOFF present The FOUR LEAF production

ANGEL, ANGEL, DOWN WE GO

STARRING

JENNIFER JONES
JORDAN CHRISTOPHER · HOLLY NEAR · LOU RAWLS CHARLES AIDMAN
DAVEY DAVISON
RODDY McDOWALL as SANTORO COLOR [R] RESTRICTED

ROBERT THOM JEROME F. KATZMAN SAM KATZMAN ROBERT THOM BARRY MANN CYNTHIA WEIL · AMERICAN INTERNATIONAL

Jordan Christopher portrayed an enigmatic rock star who systematically destroys
Holly Near's wealthy parents in Sam Katzman's infamous Angel, Angel, Down
We Go (AIP 1969; recut and rereleased a year later as Cult of the Damned).

The end of the 1960s was just about the end of Sam Katzman's career as well. Supposedly, he was on the verge of turning over a new leaf, promising to produce more artistic, meaningful films. *Angel, Angel, Down We Go* (1969) was the first of a proposed series of nonexploitation films. According to writer-director Robert Thom, the screenplay for the film was inspired by a series of dreams. If so, that could explain the incoherence of the plot. For reasons never divulged, enigmatic rock star Bogart Peter Stuyvesant (Jordan Christopher) and his comrades move into the estate of a wealthy, middleaged couple (Jennifer Jones and Charles Aidman) and their unloved teenage daughter, Tara (Holly Near). It is Bogart's plan to destroy Tara's parents, their lifestyle, and the hated generation they represent. He first seduces Tara's mother, Astrid, then asks the woman to join him and his friend in some skydiving. During their descent, Bogart taunts the woman by playing "keep-away" with her diamond necklace. Astrid values her jewels above all else and in her attempts to recapture the necklace she forgets to pull her rip-cord. The results are hazardous to her health and following her funeral, Bogart makes a pass at Tara's bisexual father, the next target for destruction.

Katzman's film was a mish-mash of currently fashionable clichés and cinematic devices. Like *Wild in the Streets* it featured several songs from composers Barry Mann and Cynthia Weil, but unlike the earlier film, it bombed. After an extensive advertising campaign, *Angel, Angel Down We Go* played exclusively at one of the more prestigious Hollywood theatres, an unusual achievement for an AIP film and it was obvious that the company, and Katzman, held high expectations for it. Within weeks it proved such a disaster that the film was withdrawn and shelved for one year. It returned as a second feature, recut, re-edited, and given a new title, *Cult of the Damned*, attempting to capitalize on the recent disclosures about Charles Manson's hippie murder cult. The film proved to be Sam Katzman's swan song. He died in August 1973.

There was a popular phrase in the sixties, "Never trust anyone over thirty." The obvious paradox of anyone's embracing this slogan was that one day, save for some tragedy, they too could not be trusted. And as the median age of the average American increased, the sentiment disappeared. And as the average age of moviegoers also increased, exploitation films primarily aimed at teenagers also disappeared. The great youth rebellion vanished, its members absorbed into the same mainstream establishment they had previously criticized. There was, in fact, a counter-culture bumper sticker in the sixties which read "We Are the People Our Parents Warned Us Against." An appropriate bumper sticker for the seventies would be "We Are the People *We* Warned Us Against."

In the wake of an era of major social and cultural advances, everything stopped, and we entered a period of nostalgia. The baby boom had peaked. There were fewer teenagers, ergo, fewer movies about them. The youth rebellion which had spawned so many juvenile delinquency films had spanned less than a generation, the fifteen years between 1955 and 1970.

Epilog

"The twelve year old who is dragged by his parents to see *The Love Bug* may very well be making, in his seventh grade classroom, an 8mm film on the extinction of the American Indian... — Sterling Silliphant, novelist and screenwriter.

The advertisements for *American Graffiti* asked, "Where were you in '62?" The picture, written and directed by George Lucas, was an affectionate return to what many felt was a time less entangled — happier. The film was indicative of a people's hunger to escape from the present, evidenced by the wave of nostalgia that had been building since the closing of the sixties when acid rock was on the way out and Elvis started his comeback.

The seventies had been launched by the tragedy at Ohio's Kent State University, christened with the blood of four students killed by nervous National Guardsmen while protesting President Nixon's decision to invade Cambodia. Public outrage at the incident escalated when the charges against the eight guardsmen responsible were dismissed. A shocked people looked hard at the officials in charge of their safety and found irresponsibility and corruption that spread all the way to Washington. An insignificant second lieutenant was being used as a scapegoat for all of the atrocities committed in Vietnam; Congressmen were putting their whores on the public payroll; the President was shown to be a liar and a crook.

Equally unsettling were the rash of terrorist groups, self-righteous loons with a penchant for airplane hijackings, kidnappings, and murder, all in the name of "the people." So "the people" responded with their own brand of craziness, streaking, and buying stereo units with enough power to drown out further bad news by cranking up the volume of their music. Watching Ron Howard and Richard Dreyfuss just kind of hanging around a bygone era, before all the disgrace, listening to oldies like "Rock Around the Clock" seemed like a real good idea. The police did not shoot people or bash any skulls in *American Graffiti*. They just handed out traffic citations which were promptly filed away in glove compartments already filled to overflowing with like pieces of paper. It was fun to see the direct descendants of Dick Bakalyan and Vic Morrow embodied in the Pharaohs, a tough street gang played by Bo Hopkins, Manuel Padilla,

George Lucas' American Graffiti (Universal 1973) was the most successful film to capitalize on the trend towards nostalgia. Richard Dreyfuss starred as the class intellectual who becomes involved with an outlaw car club, the Pharaohs.

Jr., and Beau Gentry. True, we knew Paul Le Mat could not last forever as king of the dragstrip, even before the epilog informed us of his death a few years later. His time had already passed.

Lucas' film spawned several nostalgic sojourns to the past, specifically to the fifties. One of the appeals of these bits of regression was that the teenagers in them could act and talk the way they actually did, never possible in the films made during the decade they were about.

The Lords of Flatbush (1974) were neighbors of the Amboy Dukes, though slightly better adjusted. Photographed in 16mm, it featured Sylvestor Stallone and Henry Winkler before they became Rocky and the Fonz, respectively. *Cooley High* (1975) was *American Graffiti* in black-face, the music on its soundtrack filled with old Motown songs. *Hometown U.S.A.* (1979) chronicled the efforts of some toughs trying to get the school nurd laid. *The Hollywood Knights* (1980) were members of a car club, wreaking havoc on those responsible for closing the last remaining drivein eatery in Beverly Hills. But as each of these pictures point out, time changes everything.

Grease (1978) finally made it to the screen, the popular Broadway play about teenage life in the 1950s. Serious liberties were taken with Jim Jacobs and Warren Casey's amusing musical, several of their songs discarded in favor of new tunes written to accommodate Olivia Newton-John, and an enigmatic disco-type dance number was inserted for her costar, John Travolta. By the time everyone had finished tampering with it, the thing became sort of an up-dated *Beach Party*, not as inane, of course, but not much better either. Granted, Olivia looked better in her tube top and skin-tight black capris than Annette ever did in her bikini, but Frankie could sing better than John and the dialogue was equally lacking in wit. Still, it was embraced by an audience largely too young to know or care that it was a misrepresentation of both the original play and the era.

For those who did recall the decade, *Let the Good Times Roll* (1973) was a wonderful celebration of old newsreel and film clips combined with new footage of Chuck Berry, Little Richard and other popular fifties rockers.

In spite of the fact that *Drive-In* (1976) was set in the present, it owed much to Lucas in its episodic structure and longing for the past, indicated by its title song which asked, "Whatever happened to Randolph Scott?" The film was otherwise light and breezy, cutting from various juveniles, some thieves, others dragsters, all tied together with gang leader Billy Milliken's efforts to do away with Glenn Morshower for stealing his girl. The individual stories come to a head at the Alamo Drive-In Theatre where scores of patrons sit watching a hilarious parody of *Airport*, *The Towering Inferno*, and *Jaws* called *Disaster '76*. Naturally, good guy Morshower ends up with the girl, Milliken only succeeding in flooding his van when he accidentally pops his waterbed.

In *Van Nuys Boulevard* (1979), another contemporary comedy, the police try to put the damper on night-time cruising and drag racing by imposing a ten o'clock curfew.

Darktown Strutters (1975), also known as *Get Down and Boogie*, had nothing to do with the past and little to do with the present. Trina Parks played the leader of a black, female cycle gang, tough enough to make quick work of any of their male counterparts. In her search for her missing mother, Trina finds her, as well as several missing black community leaders, prisoner in the southern-styled mansion of bigot Norman Bartold. Bartold has made his fortune with a string of roadside rib stands. He plans to clone, then replace his captives in some cockamamie scheme to control the black race. He ends up tarred-and-feathered and tied to the revolving plastic hog atop one of his chicken 'n' ribs stands.

Another outrageous fantasy, *Rock 'n' Roll High School* (1979) was an inexorable backlash against all those fifties films in which teenagers tried so hard to win the acceptance of their parents and other authority figures. Here they don't care. When the new pinch-butt female principal decides to burn all of their rock and roll records the kids retaliate by blowing up the school.

Although most of the J.D. films of the seventies were played for laughs, a few were grimly serious. *Badlands* (1973) was based on the real-life thrill murderer, Charles Starkweather who, together with his 14-year-old girlfriend, murdered ten people before he was caught and condemned to die in the electric chair. The fact that Richard Lyons' character in *The Todd Killings* (1971) was fictitious made the wholesale carnage in that film no less unpleasant.

There was also a few serious studies of the transitional fifties-sixties period. *The Wanderers* (1979) was concerned with the rival of various ethnic street gangs in the Bronx, to include the Ducky Boys, surrealistic nightmare figures that magically appeared during moments when other gang members became isolated. *Quadrophenia* (1979) showed the emergence of the new era by recreating the battle in England between the Rockers, leather jacketed fifties-type bikers, and the Mods, sharply dressed Beatle fans.

Big Wednesday (1978), which featured some breath-taking surfing sequences, showed what happened when the "Beach Party" gang grew up, a bitter portrait of people clearly out of step.

Definitely *in* step, John Travolta strutted his stuff in *Saturday Night Fever* (1977). As Tony Manero, Travolta makes his drab home and work life tolerable by developing his abilities on the dance floor where every weekend he becomes king of the local disco. But after a while the week days in the paint store grow too long and Tony wants more out of his life. In a symbolic gesture of his accepted futility, he hands a coveted dance trophy that he won to another couple and leaves the disco scene to find himself.

On the lighter side, and capitalizing on the popular disco craze, *Thank God It's Friday* (1978), another *Graffiti* set to disco music, jumped from character to character during one night in a discotheque. It featured a stand-out dance number by "Marv, the Leatherman." Similarly, *Skatetown U.S.A.* (1979) put the whole business on roller skates, the film structured like a variety show. Not altogether successful,

Rock 'n' Roll High School (New World Pictures 1979) took the antiauthoritarian attitude of the fifties to its anarchistic conclusion. At the end of the film, the students blow up the school and rock off into the night.

it was far better than *Roller Boogie* (1979), about a bunch of kids joining forces to keep "the mob" out of the rink. It looked like something old "Jungle Sam" might have cooked up on one of his less creative days.

When *West Side Story* was shown to a group of high school dropouts, the kids said the gangs depicted were "phony." It would have been interesting to hear their reaction to *The Warriors* (1979), one of the many no-nonsense gangs who roam the streets of New York City. There were certainly many people who were vociferous in their opinion of the film. It caused more controversy than any motion picture since *Blackboard Jungle*, held responsible for countless violent outbursts. Eighteen-year-old Timothy Gitchel was stabbed to death when a fight broke out between blacks and whites as an Oxnard theatre and at a Palm Springs drive-in, a teenager was shot in the head while trying to get something to eat in the snack-bar. When heavy criticism was launched against Paramount for releasing the picture, one defensive studio executive pointed out that it was not the movie but the fault of the audience it attracted. "If you bring that sort of crowd into the movie house," he declared, "you will have the same trouble with *The Sound of Music.*" One confused theatre manager said, "The movie doesn't seem that bad to incite them," thinking it was the quality rather than the content that was causing the trouble. And if that were the case, violent outbursts would not be restricted to J.D. movies.

Briefly, *The Warriors* was about a charismatic hood who is gunned down while trying to organize all the New York street gangs into one mighty army which would outnumber the police two to one. His murder is erroneously pinned on a Coney Island gang called the Warriors and the majority of the film entails that group's efforts to return to their own turf before the other gangs can waste them. After running and fighting all night, the boys finally reach their destination. A tired Michael Beck looks at the drab and dreary place they call home and utters to himself, "Is this what we fought for?" It was hardly an inducement for anyone to join a street gang. And Stanley Kubrick's *Clockwork Orange* (1971), set in England, predicted things would be no better in the future.

Although the plot of *The Warriors* did not register much in the way of maturity, the gritty ugliness of the film did suggest an extreme loss of innocence since the days of *West Side Story.* Both the characters in the story and the audience watching them accepted once taboo subjects like sex, drugs, and extreme violence with casual indifference. Not that this acceptance of reality is completely negative; it certainly would not be desirable to have a world full of people whose emotions have been dulled to the point of the pod people in *The Invasion of the Body Snatchers* (1956). In a way, *Little Darlings* (1980) touched on this by exploring the sexuality of two teenaged girls, Kristi McNichol and Tatum O'Neal. Because of peer pressure, so prevalent in adolescence, the girls fear loss of status due to the burden of their virginity. A contest is devised to see who can get laid first. The stakes are high; becoming a woman and having a place in the group, not necessarily in that order. Although the contest is a reflection of their immaturity, they set out responsibly with enough rubbers for a battalion of Marines. They choose their "victims" and go for it.

Each girl has a different experience but come to the same conclusion. They learn that their sexuality is their *own* and that sex is not a game. And contrary to what Kristi's mother has told her, it is "a big deal." Both girls resolve to take the responsibility for their own bodies and lives, giving themselves permission to either have or not have sex, and in doing so each has, indeed, become a woman.

And maybe that's what the lapse into nostalgia had really been all about ... a search for our lost virginity. But despite the fact that nostalgia has its place (this book is devoted to it), it is ultimately counter-productive. It should be used in much the same way as a car's rearview mirror — an occasional glance at what is behind us to help us go forward safely.

So where are we going, or in respect to this volume, where are the J.D. films going? Statistics tell us every year that juvenile crime is increasing. Of course, they also tell us that crime in general is on the rise, so the advances in youthful delinquency may simply be proportionate. Films concerning juvenile delinquency are not popular in the early eighties, nor are films about teenage rebellion. This is subject to change without notice as there are still sufficient numbers of teenagers to support their own entertainment needs. The genre just needs a new direction and, as usual, the kids will be the ones to point the way.

Filmography

Abbreviations

Dir Director
Mus Music
Pro Producer

Sp Screenplay
(C) Color

American Graffiti (1973) Universal *(C)* 112 min. *Sp* George Lucas, Gloria Katz and Willard Huyck, *Pro* Francis Ford Coppola, *Dir* George Lucas. *Cast:* Richard Dreyfus, Ron Howard, Paul Le Mat, Charlie Martin Smith, Cindy Williams, Candy Clark, MacKenzie Phillips, Wolfman Jack, Harrison Ford, Bo Hopkins, Kathy Quinlin, Suzanne Sommers.

Angel, Angel, Down We Go (1969) American-International *(C)* 103 min. *Pro* Jerome F. Katzman, *Sp-Dir* Robert Thom. *Cast:* Jennifer Jones, Jordan Christopher, Holly Near, Roddy McDowell, Lou Rawls.

The Angel of Crooked Street (1922) Vitagraph. *Sp* C. Graham Baker from a story by Harry Dittmar, *Dir* David Smith. *Cast:* Alice Calhoun, Ralph McCullough, Scott McKee, Rex Hammel, William McCall, Nellie Anderson, Martha Mattox.

Angel Unchained (1970) American-International *(C)* 90 min. *Mus* Randy Sparks, *Sp* Jeffrey Alladin Fiskin, *Pro-Dir* Lee Madden. *Cast:* Don Stroud, Luke Askew, Larry Bishop, Tyne Daly, Neil Moran.

Angels Die Hard (1970) New World Pictures *(C)* 87 min. *Mus* Richard Hieronymous and Marcia Waldorf, *Pro* Charles Beach Dickerson, *Sp-Dir* Richard Compton. *Cast:* Tom Baker, William Smith, R.G. Armstrong, Alan De Witt, Connie Nelson, Frank Leo.

Angels from Hell (1969) American-International *(C)*. *Sp* Jerome Wish, *Pro* Kurt Neumann, *Dir* Bruce Kessler. *Cast:* Tom Stern, Arlene Martel, Jack Starrett, Ted Markland, James Murphy.

Angels Hard as They Come (1971) New World Pictures *(C)* 90 min. *Mus* Richard Hieronymous, *SP* Jonathan Demme and Joe Viola, *Pro* Jonathan Demme, *Dir* Joe Viola. *Cast:* Scott Glenn, Charles Dierkop, James Inglehart, Gilda Texter, Janet Wood, Gary Busey.

Angels Wash Their Faces (1939) Warner Bros. 76 min. *Sp* Michael Fessier, Niven Bush and Robert Bukkner, *Pro* Max Siegel, *Dir* Raymond Enright. *Cast:* Ann Sheridan, Ronald Reagan, Billy Halop, Bonita Granville, Frankie Thomas, Bobbie Jordan, Huntz Hall, Leo Gorcey.

Angels with Dirty Faces (1938) Warner Bros. 97 min. *Mus* Max Steiner, *SP* John Wexley and Warren Duff, *Dir* Michael Curtiz. *Cast:* James Cagney, Pat O'Brien, Humphrey Bogart, Ann Sheridan, George Bancroft, Billy Halop, Bobby Jordan, Leo Gorcey.

Angry Breed (1969) Commonwealth United *(C)* 89 min. *Sp-Pro-Dir* David Commons. *Cast:* Jan Sterling, William Windom, James MacArthur, Jan Murray, Lori Martin.

Are These Our Children? (1931) RKO. *Mus* Max Steiner, *Pro* William LeBaron, *Sp-Dir* Wesley Ruggles. *Cast:* Eric Linden, Rochelle Hudson, Arline Judge, Ben Alexander, Robert Quirk.

As the World Rolls On (1921) Andlauer Productions. *Cast:* Jack Johnson, Blanche Thompson.

Bad Boys (1960) [Japanese Title: *Furyo Shonen*] 90 min. *Mus* Toru Takemitsu, *Sp-Dir* Susumu Hani.

Bad Girl *see* **Teenage Bad Girl**

Badlands (1974) Warner Bros. *(C)* 95 min. *Sp-Pro-Dir* Terrence Malick. *Cast:* Martin Sheen, Sissy Spacek, Warren Oates, Ramon Bieri, Alan Vent.

Beach Blanket Bingo (1965) American-International *(C)* 93 min. *Mus* Les Baxter, *Sp* William Asher and Leo Townsend, *Pro* James H. Nicholson and Samuel Z. Arkoff, *Dir* William Asher. *Cast:* Frankie Avalon, Annette Funicello, Deborah Walley, Harvey Lembeck, John Ashley, Jody McCrea, Donna Loren.

Beach Party (1963) American-International *(C)* 101 min. *Mus* Les Baxter, *Sp* Lou Rusoff, *Pro* James H. Nicholson and Samuel Z. Arkoff, *Dir* William Asher. *Cast:* Bob Cummings, Dorothy Malone, Frankie Avalon, Annette Funicello, Harvey Lembeck, Jody McCrea, John Ashley, Eva Six.

Beat Girl (1960) Renown 91 min. *Mus* John Barry, *Sp* Dail Ambler, *Pro* George Minter, *Dir* Edmon T. Granville. *Cast:* Adam Faith, Noelle Adam, Christopher Lee, David Farrar, Gillian Hills, Shirley Ann Field, Oliver Reed.

Because They're Young (1960) Columbia 102 min. *Mus* John

Williams, *Sp* James Gunn from the novel *Harrison High* by John Farris, *Pro* Jerry Bresler, *Dir* Paul Wendkos. *Cast:* Dick Clark, Michael Callan, James Darren, Doug McClure, Tuesday Weld, Warren Berlinger, Victoria Shaw.

Big Wednesday (1978) Warner Bros. *(C)* 126 min. *Mus* Basil Poledouris, *Sp* John Milius and Dennis Aaberg, *Pro* Buzz Feitshans, *Dir* John Milius. *Cast:* Jan-Michael Vincent, William Katt, Gary Busey, Patti D'Arbanville, Lee Purcell, Sam Melville, Barbara Hale.

Bikini Beach (1964) American-International *(C)* 100 min. *Mus* Les Baxter, *Sp* William Asher, Leo Townsend and Robert Dillon, *Pro* James H. Nicholson and Samuel Z. Arkoff, *Dir* William Asher. *Cast:* Frankie Avalon, Annette Funicello, Martha Hyer, Harvey Lembeck, Don Rickles, John Ashley, Jody McCrea, Candy Johnson.

Billy Jack (1971) Warner Bros. *(C)* 112 min. *Sp* Frank and Teresa Christina (Tom Laughlin and Dolores Taylor), *Pro* Mary Rose Solti, *Dir* T.C. Frank (Tom Laughlin). *Cast:* Tom Laughlin, Dolores Taylor, Bert Freed, Kenneth Tobey, Clark Howat, Julie Webb.

Black Angels (1970) Merrick International *(C)* 92 min. *Pro* Leo Rivers, *Sp-Dir* Laurence Merrick. *Cast:* Des Roberts, John King III, Linda Jackson, James Young-El.

Blackboard Jungle (1955) Metro-Goldwyn-Mayer 101 min. *Sp* Richard Brooks from the novel by Evan Hunter, *Pro* Pandro S. Berman, *Dir* Richard Brooks. *Cast:* Glenn Ford, Anne Francis, Louis Calhern, Margaret Hayes, John Hoyt, Richard Kiley, Sidney Poitier, Vic Morrow.

The Blob (1958) Paramount *(C)* 86 min. *Mus* Ralph Carmichael, *SP* Theodore Simonson and Kate Phillips, *Pro* Jack H. Harris, *Dir* Irvin S. Yeaworth Jr. *Cast:* Steve McQueen, Aneta Corseaut, Earl Rowe, Olin Howlin.

Blood of Dracula (1957) American-International 68 min. *Mus* Paul Dunlap, *Sp* Ralph Thornton (Herman Cohen and Aben Kandel), *Pro* Herman Cohen, *Dir* Herbert L. Strock. *Cast:* Sandra Harrison, Gail Ganley, Louise Lewis, Jerry Blaine, Malcolm Atterbury, Richard Devon, Thomas B. Henry.

Born Losers (1967) American-International *(C)* 112 min. *Mus* Mike Curb, *Sp* E. James Lloyd, *Pro* Donald Henderson, *Dir* T.C. Frank (Tom Laughlin). *Cast:* Tom Laughlin, Elizabeth James, Jane Russell, Jeremy Slate, William Wellman Jr.

Born Wild (1968) American-International *(C)* 100 min. *Mus* Les Baxter, *Sp* James Gordon White, *Pro-Dir* Maury Dexter. *Cast:* Tom Nardini, Patty McCormack, David Macklin, Joanna Frank, Zooey Hall, Russ Bender.

The Boys (1963) Screen Entertainment Co. 123 min. *Sp* Stuart Douglas, *Pro-Dir* Sidney J. Fury. *Cast:* Richard Todd, Robert Morley, Felix Aylmer, Dudley Sutton, Jess Conrad.

Boys Town (1938) Metro-Goldwyn-Mayer 90 min. *Sp* Dore Schary and John Meechan, *Pro* John Considine Jr., *Dir* Norman Taurog. *Cast:* Spencer Tracy, Mickey Rooney, Henry Hull, Leslie Fenton.

Bucket of Blood (1959) American-International 66 min. *Mus* Fred Katz, *Sp* Charles B. Griffith, *Pro-Dir* Roger Corman. *Cast:* Dick Miller, Barboura Morris, Antony Carbone, Julian Burton, Burt Convey, Ed Nelson.

The Burning Question *see* **Reefer Madness**

Bury Me an Angel (1973) New World Pictures *(C)* 86 min. *Mus* Richard Hieronymous, *Pro* Paul Nobert, *Sp-Dir* Barbara Peters. *Cast:* Dixie Peabody, Terry Mace, Clyde Ventura, Stephen Wittaker, Joanne Moore Jordan, Marie Denn, Dennis Peabody.

C.C. and Company (1970) Avco Embassy *(C)* 94 min. *Mus* Lenny Stack, *Sp* Roger Smith, *Pro* Allan Carr and Roger Smith, *Dir* Seymour Robbie. *Cast:* Joe Namath, Ann-Margret, William Smith, Jennifer Billingsly, Don Chastain.

The Choppers (1962) Fairway International 70 min. *Sp-Pro* Arch Hall Sr., *Dir* Leigh Jason. *Cast:* Arch Hall Jr., Bruno Ve Sota, Tom Brown, Marianne Gaba.

Chrome and Hot Leather (1971) American-International *(C)* 91 min. *Mus* Porter Jordan, *Sp* Michael Allen Haynes, David Neibel and Don Tait, *Pro* Wes Bishop, *Dir* Lee Frost. *Cast:* William Smith, Tony Young, Michael Haynes, Peter Brown, Marvin Gaye.

City Across the River (1949) Universal-International 90 min. *Mus* Walter Scharf, *Sp* Maxwell Shane and Dennis Cooper from the novel *The Amboy Dukes* by Irving Shulman, *Pro-Dir* Maxwell Shane. *Cast:* Peter Fernandez, Al Wilks, Joshua Shelley, Stephan McNally, Thelma Ritter, Louis Van Rooten, Jeff Corey, Tony Curtis, Richard Jaeckel.

Clockwork Orange (1971) Warner Bros. *(C)* 137 min. *Sp* Stanley Kubrick from the novel by Anthony Burgess, *Pro-Dir* Stanley Kubrick. *Cast:* Malcolm McDowell, Patrick MaGee, Sheila Raynor, Philip Stone.

College Confidential (1960) Universal-International 91 min. *Sp* Irving Shulman, *Pro-Dir* Albert Zugsmith. *Cast:* Steve Allen, Jayne Meadows, Mamie Van Doren, Cathy Crosby, Conway Twitty, Herbert Marshall, Ziva Rodann, Walter Winchell.

Confessions of a Sorority Girl *see* **Sorority Girl**

The Cool and the Crazy (1958) American-International 78 min. *Mus* Raoul Kraushaar, *Sp* Richard C. Sarafian, *Pro* E.C. Rhoden, Jr., *Dir* William Witney. *Cast:* Scott Marlowe, Gigi Perreau, Dick Bakalyan, Dick Jones, Shelby Storck, Marvin J. Rosen.

The Cool World (1964) Cinema V 105 min. *Sp* Shirley Clarke and Carl Lee based on the novel by Warren Miller, *Pro* Frederick Wiseman, *Dir* Shirley Clarke. *Cast:* Hampton Clanton, Yolanda Rodriguez, Carl Lee, Clarence Williams III.

Cooley High (1975) American-International *(C)* 107 min. *Mus* Freddie Perrin, *Sp* Eric Monte, *Pro* Steve Krantz, *Dir* Michael Schultz. *Cast:* Glynn Turman, Lawrence-Hilton Jacobs, Garrett Morris, Cynthia Davis, Corin Rogers.

Crime in the Streets (1956) Allied Artists 91 min. *Mus* Franz Waxman, *Sp* Reginald Rose, *Pro* Vincent Fennelly, *Dir* Don Siegel. *Cast:* John Cassavetes, James Whitmore, Sal Mineo, Mark Rydell, Malcolm Atterbury.

Crime School (1938) Warner Bros. 86 min. *Mus* Max Steiner, *Sp* Crane Wilbur and Vincent Sherman, *Dir* Vincent Sherman. *Cast:* Humphrey Bogart, Gale Page, Billy Halop, Leo Gorcey, Bobby Jordan, Huntz Hall.

Cry Baby Killer (1959) Allied Artists 62 min. *Sp* Leo Gordon and Melvin Levy, *Pro* Roger Corman, *Dir* Jus Addis. *Cast:* Harry Lauter, Jack Nicholson, Carolyn Mitchell, Brett Halsey, Lynn Cartwright, Ed Nelson.

Cult of the Damned *see* **Angel, Angel, Down We Go**

Cycle Savages (1970) American-International *(C)* 82 min. *Pro* Maurice Smith, *Sp-Dir* Bill Brame. *Cast:* Bruce Dern, Chris Robinson, Melody Patterson, Karen Ciral, Scott Brady.

Dangerous Years (1947) 20th Century-Fox 65 min. *Mus* Rudy Schrager, *Sp* Arnold Belgrad, *Pro* Sol Wurtzel, *Dir* Arthur Belgrad. *Cast:* William Halop, Ann E. Todd, Jerome Cowan, Anabel Shaw, Richard Shaw.

Dangerous Youth (1958) Warner Bros. 98 min. *Mus* Stanley Black,

Sp Jack Trevor Story, *Pro* Anna Neagle, *Dir* Herbert Wilcox. *Cast:* Frankie Vaughn, Carole Lesley, George Baker, Jackie Lane.

Darktown Strutters *see* **Get Down and Boogie**

Date Bait (1960) Filmgroup 71 min. *Sp* Robert Slaven and Ethelmae Page, *Pro* Dale Ireland, *Dir* George Reppas. *Cast:* Gary Clark, Marlo Ryan, Richard Gering.

Dead End (1937) United Artists 93 min. *Mus* Alfred Newman, *Sp* Lillian Hellman from the play by Sidney Kingsly, *Pro* Samuel Goldwyn, *Dir* William Wyler. *Cast:* Sylvia Sidney, Joel McCrea, Humphrey Bogart, Wendy Barrie, Claire Trevor, Allen Jenkins, The Dead End Kids.

The Dead End Kids on Dress Parade (1939) Warner Bros. *Sp* Tom Reed and Charles Beldon, *Pro* Bryan Foy, *Dir* William Clems. *Cast:* Billy Halop, Bobby Jordan, Leo Gorcey, Huntz Hall, Gabriel Dell, John Litel, Cissie Loftus.

The Delicate Delinquent (1957) Paramount 100 min. *Pro* Jerry Lewis, *Sp-Dir* Don McGuire. *Cast:* Jerry Lewis, Darren McGavin, Martha Hyer, Robert Ivers, Horace McMahon, Richard Bakalyan.

Delinquent Daughters (1944) Producers Releasing Corp. 72 min. *Sp* Arthur St. Claire, *Pro* Donald C. McKean and Albert Herman, *Dir* Albert Herman. *Cast:* June Carlson, Fifi D'Orsay, Teala Loring, Mary Bovaro.

Delinquent Parents (1938) Times (for Progressive). *Sp* Nick Barrows and Robert St. Clair, *Pro* B.N. Judell, *Dir* Nick Grinde. *Cast:* Helen MacKellar, Maurice Murphy, Doris Weston.

The Delinquents (1957) United Artists 71 min. *Sp-Pro-Dir* Robert Altman. *Cast:* Tommy Laughlin, Peter Miller, Richard Bakalyan, Rosemary Howard.

The Devil on Wheels (1947) Producers Releasing Corp. 65 min. *Mus* Alvin Levin, *Pro* Ben Stoloff, *Sp-Dir* Crane Wilbur. *Cast:* Noreen Nash, Darryl Hickman, Jan Ford (Terry Moore), James Cardwell, Damian O'Flynn, Lenita Lane.

Devil Rider (1971) Goldstone Film Enterprises *(C)* 75 min. *Sp* Carole McGowan, B.F. Grinter and C.G. Ward, *Pro* Brad F. Grinter and C.G. Ward, *Dir* Brad F. Grinter. *Cast:* Ross Kananza, Sharon Mahon, Ridgely Abele.

Devil's Angels (1967) American-International *(C)* 84 min. *Mus* Mike Curb, *Sp* Charles B. Griffith, *Pro* Burt Topper, *Dir* Daniel Haller. *Cast:*

John Cassavetes, Beverly Adams, Mimsy Farmer, Maurice McEndree, Salli Sachse, Leo Gordon, Russ Bender.

Dino (1957) Allied Artists 94 min. *Mus* Gerald Fried, *Sp* Reginald Rose, *Pro* Bernice Block, *Dir* Thomas Carr. *Cast:* Sal Mineo, Brian Keith, Susan Kohner, Frank Faylen, Richard Bakalyan.

The Dirt Gang (1972) American-International *(C)* 89 min. *Sp* William Mercer and Michael C. Healy, *Pro* Joseph E. Bishop and Art Jacobs, *Dir* Jerry Jameson. *Cast:* Paul Carr, Michael Forest, Ben Archibek, Michael Pataki, Nancy Harris, Nanci Beck.

Don't Knock the Rock (1957) Columbia 84 min. *Sp* Robert E. Kent and James B. Gordon, *Pro* Sam Katzman, *Dir* Fred F. Sears. *Cast:* Bill Haley and the Comets, Alan Dale, Alan Freed, Patricia Hardy, Jana Lund, Little Richard.

Dope Addict *see* **Reefer Madness**

Doped Youth *see* **Reefer Madness**

Dragstrip Girl (1957) American-International 69 min. *Mus* Ronald Stein, *Sp* Lou Rusoff, *Pro* Alex Gordon, *Dir* Edward L. Cahn. *Cast:* Fay Spain, Steve Terrell, John Ashley, Frank Gorshin, Russ Bender.

Dragstrip Riot (1958) American-International 68 min. *Mus* Nicholas Carras, *Sp* George Hodgins from a story by Dale Ireland, *Pro* Dale Ireland, *Dir* David Bradley. *Cast:* Yvonne Lime, Gary Clark, Fay Wray, Connie Stevens.

Drive-In (1976) Columbia *(C)* 96 min. *Sp* Bob Peete, *Pro* Tamara Asseyer and Alex Rose, *Dir* Rod Amateau. *Cast:* Lisa Lemole, Glenn Morshower, Gary Cavagnaro, Billy Milliken, Lee Newsom, Regan Kee.

Easy Rider (1969) Columbia *(C)* 94 min. *Sp* Dennis Hopper, Peter Fonda and Terry Southern, *Pro* Peter Fonda, *Dir* Dennis Hopper. *Cast:* Peter Fonda, Dennis Hopper, Jack Nicholson, Warren Finnerty, Luke Asken, Luana Anders, Karen Black.

Escape from Red Rock (1958) Allied Artists 75 min. *Mus* Les Baxter, *Pro* Bernard Glasser, *Sp-Dir* Edward Bernds. *Cast:* Brian Donlevy, Eilene Janssen, Garry Murray, Jay C. Flippen, William Phipps, Michael Healey, Nesdon Booth, Daniel White.

The Explosive Generation (1961) United Artists 89 min. *Sp* Joseph Landon, *Pro* Stanley Colbert, *Dir* Buzz Kulik. *Cast:* William Shatner, Patty McCormack, Lee Kinsolving, Billy Gray, Virginia Field, Steve Dunn.

For Men Only (1952) Lippert 93 min. *Mus* Laving Friedman, *Sp* Lou Morheim, *Pro-Dir* Paul Heinreid. *Cast:* Paul Henreid, Robert Sherman, Russell Johnson, Margaret Field, Kathleen Hughes, Vera Miles.

Foxes (1980) United Artists *(C)*. *Mus* Giorgio Moroder, *Sp* Gerald Ayres, *Pro* David Puttnam and Gerald Ayres, *Dir* Adrian Lyne. *Cast:* Jodie Foster, Scott Baio, Saller Kellerman, Randy Quaid.

Gas-s-s…Or It Became Necessary to Destroy the World in Order to Save It (1970) American-International *(C)* 80 min. *Sp* George Armitage, *Pro-Dir* Roger Corman. *Cast:* Robert Corff, Elaine Giftos, Pat Patterson, George Armitage, Alex Wilson, Bud Cort, Cindy Williams, Ben Vereen, Talia Coppola (Shire).

Get Down and Boogie (1975) New World Pictures *(C)* 93 min. *Sp* George Armitage, *Dir* William Witney. *Cast:* Trina Parks, Roger E. Mosley, Shirley Washington, Bettye Sweet, Stan Shaw, Dewayne Jesse, Charles Knapp, Edward Marshall.

Ghost of Dragstrip Hollow (1959) American-International 65 min. *Mus* Ronald Stein, *Sp-Pro* Lou Rusoff, *Dir* William Hole, Jr. *Cast:* Jody Fair, Martin Braddock, Russ Bender, Paul Blaisdell.

Girls in the Night (1953) Universal-International 83 min. *Pro* Albert J. Cohen, *Sp* Ray Buffum, *Dir* Jack Arnold. *Cast:* Joyce Holden, Harvey Lembeck, Glenda Farrell, Glen Roberts, Patricia Hardy.

Girls on Probation (1938) Warner Bros. 63 min. *Sp* Crane Wilbur, *Pro* Bryan Foy, *Dir* William McGann. *Cast:* Ronald Reagan, Jane Bryan, Anthony Averill, Sheila Bromley, Henry O'Neill, Elisabeth Risdon, Sig Rumann.

Girl's Town (1959) Metro-Goldwyn-Mayer 92 min. *Mus* Van Alexander, *Sp* Robert Smith from a story by Robert Hardy Andrews, *Pro* Albert Zugsmith, *Dir* Charles Haas. *Cast:* Mamie Van Doren, Mel Torme, Paul Anka, Ray Anthony, Gigi Perreau, Margaret Hayes, Elinore Donahue, Sheilah Graham, Gloria Talbott, The Platters.

The Glory Stompers (1968) American-International *(C)* 85 min. *Sp* James Gordon White and John Lawrence, *Pro* John Lawrence, *Dir* Anthony Lanza. *Cast:* Dennis Hopper, Jody McCrea, Chris Noel, Jock Mahoney.

Grease (1978) Paramount *(C)* 110 min. *Sp* Bronte Woodard, adapted by Allan Carr from the play by Jim Jacobs and Warren Casey, *Pro* Robert Stigwood and Allan Carr, *Dir* Randal Kleiser. *Cast:* John Travolta, Olivia Newton-John, Stockard Channing, Eve Arden, Sid Caesar, Frankie Avalon, Joan Blondell, Edd Byrnes.

Halls of Anger (1970) United Artists *(C)* 100 min. *Mus* Dave Grushin, *Sp* John Shaner and Al Ramrus, *Dir* Paul Bogart. *Cast:* Calvin Lockhart, Janet MacLaclalan, James Watson, Jr., Jeff Bridges, Rob Reiner.

Hallucination Generation (1966) Trans-America (American-International) 90 min. *Pro* Nigel Cox, *Sp-Dir* Edward Mann. *Cast:* George Montgomery, Danny Stone, Renate Kasche, Tom Baker.

The Hard Ride (1971) American-International *(C)* 93 min. *Pro* Charles Hanawatt, *Sp-Dir* Burt Topper. *Cast:* Robert Fuller, Sherry Bain, Tony Russell.

The Hellcats (1968) Crown-International *(C)* 90 min. *Sp* Tony Huston and Robert F. Slatzer, *Pro* Anthony Cardoza, *Dir* Robert F. Slatzer. *Cast:* Ross Hagen, Dee Duffym, Sharyn Kinzie, Sonny West.

Hell's Angels on Wheels (1967) American-International *(C)* 95 min. *Mus* Stu Phillips, *Sp* R. Wright Campbell, *Pro* Joe Solomon, *Dir* Richard Rush. *Cast:* Adam Roarke, Jack Nicholson, Sabrina Scharf, Jana Taylor, Joan Garwood, Sonny Barger and the Oakland Hell's Angels.

Hell's Angels '69 (1969) American-International *(C)* 97 min. *Mus* Tony Bruno, *Sp* Don Tait from a story by Tom Stern and Jeremy Slate, *Pro* Tom Stern, *Dir* Lee Madden. *Cast:* Tom Stern, Jeremy Slate, Conny Van Dyke, Steve Sandor, Sonny Barger, Terry the Tramp, and the Original Oakland Hell's Angels.

Hell's Belles (1969) American-International *(C)* 98 min. *Sp* James Gordon White and R.G. McMullen, *Pro-Dir* Maury Dexter. *Cast:* Jeremy Slate, Adam Roarke, Jocelyn Lane, Angelique Pettyjohn, Michael Walker.

Hell's Kitchen (1939) Warner Bros. 82 min. *Sp* Crane Wilbur and Fred Niblo Jr., *Pro* Bryan Foy, *Dir* Lewis Seiler and E.A. Dupont. *Cast:* Billy Halop, Bobby Jordan, Leo Gorcey, Huntz Hall, Gabriel Dell, Margaret Lindsay, Ronald Reagan.

High School Big Shot (1958) Filmgroup 70 min. *Pro* Stan Bickman, *Sp-Dir* Joel Rapp. *Cast:* Tom Pittman, Virginia Aldridge, Howard Viet, Malcolm Atterbury, Stanley Adams.

High School Caesar (1960) Filmgroup 63 min. *Sp* Ethelmae Page and Robert Slaven, *Pro-Dir* Dale Ireland. *Cast:* John Ashley, Gary Vinson, Lowell Brown, Steve Stevens, Judy Nugent, Daria Massey.

High School Confidential (1958) Metro-Goldwyn-Mayer 85 min. *Sp* Lewis Meltzer and Robert Blees, *Pro* Albert Zugsmith, *Dir* Jack Arnold.

Cast: Russ Tamblyn, Mamie Van Doren, Jan Sterling, Jackie Coogan, John Drew Barrymore, Jerry Lee Lewis, Michael Landon, Ray Anthony.

High School Hellcats (1958) American-International 68 min. *Sp* Mark and Jan Lowell, *Pro* Charles "Buddy" Rogers, *Dir* Edward Bernds. *Cast:* Yvonne Lime, Bret Halsey, Jana Lund, Suzanne Sidney, Heather Ames, Nancy Kilgas.

The Hollywood Knights (1980) Columbia *(C)*. *Pro* Richard Lederer, *Sp-Dir* Floyd Mutrux. *Cast:* Fran Drescher, Leigh French, Randy Gornel.

The Hoodlum Priest (1961) United Artists 101 min. *Sp* Don Deer and Joseph Landon, *Pro* Don Murray and Walter Wood, *Dir* Irvin Kershner. *Cast:* Don Murray, Larry Gates, Cindi Wood, Keir Dullea, Logan Ramsay.

Hot Car Girl (1958) Allied Artists 71 min. *Mus* Cal Tjader, *Sp* Leo Gordon, *Pro* Gene Corman, *Dir* Bernard Kowalski. *Cast:* Richard Bakalyan, June Kenney, John Brinkley, Sheila McKay, Jana Lund, Bruno Ve Soto.

Hot Rod (1950) Monogram 61 min. *Mus* Edward J. Kay, *Sp* Dan Ullman, *Pro* Jerry Thomas, *Dir* Lewis D. Collins. *Cast:* James Lydon, Art Baker, Gil Straton, Jr., Gloria Winter.

Hot Rod Gang (1958) American-International 72 min. *Mus* Ronald Stein, *Sp-Pro* Lou Rusoff, *Dir* Lew Landers. *Cast:* John Ashley, Jody Fair, Gene Vincent, Steve Drexel, Henry McCann, Maureen Arthur.

Hot Rod Girl (1956) American-International 75 min. *Sp* John McGreevey, *Pro* Norman Herman, *Dir* Leslie Martinson. *Cast:* Lori Nelson, John Smith, Chuck Connors, Roxanne Arlen, Mark Andrews, Frank Gorshin, Dabbs Greer.

Hot Rod Hullabaloo (1966) Allied Artists 81 min. *Mus* Elliot Lawrence, *Sp* Stanley Schreider, *Pro* Martin L. Low and William Naud, *Dir* William Naud. *Cast:* John Arnold, Kendra Kerr, Val Bisoglio, William Hunter, Arlen Dean Snyder, Ron Cummins, Marsha Mason.

Hot Rod Rumble (1957) Allied Artists 79 min. *Mus* Alexander Courage, *Sp* Meyer Dolinsky, *Pro* Norman T. Herman, *Dir* Leslie H. Martinson. *Cast:* Leigh Snowden, Richard Hartunian, Joey Forman, Brett Halsey, Wright King.

Hot Rods to Hell (1967) Metro-Goldwyn-Mayer *(C)* 92 min. *Sp* Robert E. Kent from a story by Alex Gaby, *Pro* Sam Katzman, *Dir* John Brahm. *Cast:* Dana Andrews, Jeanne Crain, Laurie Mock, Mimsy Farmer, Tim Rooney.

How to Stuff a Wild Bikini (1965) American-International *(C)* 90 min. *Mus* Les Baxter, *Sp* William Asher and Leo Townsend, *Pro* James H. Nicholson and Samuel Z. Arkoff, *Dir* William Asher. *Cast:* Annette Funicello, Dwayne Hickman, Brian Donlevy, Harvey Lembeck, Beverly Adams, Jody McCrea, John Ashley, Buster Keaton.

I Accuse My Parents (1944) Producers Releasing Corporation 70 min. *Sp* Harry Fraser and Marjorie Dudley, *Pro* Max Alexander, *Dir* Sam Newfield. *Cast:* Mary Beth Hughes, Robert Lowell, John Miljan, Vivienne Osborne, George Meeker.

I Was a Teenage Werewolf (1957) American-International 70 min. *Mus* Paul Dunlap, *Sp* Ralph Thornton (Herman Cohen and Aben Kandel), *Dir* Gene Fowler Jr. *Cast:* Michael Landon, Yvonne Lime, Whit Bissell, Tony Marshall, Malcolm Atterbury, Guy Williams, Louise Lewis.

The Incident (1967) 20th Century-Fox 107 min. *Sp* Nicholas E. Baehr, *Pro* Monroe Sachson, *Dir* Larry Pierce. *Cast:* Tony Musante, Martin Sheen, Beau Bridges, Jack Gilford, Thelma Ritter, Jan Sterling, Gary Merrill, Diane Van Der Vlis, Ed MacMahon, Brock Peters, Ruby Dee.

Jacktown (1962) Picotrial International Products. *Sp-Pro-Dir* William Martin. *Cast:* Patty McCormack, Richard Meade, Donald Rutherford.

Jailhouse Rock (1957) Metro-Goldwyn-Mayer 96 min. *Sp* Guy Trsoper, *Pro* Pandro Berman, *Dir* Richard Thorpe. *Cast:* Elvis Presley, Judy Tyler, Mickey Shauhnessy, Dean Jones.

Joy Ride (1958) Allied Artists 60 min. *Sp* Christopher Knopf from a story by C.B. Gilford, *Pro* Ben Schwalb, *Dir* Edward Bernds. *Cast:* Rad Fulton, Ann Doran, Regis Toomey, Nicholas King, Robert Levin.

Juvenile Court (1938) Columbia 60 min. *Sp* Michael L. Simmons, Robert E. Kent and Henry Taylor, *Pro* Ralph Cohn, *Dir* D. Ross Lederman. *Cast:* Paul Kelly, Rita Hayworth, Frankie Darrow, Hally Chester, Don Latorre.

Juvenile Jungle (1958) Republic 69 min. *Mus* Gerald Roberts, *Sp* Arthur T. Horman, *Pro* Sidney Picker, *Dir* William Witney. *Cast:* Richard Bakalyan, Corey Allen, Anne Whitfield, Rebecca Welles, Joe Di Reda.

King Creole (1958) Paramount 116 min. *Sp* Herbert Baker and Michael Vincente Gazzo based on the novel *A Stone for Danny Fisher* by Harrold Robbins, *Pro* Hal B. Wallis, *Dir* Michael Curtiz. *Cast:* Elvis Presley, Carolyn Jones, Walter Mathau, Dolores Hart, Dean Jagger, Vic Morrow, Paul Stewart.

Kitten with a Whip (1964) Universal 83 min. *Sp* Douglas Heyes from the novel by Wade Miller, *Pro* Harry Keller, *Dir* Douglas Heyes. *Cast:* Ann-Margret, John Forsythe, Peter Brown, Patricia Barry, Richard Anderson, James Ward.

Knock on Any Door (1949) Columbia 100 min. *Mus* George Antheil, *Sp* Daniel Taradash and John Monks, Jr., from the novel by Willard Motley, *Pro* Robert Lord, *Dir* Nicholas Ray. *Cast:* Humphrey Bogart, John Derek, George Macready, Allene Roberts, Susan Perry, Mickey Knox.

Little Darlings (1980) Paramount *(C)*. *Mus* Charles Fox, *Sp* Kimi Peck and Darlene Young, *Pro* Stephen J. Friedman, *Dir* Ronald F. Maxwell. *Cast:* Tatum O'Neal, Kristy McNichol, Armand Assante, Matt Dillon, Maggie Blye.

Little Tough Guy (1938) Universal 83 min. *Sp* Gildson Brown and Brenda Weisberg, *Pro* Ken Goldsmith, *Dir* Harold Young. *Cast:* Billy Halop, Helen Perrish, Robert Wilcox, Marjorie Main, Huntz Hall, Gabriel Dell.

Live Fast, Die Young (1958) Universal-International 82 min. *Sp* Allen Rivkin and Ib Melchior, *Pro* Harry Rybnick and Gordon Kay, *Dir* Paul Henreid. *Cast:* Mary Murphy, Norma Eberhardt, Sheridan Comerate, Michael Connors, Troy Donahue, Dorothy Provine.

Loneliness of the Long Distance Runner (1962) Continental 103 min. *Mus* John Addison, *Sp* Alan Sillitoe, *Pro-Dir* Tony Richardson. *Cast:* Tom Courtenay, Michael Redgrave, Avis Brunnage, James Bolam, Derris Ward, Peter Madden, James Fox, Julia Foster.

Lord of Flatbush (1974) Columbia *(C)* 85 min. *Mus* Joe Brooks, *Sp* Stephen Verona, Gayle Glecker and Martin Davidson, *Pro* Steve Verona, *Dir* Stephen Verona and Martin Davidson. *Cast:* Perry King, Sylvester Stallone, Henry Winkler, Paul Mace, Susie Blakely, Maria Smith.

The Losers (1972) Fanfare *(C)* 95 min. *Mus* Stu Phillips, *Sp* Alan Caillou, *Pro* Joe Solomon, *Dir* Jack Starrett. *Cast:* William Smith, Bernie Hamilton, Adam Roarke, Houston Savage, Gene Cornelius.

Love Madness *see* **Reefer Madness**

The Love-Ins (1967) Columbia *(C)* 86 min. *Sp* Hal Collins and Arthur Dreifuss, *Pro* Sam Katzman, *Dir* Arthur Dreifuss. *Cast:* Richard Todd, James MacArthur, Susan Olivor, Mark Goddard, Joe Pyne.

Marijuana (1936) Roadshow Attractions Corp. *Sp* Hildagarde Stadie and Rex Elgin, *Dir* Dwain Esper. *Cast:* Harley Wood, Hugh McArthur, Pat Carlyle, Paul Ellis.

Maryjane (1968) American-International *(C)* 95 min. *Mus* Mike Curb, *Sp* Richard Gautier and Peter J. Marshall, *Pro-Dir* Maury Dexter. *Cast:* Fabian, Diane McBain, Kevin Coughlin, Patty McCormack, Michael Margotta, Russ Bender.

The Mayor of Hell (1933) Warner Bros. 80 min. *Sp* Edward Chodorou from a story by Islin Auster, *Pro* Lucien Hubbard, *Dir* Archie Mayor. *Cast:* James Cagney, Frankie Darro, Madge Evens.

Men of Boy's Town (1948) Metro-Goldwyn-Mayer 106 min. *Sp* James K. McGinness, *Pro* John Considine, Jr., *Dir* Norman Taurog. *Cast:* Spencer Tracy, Mickey Rooney, Bob Watson, Larry Nunn, Darryl Hickman, Lee J. Cobb.

Mini-Skirt Mob (1968) American-International *(C)* 82 min. *Mus* Les Baxter, *Sp* James Gordon White, *Pro-Dir* Maury Dexter. *Cast:* Jeremy Slate, Diane McBain, Sherry Jackson, Patty McCormack, Ross Hagen, Harry Dean Stanton.

Motorcycle Gang (1957) American-International 78 min. *Mus* Albert Glasser, *Sp* Lou Rusoff, *Pro* Alex Gordon, *Dir* Edward L. Cahn. *Cast:* Anne Neyland, Steve Terrell, John Ashley, Carl Switzer, Raymond Hatton, Russell Bender, Paul Blaisdell.

Muscle Beach Party (1964) American-International *(C)* 94 min. *Mus* Les Baxter, *Sp* William Asher and Robert Dillon, *Pro* James H. Nicholson and Samuel Z. Arkoff, *Dir* William Asher. *Cast:* Frankie Avalon, Annette Funicello, Morey Amsterdam, Buddy Hackett, Luciana Paluzzi, Donna Loren, Candy Johnson.

Pajama Party (1964) American-International *(C)* 85 min. *Sp* Louis M. Heyward, *Pro* James H. Nicholson and Samuel Z. Arkoff, *Dir* Don Weis. *Cast:* Tommy Kirk, Annette Funicello, Elsa Lanchester, Harvey Lembeck, Jesse White, Jody McCrea, Donna Loren, Susan Hart.

Panic in Year Zero (1962) American-International 92 min. *Mus* Les Baxter, *Sp* Jay Simms and John Morton, *Pro* Arnold Houghland and Lou Rusoff, *Dir* Ray Milland. *Cast:* Ray Milland, Jean Hagen, Frankie Avalon, Mary Mitchell, Joan Freeman, Richard Garland, Richard Bakalyan.

The Party Crashers (1958) Paramount 78 min. *Sp* Bernard Girard and Dan Lundberg, *Pro* William Alland, *Dir* Bernard Girard. *Cast:* Mark Damon, Bobby Driscoll, Connie Stevens, Frances Farmer, Doris Dowling, Walter Brooke.

Platinum High School (1960) Metro-Goldwyn-Mayer 93 min. *Sp* Robert Smith, *Pro* Red Doff, *Dir* Charles Haas. *Cast:* Mickey Rooney,

Terry Moore, Dan Duryea, Yvette Mimieux, Warren Berlinger, Conway Twitty, Jimmy Boyd, Richard Jaeckel, Elisha Cook.

The Plunderers (1960) Allied Artists 94 min. *Mus* Leonard Rosenman, *Sp* Bob Barbash, *Pro-Dir* Joseph Pevney. *Cast:* Jeff Chandler, John Saxon, Dolores Hart, Marsha Hunt, Jay C. Flippen, Ray Stricklyn, James Westerfield, Dee Pollock.

Psych-Out (1968) American-International *(C)* 101 min. *Sp* E. Hunter Willett and Betty Ulius, *Pro* Dick Clark, *Dir* Richard Rush. *Cast:* Susan Strasberg, Dean Stockwell, Jack Nicholson, Bruce Dern, Adam Roarke.

The Rebel Breed (1960) Warner Bros. *Sp* Morris Lee Green from a story by William Rowland and Irma Beck, *Pro* William Rowland, *Dir* Richard L. Bare. *Cast:* Mark Damon, Rita Moreno, Richard Rust, Diane Cannon.

Rebel Rousers (1967) Paragon International *(C)* 78 min. *Sp* Abe Folsky and Michael Kars, *Pro* Martin B. Cohen and Rex Carlton, *Dir* Martin B. Cohen. *Cast:* Cameron Mitchell, Jack Nicholson, Bruce Dern, Diane Ladd, Harry Dean Stanton.

The Rebel Set (1959) Allied Artists 72 min. *Mus* Paul Dunlap, *Sp* Louis Vittes and Bernard Girard, *Pro* Eagle Lyon, *Dir* Gene Fowler, Jr. *Cast:* Gregg Palmer, Kathleen Crowley, Edward Platt, Ned Glass, John Lupton, Don Sullivan.

Rebel Without a Cause (1955) Warner Bros. *(C)* 111 min. *Mus* Leonard Rosenman, *Sp* Stewart Stern, Adapted by Irving Shulman, *Pro* David Weisbart, *Dir* Nicholas Ray. *Cast:* James Dean, Natalie Wood, Jim Backus, Ann Doran, Sal Mineo, Corey Allen, Edward Platt, Dennis Hopper, Nick Adams, William Hopper.

Rebellious Daughters (1938) Progressive 65 min. *Sp* John W. Kraft, *Pro* B.N. Judell, *Dir* Jean Yarborough. *Cast:* Marjorie Reynolds, Verna Hillie, Sheila Bromley, George Douglas, Dennis Moore.

Reefer Madness (1936?) G&H Productions 48 min. *Sp* Arthur Hoerl, *Pro* George A. Hirliman, *Dir* Louis Gasnier. *Cast:* Dave O'Brien, Lillian Miles, Warren McCollum, Dorothy Short, Carleton Young.

Reform School Girl (1957) American-International 71 min. *Pro* Robert J. Gurney and Samuel Z. Arkoff, *Sp-Dir* Edward Bernds. *Cast:* Gloria Castillo, Ross Ford, Edd Byrnes, Sally Kellerman, Ralph Reed, Jack Kruschen, Yvette Vickers, Luana Anders.

Reformatory (1938) Columbia. *Sp* Gordon Rigby, *Pro* Larry Darmour, *Dir* Lewis D. Collins. *Cast:* Jack Holt, Bobby Gordon, Charlotte Wynters, Frankie Darro, Ward Bond.

The Restless Years (1958) Universal-International 86 min. *Sp* Edward Anhalt from the play *Teach Me How to Cry* by Patricia Joudry, *Pro* Ross Hunter, *Dir* Helmut Kautner. *Cast:* John Saxon, Sandra Dee, Margaret Lindsay, Teresa Wright, James Whitmore.

Riot in Juvenile Prison (1959) United Artists 71 min. *Sp* Orville H. Hampton, *Pro* Robert E. Kent, *Dir* Edward L. Cahn. *Cast:* Jerome Thor, Marcia Henderson, Scott Marlowe, John Hoyt, Dick Tyler, Dorothy Provine, Ann Doran.

Riot on Sunset Strip (1967) American-International *(C)* 83 min. *Mus* Fred Karger, *Sp* Orville H. Hampton, *Pro* Sam Katzman, *Dir* Arthur Dreifuss. *Cast:* Aldo Ray, Mimsy Farmer, Michael Evans, Laurie Mock, Tim Rooney.

Rock 'n' Roll High School (1979) New World Pictures *(C)* 92 min. *Sp* Richard Whitley, Russ Dvonch and Joseph McBride from a story by Alan Arkush and Joe Dante, *Pro* Michael Finnell, *Dir* Alan Arkush. *Cast:* P.J. Soles, Vincent Van Patten, Clint Howard, Dey Young, Mary Woronov, Dick Miller, Paul Bartel.

Roller Boogie (1979) United Artists *(C)*. *Sp* Barry Schneider, *Pro* Bruce Cohn Curtis, *Dir* Mark L. Lester. *Cast:* Linda Blair, Jim Bray, Beverly Garland, Roger Perry, Jimmy Van Patten.

The Romance of a Million Dollars (1926) Preferred Pictures. *Sp* Arthur Hoerl, *Dir* Tom Teriss. *Cast:* Glenn Hunter, Alyce Mills, Gaston Glass, Jane Jennings, Bobby Watson, Lea Penman, Thomas Brooks.

Rumble on the Docks (1956) Columbia 82 min. *Sp* Lou Morheim and Jack DeWitt based on the novel by Frank Ray, *Pro* Sam Katzman, *Dir* Fred F. Sears. *Cast:* James Darren, Laurie Carroll, Michael Granger, Jerry Janger, Robert Blake, Edgar Barrier.

Run Angel, Run (1969) Fanfare *(C)* 94 min. *Mus* Stu Phillips, *Sp* Jerry Wise and V.A. Furlong, *Pro* Joe Solomon, *Dir* Jack Starrett. *Cast:* William Smith, Valerie Starrett, Gene Shane, Le De Broux, Eugene Cornelius Harper.

Runaway Daughters (1956) American-International 90 min. *Mus* Ronald Stein, *Sp* Lou Rusoff, *Pro* Alex Gordon, *Dir* Edward L. Cahn. *Cast:* Marla English, Anna Sten, John Litel, Lance Fuller, Adele Jergens, Mary Ellen Kaye, Gloria Castillo, Steve Terrell.

Running Wild (1955) Universal-International 81 min. *Sp* Leo

Townsend based on the novel by Ben Benson, *Pro* Howard Pine, *Dir* Abner Biberman. *Cast:* William Campbell, Mamie Van Doren, Keenan Wynn, Kathleen Chase, Jan Merlin, John Saxon.

Saturday Night Fever (1977) Paramount *(C)* 119 min. *Mus* Barry and Maurice Gibb, *Sp* Norman Wexler based on a story by Kik Cohn, *Pro* Robert Stigwood, *Dir* John Badham. *Cast:* John Travolta, Karen Lynn Gorney, Barry Miller, Joseph Call, Paul Pape, Donna Pescow.

Savage Seven (1968) American-International *(C)* 97 min. *Sp* Michael Fisher, *Pro* Dick Clark, *Dir* Richard Rush. *Cast:* Robert Walker, Larry Bishop, Joanna Frank, Adam Roarke, John Garwood, Duane Eddy, Penny Marshall.

School for Violence *see* **High School Hellcats**

Shake, Rattle and Rock (1956) American-International 74 min. *Sp* Lou Rusoff, *Pro* James H. Nicholson, *Dir* Edward L. Cahn. *Cast:* Touch (Michael) Connors, Lisa Gaye, Sterling Holloway, Raymond Hatton, Margaret Dumont, Fats Domino, Big Joe Turner.

Skatetown U.S.A. (1979) Columbia *(C)* 98 min. *Mus* Miles Goodman, *Sp* Nick Castle, *Pro* William Levey and Lorin Dreyfuss, *Dir* William A. Levey. *Cast:* Scott Baio, Flip Wilson, Ron Palillo, Ruth Buzzi, Dave Mason, Greg Bradford, Kelly Land, Billy Barty.

So Young, So Bad (1950) United Artists 91 min. *Mus* Robert W. Stringer, *Sp* Jean Rouverol and Bernard Vorhaus, *Pro* Edward J. Danziger and Harry Lee Danziger, *Dir* Bernard Vorhaus. *Cast:* Paul Henreid, Catherine McLeod, Grace Coppin, Cecil Clovelly, Anne Francis, Rosita Moreno, Anne Jackson, Enid Pulver.

Some People (1962) American-International *(C)* 92 min. *Mus* Ron Grainer, *Sp* John Eldridge, *Pro* James Archibald, *Dir* Clive Donner. *Cast:* Kenneth More, Ray Brooks, Annika Wills, David Andrews, Angela Douglas, David Hemmings.

Sorority Girl (1957) American-International 60 min. *Mus* Ronald Stein, *Sp* Ed Walters and Leo Lieberman, *Pro-Dir* Roger Corman. *Cast:* Susan Cabot, Dick Miller, Barboura O'Neill (Morris), June Kenny, Barbara Crane, Fay Baker.

Speed Crazy (1959) Allied Artists 75 min. *Mus* Richard La Salle, *Sp* Richard Bernstein and George Walters, *Pro* Richard Bernstein, *Dir* William Hole, Jr. *Cast:* Brett Halsey, Yvonne Lime, Charles Wilcox, Slick Slaven.

Stakeout on Dope Street (1958) Warner Bros. 83 min. *Sp* Irvin

Kershner, Irving Schwart and Andrew J. Fenady, *Pro* Andrew J. Fenady, *Dir* Irvin Kershner. *Cast:* Yale Wexler, Jonathan Haze, Morris Miller, Audrey Dalton, Herschel Bernardi.

Studs Lonigan (1961) United Artists 103 min. *Pro-Sp* Philip Yordan from the trilogy by James T. Farrell, *Dir* Irving Lerner. *Cast:* Christopher Knight, Frank Gorshin, Venetia Stevenson, Carolyn Craig, Jack Nicholson.

T-Bird Gang (1959) Filmgroup 75 min. *Mus* Shelley Manne, *Sp* John Brinkley and Tony Miller, *Pro* Stan Bickman, *Dir* Richard Horberger. *Cast:* John Brinkley, Ed Nelson, Pat George, Beach Dickerson, Tony Miller.

The Tall Lie *see* **For Men Only**

Teenage Bad Girl (1957) DCA 100 min. *Pro-Dir* Herbert Wilcox. *Cast:* Sylvia Sims, Anna Neagle, Norman Wooland.

Teenage Crime Wave (1955) Columbia 77 min. *Sp* Harry Essex and Ray Buffum, *Pro* Sam Katzman, *Dir* Fred F. Sears. *Cast:* Tommy Cook, Mollie McCart, Sue England, Frank Griffin, James Bell.

Teenage Doll (1957) Allied Artists 68 min. *Mus* Walter Greene, *Sp* Charles B. Griffith, *Pro-Dir* Roger Corman. *Cast:* June Kenny, Fay Spain, John Brinkley, Ziva Rodann, Barboura Morris, Richard Devon.

Teenage Rebel (1956) 20th Century-Fox 94 min. *Mus* Leigh Harline, *Sp* Walter Reisch and Charles Bracket from the play *A Roomful of Roses* by Edith Sommer, *Pro* Charles Brackett, *Dir* Edmund Goulding. *Cast:* Ginger Rogers, Michael Rennie, Mildred Natwick, Rusty Swope, Lili Gentle, Louis Beavers, Warren Berlinger.

Teenage Thunder (1957) Howco-International. *Sp* Ray Buffum, *Pro* Jacques Marquette, *Dir* Paul Hemlick. *Cast:* Charles Courtney, Melinda Byron, Robert Fuller.

Teenage Wolfpack (1956) DCA 89 min. *Mus* Martin Boettcher, *Sp* Will Tremper, *Pro* Wenzel Luedecke, *Dir* Georg Tressler. *Cast:* Henry Bookholt (Horst Bucholz), Karen Baal, Christian Derner.

Teenagers from Outer Space (1959) Warner Bros. 87 min. *Sp-Pro-Dir* Tom Graeff. *Cast:* David Love, Dawn Anderson, Harvey B. Dunn, Bryan Grant.

Tell Your Children *see* **Reefer Madness**

These Dangerous Years *see* **Dangerous Youth**

To Sir, with Love (1967) Columbia *(C)* 105 min. *Sp* James Clavell from the novel by E.R. Braithwaite, *Pro-Dir* James Clavell. *Cast:* Sidney Poitier, Judy Geeson, Christian Roberts, Suzy Kendall, Lulu.

Too Soon to Love (1960) Universal-International 85 min. *Mus* Ronald Stein, *Sp* Laszlo Gorog and Richard Rush, *Pro-Dir* Richard Rush. *Cast:* Jennifer West, Richard Evans, Warren Parker, Ralph Manza, Jack Nicholson.

Trouble at 16 *see* **Platinum High School**

The Unguarded Moment (1956) Universal-International *(C)* 95 min. *Mus* Herman Stein, *Sp* Herb Meadows and Larry Marcus from a story by Rosalind Russell, *Pro* Gordon Kay, *Dir* Harry Keller. *Cast:* Esther Williams, George Nader, John Saxon, Edward Andrews, Les Tremayne, Jack Albertson.

Untamed Youth (1957) Warner Bros. 80 min. *Mus* Les Baxter, *Sp* John C. Higgins, *Pro* Aubrey Schenck, *Dir* Howard W. Koch. *Cast:* Mamie Van Doren, Lori Nelson, John Russell, Eddie Cochran, Lurene Tuttle, Yvonne Lime, Michael Emmett.

Up the Down Staircase (1967) Warner Bros *(C)* 123 min. *Mus* Fred Karlin, *Sp* Tad Mosel, from the novel by Bel Kaufman, *Pro* Alan J. Pakula, *Dir* Robert Mulligan. *Cast:* Sandy Dennis, Patrick Bedford, Eileen Heckart, Ruth White, Jean Stapleton.

Van Nuys Boulevard (1979) Crown-International *(C)*. *Pro* Marilyn J. Tenser, *Sp-Dir* William Sachs. *Cast:* Bill Adler, Cynthia Wood, Dennis Bowen, Melissa Prophet, David Hayward, Tara Strohmeier.

Village of the Giants (1965) Avco Embassy *(C)* 80 min. *Sp* Alan Caillou from a story by Bert I. Gordon based on H.G. Wells' novel *Food of the Gods*, Pro-Dir Bert Ira Gordon. *Cast:* Tommy Kirk, Johnny Crawford, Beau Bridges, Ron Howard, Joi Harmon, Freddie Cannon, Tim Rooney, The Beau Brummells.

The Wanderers (1979) Warner Bros. *Sp* Rose and Phillip Kaufman from the novel by Richard Price, *Pro* Martin Ransonoff, *Dir* Phillip Kaufman. *Cast:* Ken Wahl, Karen Allen, John Freidrich, Toni Kalem, Alan Rosenberg.

The Warriors (1979) Paramount *(C)* 90 min. *Mus* Barry DeVorzan, *Sp* David Shaber from the novel by Sol Yurick, *Pro* Lawrence Gordon, *Dir* Walter Hill. *Cast:* Michael Beck, James Remar, Thomas Waites, Dorsey Wright, Brian Tyler, David Harris.

West Side Story (1961) United Artists *(C)* 155 min. *Mus* Leonard

Bernstein and Stephen Sondheim, *Sp* Ernest Lehman based on the play by Leonard Bernstein, Stephen Sondheim and Arthur Laurents, *Pro* Robert Wise, *Dir* Robert Wise and Jerome Robbins. *Cast:* Natalie Wood, Richard Beymer, George Chakiris, Rita Moreno, Russ Tamblyn, Simon Oakland, Ned Glass.

Where Are Your Children? (1944) Monogram 73 min. *Sp* Hilary Lynn, *Pro* Jeffrey Bernard, *Dir* William Nigh. *Cast:* Jackie Cooper, Gale Storm, Patricia Morison, John Litel, Gertrude Michael.

The Wild Angels (1966) American-International *(C)* 90 min. *Mus* Mike Curb, *Sp* Charles B. Griffith, *Pro-Dir* Roger Corman. *Cast:* Peter Fonda, Nancy Sinatra, Bruce Dern, Diane Ladd, Lou Procopio, Coby Denton, Marc Norm Alden, Michael J. Pollard, Dick Miller, The Hell's Angels of Venice, California.

Wild Boys of the Road (1933) Warner Bros. 68 min. *Sp* Earl Baldwin from a story by Daniel Ahearn, *Dir* William Wellman. *Cast:* Frankie Darro, Dorothy Coonan, Edwin Phillips, Rochelle Hudson, Sterling Holloway.

Wild Company (1930) 20th Century Fox 73 min. *Sp* John Stone and Bradley King, *Dir* Leo McCarey. *Cast:* Frank Albertson, H.B. Warner, Sharon Lynn, Joyce Compton, Claire McDowell, Bela Lugosi.

Wild for Kicks *see* **Beat Girl**

Wild in the Streets (1968) American-International *(C)* 97 min. *Mus* Les Baxter, *Sp* Robert Thom, *Pro* James H. Nicholson and Samuel Z. Arkoff, *Dir* Barry Shear. *Cast:* Shelley Winters, Christopher Jones, Diane Varsi, Hal Holbrook, Millie Perkins, Richard Pryor, Bert Freed, Kevin Coughlin, Ed Begley.

The Wild One (1954) Columbia 79 min. *Mus* Leith Stevens, *Sp* John Paxton from a story by Frank Rooney, *Pro* Stanley Kramer, *Dir* Laslo Benedek. *Cast:* Marlon Brando, Mary Murphy, Robert Keith, Lee Marvin, Jay C. Flippen, Peggy Maley, Bruno Ve Sota.

Wild Rebels (1967) Crown International *(C)* 90 min. *Mus* Al Jacobs, *Sp-Dir* William Grefe. *Cast:* Steve Alaimo, Willie Pastrano, John Vella, Bobbie Byers.

The Wild Ride (1960) Filmgroup 86 min. *Sp* Ann Porter and Marion Rothman, *Pro-Dir* Harvey Berman. *Cast:* Jack Nicholson, Georgianna Carter, Robert Dean.

Wild Youth (1961) Cinema Associates 73 min. *Sp* Robert J. Black, Jr., Lester William Burke and Dean Romano, *Pro* John Bushelman, *Dir* John Schreyer. *Cast:* Robert Hutton, John Goddard, Carol Ohmart.

Young and Wild (1958) Republic 69 min. *Sp* Arthur T. Horman, *Pro* Sidney Picker, *Dir* William Witney. *Cast:* Gene Evans, Scott Marlowe, Carolyn Kearney, Robert Arthur, Morris Ankrum.

Young Runaways (1968) Metro-Goldwyn-Mayer *(C)* 91 min. *Mus* Fred Karger, *Sp* Orville H. Hampton, *Pro* Sam Katzman, *Dir* Arthur Dreifuss. *Cast:* Brook Bundy, Kevin Coughlin, Lloyd Bochner, Patty, McCormack, Lynn Bari, Richard Dreyfuss.

The Young Savages (1961) United Artists 110 min. *Mus* David Amram, *Sp* Edward Anhalt and J.P. Miller from the novel *A Matter of Conviction* by Evan Hunter, *Pro* Pat Duggan, *Dir* John Frankenheimer. *Cast:* Burt Lancaster, Dina Merrill, Shelley Winters, Edward Andrews, Vivian Nathan, Larry Gates, Telly Savalas, Jody Fair, Chris Robinson.

The Young Sinner (1965) United Screen Arts. *Sp-Pro-Dir* Tom Laughlin. *Cast:* Tom Laughlin, Stefanie Powers, William Wellman Jr., Jack Starrett, Chris Robinson.

The Young Stranger (1957) RKO 84 min. *Mus* Leonard Rosenman, *Sp* Robert Dozier, *Pro* Stuart Miller, *Dir* John Frankenheimer. *Cast:* James MacArthur, Kim Hunter, James Daly, James Gregory, Marian Seldes, Whit Bissell.

Youth Runs Wild (1944) RKO 67 min. *Mus* Paul Sawtell, *Sp* John Fante and Ardel Wray, *Pro* Val Lewton, *Dir* Mark Robson. *Cast:* Bonita Granville, Kent Smith, Jean Brooks, Glenn Vernon, Tessa Brind, Ben Bard, Mary Servoss, Arthur Shields.

Selected Bibliography

Allen, Frederick Lewis. *Only Yesterday*. New York: Harper & Row, 1964.

Brode, Douglas. *The Films of the Fifties*. Secaucus, N.J.: Citadel, 1976.

Crane, Robert David, and Christopher Fryer. *Jack Nicholson: Face to Face*. Philadelphia: M. Evans, 1975.

Dalton, David. *James Dean; The Mutant King*. San Francisco: Straight Arrow, 1974.

_____, editor. *The Rolling Stones*. New York: Amsco Music Pub., 1972.

De Franco, J. Philip. *The Movie World of Roger Corman*. New York: Chelsea House, 1979.

Dickens, Norman. *Jack Nicholson; The Search for a Superstar*. New York: Signet, 1975.

Didion, Joan. "The Hippie Generation." *Saturday Evening Post*, Sept. 23, 1967.

Dowdy, Andrew. *The Films of the Fifties*. New York: William Morrow, 1973.

Eames, John Douglas. *The MGM Story*. New York: Crown, 1979.

Fonda, Peter, Dennis Hopper and Terry Southern. *Easy Rider*. New York: New American Library, 1969.

Goldman, Eric F. *The Crucial Decade America 1945-1960*. New York: Random House, 1960.

Goldstein, Ruth M., and Edith Zornow. *The Screen Image of Youth: Movies About Children and Adolescents*. Metuchen, N.J.: Scarecrow Press, 1980.

Halliwell, Leslie. *The Filmgoer's Companion*. New York: Avon, 1978.

Hirschhorn, Clive. *The Warner Brothers Story*. New York: Crown, 1979.

Hitchens, Gordon. "The Truth, The Whole Truth, and Nothing But the Truth About Exploitation Films." *Film Comment*, 2, No. 2, 1964.

Hopkins, Jerry. *Elvis; A Biography*. New York: Warner Books, 1971.

Howlett, John. *James Dean; A Biography*. New York: Simon & Schuster, 1975.

Jenkinson, Philip, and Alan Warner. *Celluloid Rock — Twenty Years of Movie Rock*. London: Lorrimer, 1974.

Kakinsky, Stuart. *Don Siegel: Director*. New York: Curtis Books, 1974.

Kaufman, William. *Great Television Plays*. New York: Dell, 1969.

Keylin, Arleen, and Christine Bent. *The New York Times at the Movies.* New York: Arno Press, 1979.
Krafsur, Richard P. *The American Film Institute Catalog of Motion Pictures — Feature Films 1961-1970.* New York: R.R. Bowker Co.
Kreidl, John Francis. *Nicholas Ray.* Boston: Twayne, 1977.
Lichter, Paul. *Elvis in Hollywood.* New York: Simon & Schuster, 1975.
MacCann, Richard Dyer. *Film and Society.* New York: Scribner's, 1964.
McCarthy, Clifford. *Bogey.* Secaucus, N.J.: Citadel, 1973.
McCarthy, Todd, and Charles Flynn. *Kings of the Bs.* New York: Dutton, 1975.
Maltin, Leonard. *TV Movies 1981-82 Edition.* New York: New American Library, 1980.
Manvell, Roger. *New Cinema in the U.S.A.* New York: Dutton, 1968.
Marx, Arthur. *Goldwyn, A Biography of the Man Behind the Myth.* New York: Ballantine, 1976.
Michael, Paul. *The American Movies Reference Book, The Sound Era.* Englewood Cliffs, N.J.: Prentice-Hall, 1969.
Morella, Joe, and Edward Epstein. *Rebels — The Rebel Hero in Films.* New York: Citadel, 1971.
Pretley, Gerald. *The Cinema of John Frankenheimer.* Cranbury, N.J.: A.S. Barnes, 1969.
Rooney, Frank. "Cyclist's Raid," in *Fiction from the Fifties.* Garden City, N.Y.: Doubleday, 1959.
Sann, Paul. *Fads, Follies and Delusions of the American People.* New York: Crown, 1967.
Schulman, Irving. *The Amboy Dukes.* Garden City, N.Y.: Doubleday, 1947.
Schumach, Murray. *Face on the Cutting Room Floor.* New York: William Morrow, 1964.
Siegel, Joel E. *Val Lewton; The Reality of Terror.* New York: Viking, 1973.
Spoto, Donald. *Stanley Kramer, Film Maker.* New York: Putnam, 1978.
Stoehling, Richard. *From Rock Around the Clock to The Trip: The Truth About Teen Movies.* San Francisco: Straight Arrow, 1969.
Swindell, Larry. *Spencer Tracy.* New York: Signet, 1971.
Thomas, Bob. *Joan Crawford.* New York: Simon & Schuster, 1978.
————. *Thalberg: Life and Legend.* Garden City, N.Y.: Doubleday, 1969.
Thomas, Tony. *The Films of Ronald Reagan.* Secaucus, N.J.: Citadel, 1980.
Thompson, Howard. *The New York Times Guide to Movies on TV.* Chicago: Quadrangle Books, 1970.
Vreeland, Frank. *Foremost Films of 1938 — A Yearbook of the American Screen.* New York: Pitman, 1939.
Wecter, Dixon. *The Age of the Great Depression.* New York: Macmillan, 1949.
Whitehead, Donald. *The F.B.I. Story.* New York: Random House, 1956.
Zinman, David. *Fifty Films from the Fifties.* New York: Arlington House, 1979.

Index

1757